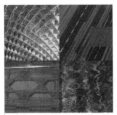

web
developer's guide to
Visual J++
& ActiveX

web developer's guide to Visual J++ & ActiveX

Trevor Harmon

CORIOLIS GROUP BOOKS

PUBLISHER	**KEITH WEISKAMP**
PROJECT EDITOR	**TONI ZUCCARINI**
COVER ARTIST	**GARY SMITH**
COVER DESIGN	**TONY STOCK**
INTERIOR DESIGN	**NICOLE BIRNEY**
LAYOUT PRODUCTION	**KIM EOFF**
COPYEDITOR	**SUSAN HOLLY**
PROOFREADER	**CHARLOTTE ZUCCARINI**
INDEXER	**KIRSTEN DEWEY**

Trademarks: Any brand names and product names included in this book are trademarks, registered trademarks, or trade names of their respective holders.
Text copyright © 1996 Coriolis Group, Inc. All rights under copyright reserved. No part of this book may be reproduced, stored, or transmitted by any means, mechanical, electronic, or otherwise, without the express written consent of the publisher.

Copyright © 1996 by The Coriolis Group, Inc.
All rights reserved.

Reproduction or translation of any part of this work beyond that permitted by section 107 or 108 of the 1976 United States Copyright Act without the written permission of the copyright owner is unlawful. Requests for permission or further information should be addressed to The Coriolis Group, 7339 E. Acoma Drive, Suite 7, Scottsdale, Arizona 85260.

The Coriolis Group, Inc.
7339 E. Acoma Drive, Suite 7
Scottsdale, AZ 85260
Phone: (602) 483-0192
Fax: (602) 483-0193
Web address: http://www.coriolis.com

ISBN 1-57610-062-6 : $39.99

Printed in the United States of America
10 9 8 7 6 5 4 3 2 1

To Clara

Contents

Introduction xvii

Chapter 1 The Fourth Dimension 1

Whims, Webs, And Words 2
CGI To The Rescue 2
Flashback To Yesterday 4
    Those Kids In Redmond 5
Sun Gets Java Jumpin' 7
Enter The Fourth Dimension 7
Microsoft Makes A Mistake 9
    Never Fear, The Underdog Is Here 10
    Microsoft Surrenders 10
ActiveX Powers Up 11
    ActiveX Controls 11
    The Portability Problem 12
Integration 13
Visual J++ 14
    First, The Bad News 15
    And Now, The Good News 15

Chapter 2 Learn *More* Java Now 17

Why Java? 19
    Pricing Model 19
    The Microsoft Empire 20

Java Overview   21
Strengths   21
Weaknesses   22

A Peek Under The Hood   23
The Virtual Machine   24
The Bytecode Interpreter   25
Just-In-Time Compilers   27
Sanitation Engineering 101   27
The Native Code Interface   30
The <APPLET> tag   30

Java On Windows   33
The Windows VM Today   34
The Feature Set   35

Advanced Graphics   36
Double-buffering   36
Palette-based Images   38
Direct Image Manipulation   42

Continuing On   44

Chapter 3   Visual J++   47

Visual J++ Profile   48
Highlights   49
ActiveX Integration   50
Missing Features   51

The Grand Tour   52
Project Workspace   52
Text Editor   55
Output Window   56
Tools   56

Starting From Scratch   58
Creating A Java Workspace   58

Importing A Java Workspace 59
The Java Applet Wizard 60

Build Settings 65

General Tab 65
Debug Tab 65
Java Tab 66

Resource Wizardry 67

Creating Resources 68
Importing Resources 71

Debugging With Visual J++ 74

Setting Breakpoints 74
Controlling Program Flow 76
The Call Stack Window 77
The Variables Window 77
The Watch Window 78
Debugging Exceptions 79
Debugging Threads 81
Disassembly 82

Sample Code 82

Java Lava Lamp 83
Magnifying Glass 89

A Look At The Competition 97

Summary 99

Chapter 4 ActiveX Fundamentals 101

What Is ActiveX? 102

My ActiveX Analogue 102
ActiveX Containers 103

ActiveX Controls Vs. Java Applets 105

Similarities   105
Differences   106
The Portability Problem   107
File Access   109
OLE Support   109
Legacy Code   109
Support For Non-Internet Applications   110
Compilation   110
Execution   111

ActiveX Controls And The Web Browser   111

The <OBJECT> Tag   111
Loading The Control   114

ActiveX Control Pad   116

Inserting ActiveX Controls   117

Chapter 5   Building ActiveX Controls   123

Visual C++   124

Building An ActiveX Control   125

The ClassWizard   127
Properties   129
Methods   138
Events   139

Debugging ActiveX Controls   140

Prefabricated Containers   141
Custom Containers   141
Just-In-Time Debugging   143

Preparing Your Control For Visual J++   144

Feature Limitations   145
Creating Nonvisual Controls   145
Version Stamping   146

Sample Code 147
Fire Animation 147
Plasma Animation 148
Bitmap Twirl 149

Moving On 150

Chapter 6 Interfaces 151

Interface? What's That? 152

Java Interfaces 152
Declaring An Interface 152
Using An Interface 154
Why Are They Necessary? 155

ActiveX Interfaces 158
Binary Functions 158
IUnknown: The Mother Of All Interfaces 160
IDispatch: The Property Provider 160

Calling ActiveX Interfaces From Java 161
Advantages Of ActiveX Integration 161
Calling ActiveX Functions 163
Accessing ActiveX Properties 164
Handling Errors 165

Summary 169

Chapter 7 Activating ActiveX 171

ActiveX Controls In Visual J++ 172
ActiveX Controls Redefined 172
Why Integrate? 173
The Portability Problem 173
The Security Problem 174

The Java Type Library Wizard 175

Harnessing The Wizard's Magic 176
Creating The Object 177
Calling Its Methods 179
Accessing Its Properties 180

Integrating OLE Automation Servers 181

Integrating Visual Controls 188
Passing Controls As Parameters 189
The Video Playback Control 190

Integrating Licensed Controls 197
The ILicenseMgr Interface 197
The Licensing Demo 198

Putting It All Together: The Taskbar Tray Example 199

Summary 202

Chapter 8 Java Controls 205

What Are Java Controls? 206
Java Controls Vs. ActiveX Controls 206
Limitations Of Java Controls 206
How Is Integration Possible? 207

Creating Java Controls 208
Step 1: Write The Java Source Code 208
Step 2: Create The Object Description 212
Step 3: Build The Type Library 219
Step 4: Rebuild The Java Class 220
Step 5: Register The Java Class 220

Driving Java Controls 222
Driving From Visual Basic 222
Driving From C++ 224

Putting It All Together: The Lingo Maker Example 229

Summary 240

Chapter 9 Scripting 241

Back To Script School 243
What's A Script? 243
The Basics 244
Functions 248
Events 249

The ActiveX Control Pad 250
Electing Your Events 251
Adding Your Actions 253

Scripting ActiveX Controls 254
Calling Methods 255
Setting Properties 256
Handling Events 256

Scripting Java Applets 258
Handling Events 259

Putting It All Together: The City Selector Example 262

Summary 270

Chapter 10 OLE Automation 271

OLE Automation In Visual J++ 272
Late-binding Vs. Early-binding 273
The Portability Problem 275
The Battle Of The Beans 276

Creating Early-binding Automation Controllers 276
Case Study: Entisoft Tools 277
Case Study: Microsoft Access 280

Creating Late-binding Automation Controllers 288
ActiveX To The Rescue 288
Case Study: Microsoft Word 290

Summary 294

Chapter 11   Data Access Objects   295

Database Support In Visual J++   296
Data Access Objects   296
Remote Data Objects   298
JDBC   300

DAO Basics   301
Before You Begin   301
Connecting To The Database   302
Browsing Records   304
Getting And Setting Fields   306
Adding And Deleting Records   307
Searching For Records   308

Putting It All Together: The Harmon Optical Example   311

Chapter 12   Security   333

Sandboxing   334
How To Play In A Sandbox   335
Applet Restrictions   337
Applet Privileges   340
The Internals Of Java Security   341
Java's Future Security   343

Code-signing   344
Why Is Code-signing Important?   344
How Code-signing Works   345
Microsoft Authenticode   348

How To Sign ActiveX Controls   356
Obtaining A Certificate From VeriSign   356
Running The Authenticode Utilities   361

How To Sign Java Applets   366

Signing Standard Java Classes 367
Signing ActiveX-enabled Java Classes 368

Summary 372

Appendix A   Online Resources   373

Appendix B   com.ms.com Reference   383

Appendix C   WHERE Reference   391

Index   397

Acknowledgments

I never thought I would survive the stress of this project. But thanks to the support of my editor, Toni Zuccarini, my book was published pre-posthumously.

I'd also like to thank the staff at Coriolis who helped turn my ideas into realities: Susan Holly, Anthony Potts, Keith Weiskamp, Dave Friedel, Jeff Duntemann, and many other hard workers I never had the chance to contact directly.

Assistance for this project came from the Internet, too. Tientien Li, Steve Horne, and Kerry Ryan answered my tough questions in return for a simple thank you.

Chip Anderson of Microsoft and Mahi de Silva of VeriSign deserve special mention. They took time away from their busy schedules just to answer phone calls from some kid in Kansas.

Finally, I want to thank Mom and Dad. Their years of support (emotional *and* financial) made this book possible.

Introduction

The Web Developer's Guide to Visual J++ & ActiveX is ideal for anyone who wants to get more out of Visual J++. Whether you're a Webmaster, a corporate intranet developer, or just a casual programmer looking to become a Java expert, this book is for you.

What This Book Is Not

This book is not a Java tutorial. It assumes that you already know the basics of Java and are somewhere between the novice and intermediate stages. If you need an introduction to Java, check out *Learn Java Now*, the printed tutorial that ships with Visual J++.

Once you've read *Learn Java Now* or some other tutorial, *The Web Developer's Guide to Visual J++ & ActiveX* will transform you into a Java expert and provide you with some practical examples along the way. It will also show you how to combine the power of ActiveX with the ease of Java.

Organization Of This Book

Part 1 introduces you to the basics of Java and ActiveX with an eye towards Microsoft's development tools. It covers every nook and cranny of Visual J++ including:

- The user interface
- The Applet Wizard
- The ClassView
- The integrated debugger
- The Resource Wizard
- The Type Library Wizard
- ActiveX support

The book also includes a chapter on ActiveX controls and how to create them using Visual C++.

Part 2 is the meat and potatoes of this work. It begins with a chapter on interfaces—what they are and how to use them—then moves on to encapsulating ActiveX controls within Java applets. It also explains how to write ActiveX controls with Java, and it concludes with a chapter on how to manipulate controls and applets with HTML scripts.

Part 3 moves on to more advanced topics, such as:

- Automating Microsoft Word and other OLE applications
- Accessing databases on a back-end server
- A comparison of security issues in ActiveX and Java

Online Support

To report errors, ask questions, or offer comments, contact the author at:
visualj@TrevorHarmon.com

Or visit his home page at:
http://TrevorHarmon.com/visualj

Chapter 1

- The Web as a book
- The CGI problem
- The birth of Java and ActiveX
- A marriage of technologies
- Visual J++ overview

The Fourth Dimension

A mighty bad dream woke me up at five o'clock in the morning. Not able to fall back asleep, I walked barefoot out to the front yard and fetched the morning paper. Lying on the driveway was a sharp rock, and, of course, I stepped on it. My tongue curled around the worst kind of language.

Feeling sober and down in the mouth, I walked back inside for a half-pint of O.J. and to find out who shot who last night. On page 3, I came across a scoop that was a bit out of the ordinary: Scientists in Antarctica had hooked up their computers to the World Wide Web. All of their research, their notes, their discoveries—they were all on the Web.

"Well, now, how about that?" I said. "I guess it's official. The World Wide Web really is worldwide."

All that reading had tired me out, so I trudged back to bed. I didn't fall asleep right away, partly because of the juice jolt and partly because I couldn't stop thinking about where Moses was when the light went out. Maybe those Web-surfing scientists would know. I decided to send them an email.

Whims, Webs, And Words

I woke up at the crack of noon. Over a bowl of cold cereal, I thought some more about those scientists in Antarctica and this whole World Wide Web thing. I couldn't figure out why the Web had become so popular. Everyone was galloping for it, like horses on their way back to the stable. It was in the news and the magazines, on TV and in the movies...even Kmart had its own site on the Web. I didn't know why this mad rush was happening.

The Web, I said to myself, is nothing more than a really big book. It has pictures, and it has words. Yes, it has videos and sounds, too, but those are just extra glitz and glitter. Okay, okay, so it's a really big, fancy book. But it's still just a two-dimensional piece of electronic paper.

Wait a minute, I said, suddenly arguing with myself. It's not two-dimensional at all. It has a third dimension: hyperlinks. You know, those blue underlined words in a Web page. Clicking on them with your mouse brings you to another page, anywhere on the Internet. Even Antarctica.

That's right, I conceded to myself. Hypertext gives the Web depth—a third dimension. Whoa! I just experienced Net nirvana! I'm beginning to understand why the Web is so popular. With hyperlinks, you almost never have to seek out more information; you just click your mouse.

Yes, I replied, hoping this conversation wasn't a symptom of schizophrenia, it's quicker to look up references and follow footnotes if the searching has already been done for you. You can have as easy a time as Huck and Jim as they floated down the Mississippi River.

CGI To The Rescue

I can see pretty plainly that the Web deserves the attention it receives. Yet it still seems like nothing more than a monstrous, computerized library. That's cool, all right, but there's a problem: The information in this library travels in only one direction. The Internet is about communication—not libraries—and communication doesn't exist in just one direction, it demands a two-way street. So where's the second lane on the Information Superhighway?

That second lane is called the *Common Gateway Interface*, better known as CGI. Invented in 1993, this technology allows Web servers to run external programs. More importantly, CGI provides a connection between these programs and a Web page. Users can type data into the page and then send the data back to the programs.

CGI isn't pretty, but it gets the job done. Millions of Web surfers use CGI for sending email, searching databases, or even ordering a pizza, as shown in Figure 1.1.

Despite its widespread acceptance, CGI has a hefty helping of problems. The biggest drawback is its overhead. Even the tiniest bit of interaction through CGI requires a new connection with the Web server. The constant chitchat between the user and the server slows everything down and makes immediate feedback impossible. This two-way method of communication is shown in Figure 1.2.

Another disadvantage is CGI's reliance on the Web server. Because CGI programs run only on the server, the speed and capabilities of these programs are, of course, limited by the speed and capabilities of the server. And with the explosive growth of the Internet, most servers can't handle the increased demand placed on them each day.

Security holes are yet another problem with CGI. The first few years of its existence brought a steady stream of hackers looking to exploit its

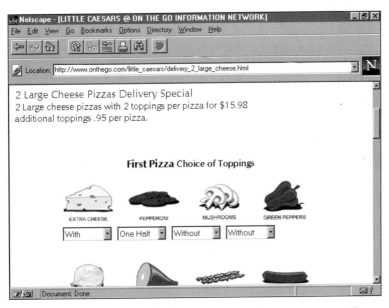

Figure 1.1 The Little Caesars Web site is perfect for anyone too lazy to pick up the phone.

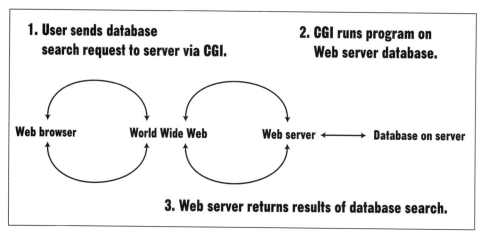

Figure 1.2 The two-way path of CGI.

design flaws. They were able to sneak inside a Web server, execute commands, and look at sensitive data. Fortunately, most of the holes have been patched up by now, but trusting CGI's security measures is still risky.

Flashback To Yesterday

Let's forget about the Web for a moment and travel back to the year 1992. Under the code name Oak, a team of programmers at Sun Microsystems is attempting to create a new consumer electronics device known as the *set-top box*. It looks much like the cable box that perches atop so many televisions, but this little box has a special ability: It speaks a digital tongue. Wearing a target price of $300, the Oak box can communicate with all sorts of electronic devices in your home—TVs, VCRs, CDs, and a few other acronyms.

With so many different gadgets from so many different companies, things could get mighty confusing if they all try to talk to one another. Sun decides that the only way to keep everything under control is to give those electronic devices a common language. But which language?

Sun's first choice is C++. It's popular and mature, but unfortunately it just doesn't fit into the world of set-top boxes. The language is fat, tough to learn, and not highly portable.

The Oak team then decides to craft a new language based on C++. They keep the cool stuff that C++ has to offer—object orientation, class inheritance, and clean syntax—and they take out the features that make

C++ the child of calamity—pointers, multiple inheritance, and platform dependence. They also add a few sweet treats such as built-in multithreading, garbage collecting of unused memory, and a thoughtfully designed class library.

In 1993, members of the Oak team had a chance to look back on their accomplishments, and they're mighty pleased. They had built a language that was uncommonly elegant.

Those Kids In Redmond

Way up north in Redmond, Washington, Microsoft Corporation was working on some major projects, as well. Their Windows operating system had begun to take off, and the company desperately wanted every software maker in the country to migrate to Windows. To that end, Microsoft was plopping powerful features into the increasingly popular operating system.

OLE Is Born

One such technology had sprung from Microsoft's R&D department. Called Object Linking and Embedding, or OLE, it was advertised as a method for creating compound documents—those that can hold any type of data from any type of Windows application. The advertising didn't have much effect, though, because few developers really understood what OLE was all about.

Not until the next revision of OLE, titled simply OLE 2, did Windows programmers really start to take notice. This new version was a more ambitious technology, providing a drag-and-drop protocol, a foundation for document-centric software, a method for applications to communicate with each other, and more. The combination of these new object-oriented features met a warm reception in the Windows developer community. (See Chapter 10 for a detailed overview of OLE.)

The Visual Basic Revolution

At about the same time, Windows developers were discovering another Microsoft technology that was quickly becoming more popular than OLE and OLE 2 combined. The idea was relatively simple: Developers take a Windows application, add a few dozen lines of code, and instantly transform it into a component that plugs directly into Visual Basic, Microsoft's trendy development environment, shown in Figure 1.3.

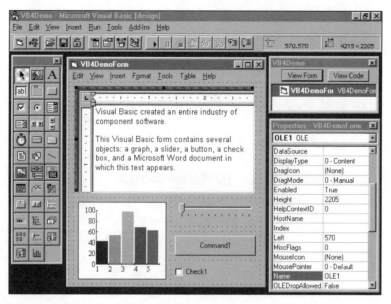

Figure 1.3 Visual Basic created an entire industry of component software.

The developers loved the idea. The growing acceptance of Visual Basic created a huge and hungry market for these ready-made software components, called *custom controls*. Visual Basic programmers loved them, too. They could purchase specialized, prefabricated code that added extra value to their applications.

As the demand for Visual Basic custom controls soared, flaws in the design grew more prominent. The custom controls were not suited for the new 32-bit version of Windows, they could be created only with C, and they were compatible only with Visual Basic. Developers complained to Microsoft that the design needed a major update.

Instead of fixing the original design, Microsoft trashed it and started over. This time, the company borrowed from their experience and centered the new design around OLE technology. The reincarnated custom controls, known simply as *OLE controls*, worked well in either 16- or 32-bit Windows; they could be created by virtually any compiler; and they could be used with any OLE-enabled program.

Microsoft was so busy inventing these newfangled features that they didn't notice a crisis developing in sunny Mountain View, California.

Sun Gets Java Jumpin'

The set-top box, as it turned out, was a dud. The nonexistent market for the devices had been hyped beyond belief, and interactive television was years ahead of its time. No matter how hard Sun tried, the company couldn't get anyone to license the Oak language.

In desperation, Sun repositioned Oak as a tool matched perfectly with the latest fad: the Personal Digital Assistant (PDA). PDAs were hot at the time, and Sun knew that Oak's virtues—a small footprint (only 45 K), platform independence, and networking features—were ideal for the swelling PDA market. But after Apple's Newton fiasco, Sun still couldn't sell Oak. The company would've had an easier time convincing the general population that dogs have thumbs.

By 1994, Oak seemed destined for ruin. Nobody wanted interactive TV; nobody wanted PDAs; and nobody, but nobody, wanted Oak. Instead, everyone wanted the next big thing: the World Wide Web. James Gosling, the team leader of the Oak project, had a brainstorm.

"We realized we could build a really cool browser," said Gosling in an interview with Sun World Online. "[The Web] was one of the few things in the client/server mainstream that needed some of the weird things we'd done [with Oak].... So we built a browser." The HotJava Browser, shown in Figure 1.4, was born.

The browser showed Oak in a new light. It caught the eye of Eric Schmidt, Sun's chief technology officer, and Scott McNealy, Sun's CEO. They saw a potential renaissance for Oak and, together with Gosling and his team, began to redefine the language. Over the next few months, they morphed it into a tool for creating programs that live inside the Web. They also gave it a catchier, more exotic name: Java.

Enter The Fourth Dimension

Although the company may not have realized it at the time, Sun had transformed not just Oak, but the entire World Wide Web. With the power of Java, the Web now has a fourth dimension—motion. Web pages are no longer static pieces of paper. They are living, breathing computer programs.

These programs, called Java *applets*, are a new type of computer software. They're not shackled to a single type of machine or even a single

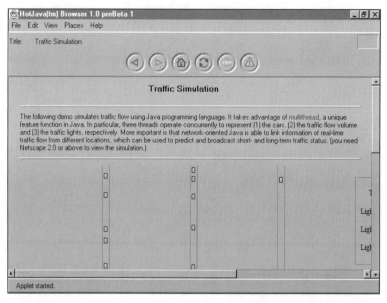

Figure 1.4 HotJava was one of the first Java-enabled Web browsers.

location. They can reside anywhere on the Web and, thanks to Java's cross-platform abilities, can be executed by any computer attached to the Internet.

Unlike typical computer software, Java programs do not require installation. The nomadic applets install themselves automatically when they are downloaded into a Web browser. This means that computer users must no longer own every piece of software that they run. They can simply point their Web browser to a new site and enjoy the features of whatever applet happens to reside there. (See Chapter 2 for details on how this feature affects the business model for selling software.)

Once downloaded into a browser, Java applets can do just about anything. They can show animation, display up-to-the-minute stock quotes, access databases on the server, perform an automatic search of the Internet...anything the programmer can think of. And they can do all of this without any help (or hindrance) from the CGI. The only task they can't do, for security reasons, is access files on your system. (See Chapter 12 for information on Java security.)

To put it simply, Java makes the Web less like reading a book and more like an interactive experience.

Microsoft Makes A Mistake

The first major company to understand the new shape of the Web was Netscape Communications, makers of the ubiquitous Netscape Navigator. Netscape realized that Java would make a nifty addition to their browser. The company licensed Java from Sun and announced that version 2.0 of Navigator would be fully Java-compatible, as shown in Figure 1.5. Industry pundits declared Java a success.

While the pundits were singing praises to Netscape and Sun, Microsoft was still concentrating on OLE, Visual Basic, and the rest of the Windows universe. The company seemed unaware of the Web and focused its efforts on bringing Windows 95, the overly hyped next generation of Windows, and the Microsoft Network, a proprietary online service, to the masses.

Meanwhile, fueled by Netscape's Navigator and Sun's Java, the Web seemed unstoppable. The international network, originally designed to link some 2,000 scientists to a tiny number of supercomputers, was now spread across 2 million computers and 18 million users. It was a huge market for any company fast enough to catch it. But Microsoft, taken completely by surprise, was standing still.

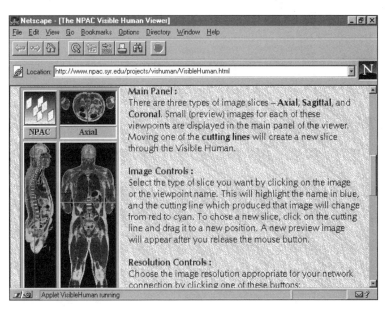

Figure 1.5 Netscape placed Java in the limelight.

Never Fear, The Underdog Is Here

The company soon found itself in a game of catch-up. Bill Gates and his clan scrambled to announce Web products, hold press conferences, and develop an Internet strategy. Hoping to maintain a focused public image, Microsoft tried to appear calm and confident. On the inside, however, the company was about as mixed up as a crazy quilt caught in a cyclone. Microsoft, with virtually no Web experience, was way out of their league.

Microsoft was playing the role of the underdog. Netscape and Sun had a tremendous lead; Microsoft seemed years behind. Normally when caught in this situation, the company would leverage their controversial dominance of the personal computer industry to catch up with the competition. This time, however, Microsoft's deadly garrote on the desktop market was of little help. The Web rendered operating systems, and hence Windows, obsolete. Microsoft needed something—anything—to turn the tide in their favor.

Microsoft Surrenders

So desperate was the software giant that they proclaimed the unthinkable: endorsement of another company's technology. On December 7, 1995, Microsoft announced that they would license Java from Sun Microsystems. This move was a big gulp of pride for Microsoft, but it was also a shot in the arm. Access to Java allowed the company to move quickly into direct competition with Netscape and Sun. Some critics, however, suggested that the announcement was nothing more than a public-relations ploy to prevent Microsoft from openly flouting a popular and inevitable trend.

Regardless of the motives, Microsoft immediately began to integrate Java with their product line. As a first step, the company announced plans for enabling Internet Explorer, Microsoft's immature Web browser, for Java applets. They also declared that future versions of Windows would provide internal support for Java. These events were a stride toward placing Microsoft on equal footing with Netscape, but they still would not give the company the same power over the Web that they had enjoyed with the desktop market. Never satisfied, Microsoft searched for ways to get an imperious edge on the competition.

ActiveX Powers Up

Eventually, Microsoft came across the idea of adapting OLE for the Web. They quickly added a few Internet features to OLE and slapped a new name on it: ActiveX. This shortcut allowed the company to throw some juicy buzzwords to the media hounds and to turn the public's attention away from Sun and Netscape. True to form, Microsoft had generated industry hype without actually doing anything.

The "new" ActiveX architecture, as shown in Table 1.1, shares many features with its OLE progenitors. It allows programs to interact with each other and to embed themselves in documents. But it also offers some genuine enhancements that renew OLE for use on the Web. The most significant of these enhancements is the ActiveX control.

ActiveX Controls

A slightly modified version of OLE controls, ActiveX controls are self-contained programs that live inside the Web. They are similar to Java applets because they, too, can supercharge the Web with fancy animation, realtime display of stock quotes, easy access to corporate databases, and more. But ActiveX controls (shown in Figure 1.6) are more powerful than their Java counterparts. They can access files on the client machine; they run faster; and they have better support for legacy code. (See Chapter 4 for details on the ActiveX architecture.)

Although OLE controls experienced the least amount of change in the transition to ActiveX, they are, ironically, the most crucial part of Microsoft's strategy to control the Internet. Microsoft, secretly hoping that Java will just disappear, is trying to turn ActiveX controls into Java-killers. The company is striving to give ActiveX every possible advantage over Java. And with help from the OLE ancestry, Microsoft has the potential to do exactly that.

Table 1.1   OLE is reborn as ActiveX.

1992	1994	1996
OLE	+ Internet	= ActiveX
OLE controls	+ Internet	= ActiveX controls
OLE documents	+ Internet	= ActiveX documents
OLE object model	+ Internet	= ActiveX object model

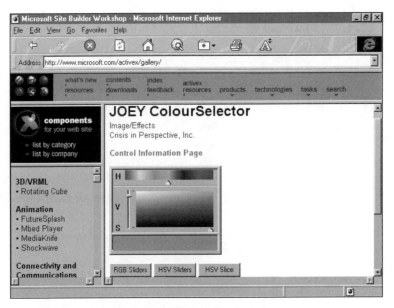

Figure 1.6 ActiveX controls supercharge the Internet.

For example, any tool that can create OLE controls can also create ActiveX controls. Programmers don't have to learn any new tricks to write them. They can use time-tested tools such as Borland Delphi, Visual C++, and Visual Basic.

Even more important in this battle for the Web is the existing market for ActiveX controls. Because ActiveX controls are just OLE controls in disguise, every third-party vendor of OLE controls (Microsoft claims more than 1,000) is also a vendor of ActiveX controls. The popularity of Java, though strong and growing, is nowhere near this volume.

Yet another Microsoft advantage is the compatibility of ActiveX controls with desktop software. Any OLE-enabled program—word processors, spreadsheets, databases, and the like—can use ActiveX controls. Java applets, in comparison, can run only inside a browser or as a stand-alone application.

The Portability Problem

The major disadvantage to ActiveX controls is that they are so closely tied to the Windows platform. Programmers who choose ActiveX are as bound to Windows as Brer Rabbit was to Tar Baby in Uncle Remus's famous folktale. Clearly, Java has a leg up in the portability arena.

This situation may change in a few short months. Microsoft has revealed that other companies, through contracts with the software Goliath, will provide ActiveX capabilities for Unix systems and the Apple Macintosh. Just how well these solutions will work, however, remains to be seen.

The solutions may turn out to be unnecessary. Not only is Windows becoming universal, but with the advent of intranets—private, corporate computer networks linked to the Internet—portability may soon become a nonissue. Corporations frequently standardize on a single platform and purchase tools and applications designed specifically for that platform. On the intranet, portability is moot.

Integration

Java evangelists would argue that their favorite language has more to offer than portability. Programmers who write in Java never have to worry about freeing memory (thanks to Java's automatic garbage collection), they have built-in exception handling, and they have access to the source code of one of the world's best class libraries.

These purists would miss the key difference between ActiveX and Java: ActiveX is an *architecture*; Java is a *language*. While Java helps programmers write software components, ActiveX allows those components to interact with each other. The two technologies are in cooperation, not competition.

The symbiotic relationship between ActiveX and Java solves problems that could not be fixed by either technology alone. Here are some examples:

- *Lower the Learning Curve*—ActiveX components can be written with any language: C++, Visual Basic—even Java. Programmers who want to create ActiveX controls, but don't want to give up the luxuries of Java, can do both. They're not required to learn a new language just to write ActiveX controls (see Chapter 8).

- *Never Reinvent the Wheel*—The Java class libraries, though powerful, can't handle every contingency. Many situations require the use of previously written or store-bought code. Java does provide an interface—known as the *native code interface*—for using C in Java programs, but it is poorly documented, difficult to use, and ruins Java's portability. A better solution is to encapsulate an ActiveX control inside a Java applet (see Chapter 7). By harnessing the power of ActiveX, Java programmers can choose from hundreds of commercial ActiveX controls to find the features they want. They can convert existing code, whether written in C, C++, or Visual Basic, to a self-contained ActiveX control. Then all they have to do is plug the control into the applet. With ActiveX, writing chunks of code from scratch is a rarity.

- *Communicate with Other Programs*—Java was never designed for OLE. It can't talk to popular software such as Microsoft Excel, Borland Paradox, or Fractal Design Painter. But with a little help from ActiveX, Java can call OLE interfaces and thus communicate with OLE-enabled software. Applets are no longer isolated; they have access to a wide range of third-party applications.

Visual J++

At the moment, only one tool allows this tight integration between ActiveX and Java. Not surprisingly, that tool comes from Microsoft. It's called Visual J++ (see Figure 1.7).

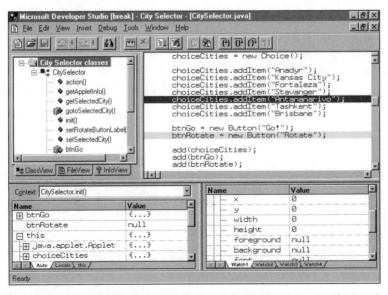

Figure 1.7 Visual J++ is Microsoft's first stab at the Java tools business.

Visual J++ is a professional development environment for creating Java applets and applications. A sibling of Microsoft's Visual C++, it runs only on Windows 95 or Windows NT 4.0. It offers a text editor, resource editor, project builder, integrated debugging, and comprehensive online help.

First, The Bad News

The name is a bit misleading. Visual J++ is actually not very visual at all. You can't draw user-interface components and link them to code as you can with Borland Delphi, Visual Basic, or Visual C++. The best that Visual J++ can do is create such basic components as menus and dialogs and import them into your Java project.

Visual J++ also omits the ClassWizard, a helpful innovation found in Visual C++. Support for the ClassWizard will not be available until version 2.0 of Visual J++. Until then, the product still has some important features going for it.

And Now, The Good News

Visual J++ is *fast*. When Microsoft released the first beta version, some testers wrote in to grumble about the buggy compiler. "It's not doing anything," said one disgruntled programmer. "When I try to compile my Java code, the thing starts and then quits without giving me any errors."

The compiler was, in fact, perfectly fine. It was just too speedy. So fast was Visual J++ that the programmers thought it was somehow skipping over their code. In reality, it was compiling at around a million lines per minute.

Visual J++ also has some nice features that make it more than just a shell for Sun's Java Development Kit:

- *ActiveX Support*—With Visual J++, you can integrate ActiveX controls in your Java applets. You can also use OLE automation to hook up with other applications (see Chapter 10).

- *Integrated Debugging*—Visual J++ is a powerful tool for debugging Java code. In addition to standard features like breakpoints and watches, the integrated debugger can browse the call stack, monitor threads, and even drop down to the bytecode level (with source code annotation) for hunting those especially nasty bugs.

- *ClassView*—Microsoft borrowed the ClassView feature from Visual C++. As its name implies, the ClassView gives a hierarchical view of every class in your project. Instead of the usual file-based view offered by older development tools, it uses icons and colors to show the logical, abstract connections between classes.

If you're anxious to get started with Visual J++, skip ahead to Chapter 3. There you'll find detailed information on all of its cool features, including a look at how the product stacks up against its competitors. Otherwise, you should continue your Java journey with Chapter 2, where you'll learn a few esoteric secrets and some advanced programming tricks.

Chapter 2

Learn *More* Java Now

- Why Java?
- Java strengths and weaknesses
- A peek under the hood
- Java on Windows
- Advanced graphics techniques

The personal computer industry can find some parallels in African history. For centuries, African tribes and their religions thrived in solitude, each with its own spiritual traditions just as unique and valuable as the twinkling stones from Africa's diamond mines. Then, in the nineteenth century, missionaries from the Western world began flocking to Africa, seeking to convert tribal members to Christianity.

Conversion to Christianity came with a price. It meant breaking away from the old lifestyle, adopting new alliances, and adjusting to new moral and religious standards. Despite the obligations, a fresh flock of believers readily paid the tax and transferred their loyalties to the Christian church, abandoning their own traditions. The unavoidable result was a breakdown in tribal structure that destroyed countless African cultures and creeds.

In truth, the Christian missionaries improved the lives of many Africans. They brought the first clinics and hospitals into rural areas, and their direct influence caused African governments to place greater emphasis on affordable health care, adequate housing, and clean water. Only late in the twentieth century have Africans begun to recapture their lost religious heritage.

In a similar fashion, the personal computer industry is returning to its roots. More and more companies long for the good old days of IBM, when compatibility was held as a religious conviction. Back then, software start-ups were primitive tribes, exquisitely unique and surprisingly innovative, yet united by the open standards of the IBM PC.

Microsoft, a sort of self-righteous missionary for the computer world, helped put an end to the innovation. With questionable business practices and the world's best marketing agents, their Windows operating system sucked part of the spirit from the software industry. The company, aided by a partnership with Intel, demanded complete and total conversion to the Windows way of life. When they could not convince a company to convert, Microsoft would simply buy faith with stock options.

To be fair, Microsoft's dominance of the computer industry has certain advantages. Nearly 80 percent market saturation means that developers can write software for Windows alone and not worry too much about compatibility. The strong competition from Microsoft also helps drive prices down.

Aside from these benefits, many companies are still wary of Microsoft. They've seen how dominance of the desktop can stifle competition and stamp out new, exciting technologies. And they're concerned that Microsoft's motto of "a computer on every desktop running Microsoft software" has secretly been changed to "a computer on every desktop running *only* Microsoft software."

When Java came along, these companies rejoiced, not so much for Java's features, but for the simple fact that the technology didn't originate at Microsoft. Word-of-mouth and sugarcoated rumors gave Java more publicity than Microsoft's money could ever buy.

As a result, we're seeing a spiritual revival that will change the computer industry forever. No longer will the features of your desktop determine the features of your software. No longer will the size of your hard drive limit the number of programs you can run. Eventually, the computer will be peripheral to the World Wide Web.

Hallelujah!

Why Java?

In a recent interview with SunWorld Online, James Gosling, creator of Java, said: "Consumers don't care which CPU is inside. They don't appreciate big or powerful RISC-based processors, which are expensive and proprietary."

Phooey. We've already been through this scenario. The age of the dumb terminal has come and gone. If history is any guide, users want power. They want control. They want a fast, self-contained computer with a high-speed link to the outside world.

So where does Java fit into this egregious need? Many Java applets have been nothing more than groovy animations or movie-style marquees. They've offered little content to please consumers.

The key to Java lies in its potential. The framework provides users with the speed of their client machine and the power of the network. Because Java applets run locally but originate at the server, users get the best of both worlds.

Nevertheless, Java still faces the possibility of failure. Some industry analysts think the language is an 18-month technology that will be replaced when something better comes along. Others fear that Java entrepreneurs, in an effort to gain market share by distributing free software, will go bankrupt.

In the long term, Sun Microsystems and their Java cohorts must allow the language to roam free. They should not hold the technology too close nor allow its capture by competitors such as Microsoft. Java needs roots *and* wings.

Pricing Model

The Java community hasn't quite figured out how to make money. The majority of applets on the Web are not designed to turn a profit, but rather to show off the author's programming skills or to teach others about Java. Today, almost all Java dollars come from three sources:

- *Tools*—Source-code editors and compilers
- *Tutorials*—Books and magazine articles
- *Consulting and authoring services*—For corporate Web sites

Only the last category actually creates profit. The other two markets are incestuous and simply feed off the hype and popularity of Java. They're already starting to die out. The only sure way to make money is to become a Java expert and sell your skills to contractors who want to spice up their Web pages. You could also solicit these services to large enterprises looking for Java-based information management tools.

If you decide to go this route, you'll find that the road is relatively free of potholes. Java is beginning to mature, so you now have access to a wide assortment of professional development tools. Also, Java's cross-platform features allow you to concentrate on the content of your applications instead of their gritty details.

Another advantage to working as a Java programmer is that you can offer your customers a convenient distribution mechanism: the World Wide Web. Your applets and applications are available immediately on demand, directly through a Web browser. Thus, users always get the most up-to-date version of your code.

The Microsoft Empire

Microsoft calls the Internet the most important single development in the entire history of computers. Strangely, Microsoft had almost nothing to do with this "most important single development." As the Web exploded, the company isolated itself in a Windows wonderland, constantly asking customers where they wanted to go today. Obviously, those customers wanted to go where Microsoft wasn't headed: to the Internet.

Windows Obsolescence

The Web and its Java companion scare Microsoft. These technologies render the company's strongest asset, the Windows operating system, obsolete. Software is truly open for the first time, and the Microsoft desktop is simply a commodity. Content is king.

Sun, Netscape, and other Java promoters see this development as an opportunity to destroy Microsoft—or at least Microsoft's domination of the desktop market. They hope that Java will place Windows in the background and turn the spotlight on Java. Windows will still be a fundamental part of the computer, just like the BIOS is a crucial component, but Java applications will hold the reins.

ADOPT IT, ADAPT IT, OWN IT, KILL IT

Ironically, ownership of the operating system could help Microsoft win the Java battle. They can provide direct support for Java through Windows, eliminating the need for customers to buy Java add-ons. This strategy is all part of what William Blundon, President and COO of SourceCraft, Inc., refers to as "adopt it, adapt it, own it, and then kill it."

Microsoft will adopt Java into their own software line, adapt it for new features such as ActiveX support, use these features to attract and own customers, and then dispose of Java as the company pleases. The end result: Sun's and Netscape's efforts to destroy Microsoft could backfire.

Regardless of what Microsoft does with Java, expect to hear them mentioning Visual J++ whenever Java is praised and citing ActiveX as an alternative whenever Java is criticized. Either way, Microsoft appears to be Java's biggest fan.

Java Overview

Java is what C++ should have been. It's a clean, strong, object-oriented language. Because it was designed from scratch, not tacked on to an existing language, Java retains most of the power of C++, but avoids controversial, hard-to-learn features, such as multiple inheritance. Also, Java's syntax is almost exactly like C++, so experienced C++ programmers will feel at home with Java.

Like all programming languages, Java is not perfect. It has specific strengths and weaknesses. Take a look at the following two sections to see if Java is right for you.

Strengths

Here are the highlights of Java's most potent features:

- *Portability*—Java programs are independent of operating systems. They run without modification on Windows, Macintosh, Unix, and future platforms.

- *Built-in networking*—Sun designed Java especially for client-server environments. Applets can exchange information and communicate with server machines. This capability makes applets ideal for the Internet, the largest client-server network on earth.

- *Supercharge the Web*—Java brings a fourth dimension to the Web. It allows users to interact with Web pages instead of just viewing them. In the old days, for example, a page about electrical components would contain descriptive text and perhaps a picture of a transistor. Today, that page could contain a Java applet that lets readers move transistors around a circuit board and see how they interact in realtime.

- *Robustness*—Java places security restrictions on applets to prevent them from harming your system. Additionally, Java code forbids memory pointers, so lockups are virtually eliminated.

- *Faster programming*—Java is object-oriented inside and out. Everything about the language encourages code reuse for more efficient programming, and thanks to Java's inherent portability, developers don't waste time porting their code to other platforms.

- *Great for the corporate enterprise*—Users don't need much computer experience to run Java applets. As long as they can handle a Web browser, users automatically know how to install any applet, no matter how complex. This no-brainer approach makes life easier for administrators of corporate computer networks. Information systems managers can develop applications in Java, put them on an in-house Web server, and instantly distribute services to everyone in the enterprise, including remote employees in distant cities. Plus, upgrading the software is a simple matter of upgrading the Java code on the server. These benefits make Java ideal for the fast-growing intranet market.

Weaknesses

Despite the tremendous hype surrounding Java, the language has a few disadvantages:

- *Poor performance*—Java code is compiled twice: once at runtime and once at design time (see the section later in this chapter, "A Peek Under The Hood"). As a result, Java programs run slower than those written in other languages. Even with modern optimization techniques, applets can be annoyingly slow. (Keep your eyes open for Java chips built into your computer's hardware. In the future, these dedicated chips could accelerate Java applets just as dedicated video cards speed up graphics-intensive programs.)

- *Steep learning curve*—Java tutorials have sold quite well—for good reason. Unless you're an experienced C++ programmer, the language can be tough to learn. Java is based on C++, so it brings some heavy baggage, such as interfaces and exception handling.

- *Security concerns*—An unwritten rule in the programming world is that applications are not allowed to spawn other applications without the user's permission. Yet Java breaks this rule by default. Even with the extreme approach that Java takes in preventing malicious code, some users worry about foreign programs sneaking into their systems.

In the name of security, Java places a number of restrictions on applets. Here's what they cannot do:

- Read or write files on the client machine
- Access memory directly
- Access other hardware directly
- Launch programs
- Make system calls
- Find out your name, email address, or IP address

With ActiveX integration, you can circumvent all of these restrictions. Don't worry: This won't eliminate Java's security model, because ActiveX controls have their own security measures (see Chapter 13). To learn how to get around the restrictions, take a look at Chapter 7.

A Peek Under The Hood

Most computer languages fall into two categories:

- *Interpreted*—An interpreted language is converted into a binary, computer-readable form as it is read from the source-code file. This process speeds development time but slows execution time. It also makes the code harder to debug because errors are not caught until the program actually runs.

- *Compiled*—A compiled language is completely converted to a binary, computer-readable form before it runs. This process slows development time but speeds execution time. It also makes the code easier to debug because most errors are caught as the program compiles.

Java fits neither of these categories; it's actually a hybrid of both types. Before running a Java program, you must first compile the source code into a form known as *bytecode*. This bytecode is then translated, or interpreted, at runtime into a true executable format. Each step of this process is orchestrated by a piece of software called the *virtual machine*.

The Virtual Machine

The virtual machine, or VM, is exactly what it sounds like, a generic, nonexistent computer. When you build a Java applet under Visual J++, your code is not targeted for Windows, but rather for an imaginary computer—the virtual machine.

PORTABLE POWER

The VM gives you a tremendous advantage: instant portability. Your Java applet will run anywhere that a virtual machine can exist (see Figure 2.1). This, of course, includes not only Windows, Macintosh, and Unix systems, but also consumer devices, such as cable boxes and Internet appliances. Who knows? Maybe toaster ovens will one day sport a "Designed for Java" logo.

With the virtual machine, you're no longer concerned with operating systems or instruction sets. All of your code runs on a single machine—the Java VM. This allows you to concentrate on the content of your applications, not their platform-specific idiosyncrasies.

WEB WONDERMENT

The true power of the virtual machine comes alive in the belly of the browser. Web browsers need only to include a Java VM to support applets. Once this support is in place, Java code from any developer can zip through the Internet and land in your Web browser.

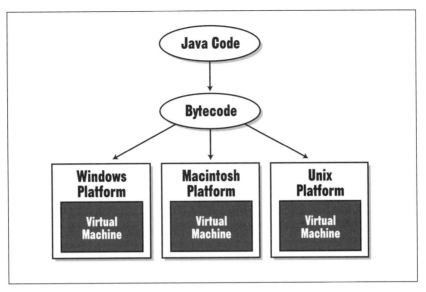

Figure 2.1 Java code, once compiled to bytecode, can run on any platform that provides a VM.

These nomadic programs are potentially dangerous, so the VMs in Web browsers have been altered to prevent file access on the client machine. Applets can't access the client machine in any way other than to draw to its screen. The VMs of some Web browsers also contain signature checkers that scan for unwanted software (such as pornographic applets) and prevent them from appearing.

The Bytecode Interpreter

The virtual machine contains a special component called the *bytecode interpreter*. This integral part of the VM loads Java bytecodes and translates them into low-level instructions, readable directly by the computer. Bytecode interpreters are fundamentally different for each platform because each one has its own proprietary instruction set.

TRANSLATION

Bytecodes are analogous to assembly language. They're a symbolic representation of low-level computer instructions. Consider, for example, the following list of bytecodes:

```
iinc      y,1     // Add 1 to the value of the integer
                  // variable y
iload     nMyVar  // Push the local variable nMyVar onto the
                  // stack
```

```
i2f                     // Pop an integer off the stack, convert it
                        // to a floating point value, and pop it
                        // back onto the stack
```

These bytecodes are harder to read than normal Java code, but they are much closer to a form that the computer can understand. Consequently, bytecodes can be translated quickly into machine language while remaining generic enough to be portable.

VERIFICATION

As the interpreter thrashes through a class file, it verifies the integrity of the bytecodes (see Figure 2.2). It ensures that they do not overflow the stack, create fake memory references, or pass invalid arguments to

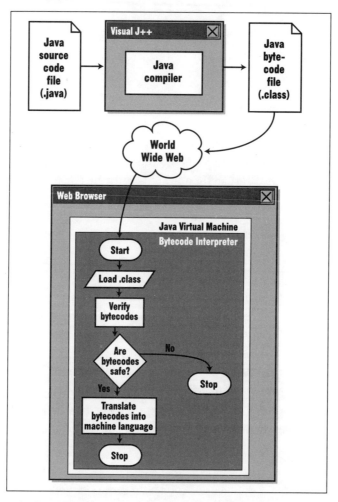

Figure 2.2 Java's journey from source to bytecode to machine language.

function calls. Only when the class file has passed all security tests does the bytecode interpreter allow it to run.

Just-In-Time Compilers

Interpreting and verifying bytecodes is a lengthy process, and Java code can run painfully slow as a result. Fortunately, vendors of Java tools have created a solution known as the Just-In-Time compiler, or JIT. Instead of interpreting bytecodes *after* they are loaded into the virtual machine, the JIT will translate them into native machine instructions *as they are loaded*. As soon as the class file has been completely read, the JIT has already compiled it...just in time.

Normally, bytecode interpreters must compile Java functions again and again, each time they are called. JIT compilers eliminate this inefficiency by saving compiled functions in memory and storing a link to their code. If a function is called again, the link is activated and the compiled code runs immediately. Thus, execution of Java code can approach (but does not match) the speed of native C++ code.

JIT compilers are real moneymakers for Java companies. Borland International, for instance, recently purchased a Java license from Sun Microsystems. They used the license to create a powerful JIT compiler that attracted the attention of Netscape Communications. In a sort of round-robin of technology, Netscape purchased the compiler for integration with their Navigator browser, transforming Borland's Java license into a profit.

Sanitation Engineering 101

You can easily tell the difference between a C++ programmer and a Java programmer. The face of the C++ programmer is all scrunched up and frowning. But if your gaze falls on the Java programmer, you'll see a face that's happy and relaxed.

The mother of misery for the C++ programmer is an overabundance of memory leaks. Memory leaks pop up whenever program code allocates memory, but forgets to free it. This type of bug appears quite often, because C++ leaves the responsibility of freeing memory entirely up to you. Eventually, you're going to forget to free some memory (as I have done more than a few times), and the result is a nasty, hard-to-find bug that could crash your program. Hence the frowning face.

You may be asking yourself: "Why didn't somebody come up with a fix for this problem a long time ago?" The answer: Somebody did. Programmers have grappled with memory leaks for decades, and they've had a solution for almost as long. It's called *garbage collection*. With garbage-collecting languages, such as Lisp or Smalltalk, you never have to worry about freeing memory. The task is handled for you automatically by the virtual machine.

Garbage Collection In Java

The tremendous popularity of Java—a garbage-collecting language—has finally brought this handy technique into focus. The mainstream programming community fully acknowledges the value of automatic garbage collection, but programmers should also recognize its minor drawbacks.

The problem with garbage collection is that it all takes place behind the scenes, so you have no control over it. As your program runs, the Java VM starts a low-priority background thread that constantly searches for unused memory blocks. This thread, of course, takes away some of the computer's processing power. Fortunately, the amount it takes (only about 3 percent) is so small that you can easily ignore it.

Another issue in collecting garbage is that the automated process is not as efficient as your manual skills. As the human programmer, you know your code intimately and can best decide when to deallocate memory. The Java garbage collector can only make guesses. Eventually, the memory heap becomes highly fragmented and oversized.

Memory Compaction

To repair this fragmentation, Java's garbage collector applies two algorithms to the memory heap:

- *Mark and sweep*—Circular memory, such as linked lists, can fool Java's garbage collector into thinking that a piece of memory is in use when it actually is not. To track down this hidden memory, the collector traces through each memory reference and *marks* the blocks it finds with a "used" tag. After reaching the final reference, the collector can quickly walk through the memory heap and *sweep* away the veil of unseen memory (see Figure 2.3).

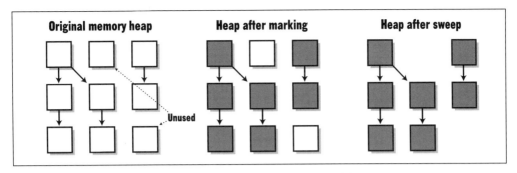

Figure 2.3 The mark-and-sweep algorithm finds hidden memory.

- *Stop and copy*—Even after a mark and sweep, the memory heap is still fragmented with holes and wasted space. The Java VM, in a manner similar to hard-disk optimizers, can *stop* its garbage collection and *copy* the memory heap to a new location. In doing so, the fragmented heap becomes a single, contiguous block of storage (see Figure 2.4).

FORCING MEMORY COMPACTION

*Java provides a system call, **System.gc()**, that forces the garbage collector to compact the memory heap. Calling this function will immediately run the mark-and-sweep and stop-and-copy algorithms. You should call this function only as a last resort when allocating huge amounts of circular data structures. In all other situations, the garbage collector's built-in intelligence will work just fine.*

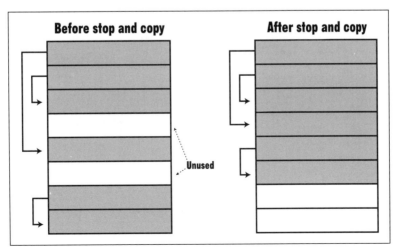

Figure 2.4 The stop-and-copy algorithm condenses memory blocks.

Learn More Java Now

The Native Code Interface

The Java class libraries are extensive and able to handle most programming chores. They offer everything from simple string manipulation to powerful multimedia command sets. But no matter how comprehensive the libraries are, they can't handle every situation. You may, for example, want to write a Java program that backs up your hard disk onto a tape drive. Or maybe you want your Java application to take advantage of the hardware acceleration features in the latest graphics cards.

These tasks are impossible in Java. Your code is limited to the capacity of the class libraries, and those libraries do not yet provide direct access to hardware. Your only recourse is the *native code interface*, which allows Java to call C or C++ code directly. In addition to solving the hardware-access problem, this interface also provides a means for using existing code in Java.

The native code interface is far from ideal. It completely ruins Java's greatest advantage—portability—and prevents your code from running within a Web browser (for security reasons). It also forces you to keep track of messy headers and to generate stub files.

An easier, safer, and more portable alternative is Microsoft's Component Object Model (COM). Just like the native code interface, COM allows you to access hardware directly and to call existing C and C++ code from within Java programs. You can even import code from Visual Basic, Delphi, and any other COM-compatible development tool. Unlike the native code interface, COM is completely compatible with Web browsers. See Chapter 7 to learn more about using COM with Java.

The <APPLET> tag

To enable a Web page for Java applets, you must first create an HTML file that contains the **<APPLET>** tag. This tag allows the Web browser to find, load, and display an applet. The format of the **<APPLET>** tag looks like this:

```
<APPLET
ALIGN=align-type
ALT=text
CODE=class-name
CODEBASE=url
```

```
HEIGHT=n
HSPACE=n
NAME=text
VSPACE=n
WIDTH=n>
<PARAM NAME=text VALUE="value">
<PARAM ... >
...
error-text
</APPLET>
```

The meaning of each line is as follows.

ALIGN sets the alignment for the applet. The *align-type* can be one of these values:

- **BASELINE**—The bottom of the applet aligns with the baseline of the surrounding text.

- **CENTER**—The applet is centered between the left and right margins; subsequent text starts on the next line after the applet.

- **LEFT**—The applet aligns with the left margin, and subsequent text wraps along the right side of the applet.

- **MIDDLE**—The middle of the applet aligns with the baseline of the surrounding text.

- **RIGHT**—The applet aligns with the right margin, and subsequent text wraps along the left side of the applet.

- **TEXTBOTTOM**—The bottom of the applet aligns with the bottom of the surrounding text.

- **TEXTMIDDLE**—The middle of the applet aligns with the midpoint between the baseline and the x-height of the surrounding text.

- **TEXTTOP**—The top of the applet aligns with the top of the surrounding text.

Some Web browsers, such as text-mode browsers, can recognize the <APPLET> tag, but are unable to display applets. These browsers will display the text following the **ALT** parameter in place of the applet.

CODE is the name of the file, such as **MyApplet.class**, that contains the Java applet's main class. This parameter is required.

The **CODEBASE** parameter contains a URL, such as **http://MyServer.com/MyDirectory/**, that tells the browser where to find the applet. You must use this parameter whenever your applet is not located in the same directory as your HTML file. The **CODEBASE** parameter is also useful for inserting public-domain applets from anywhere in the world. For instance, a Web surfer in Australia could view an HTML file in Germany that contains a Java applet from Japan.

HEIGHT specifies the suggested height for the applet. This parameter is required.

HSPACE specifies the horizontal gutter. This is the extra, empty space between the applet and any text or images to the left or right of the applet.

NAME sets the name of the applet. You can use this name in forms and scripts as a mnemonic reference to the applet.

VSPACE specifies the vertical gutter. This is the extra, empty space between the applet and any text or images above or below the applet.

WIDTH specifies the suggested width for the applet. This parameter is required.

The **<PARAM>** parameter allows you to set properties of the applet immediately after it is loaded. For example, if your applet displays the contents of a JPEG image, you could pass the name of the JPEG file to the applet via a **<PARAM>**. The applet tag would look something like this:

```
<APPLET
   CODE=My_JPEG_Viewer.class
   WIDTH=100
   HEIGHT=200>
   <PARAM NAME=JPEG_File_Name VALUE="My_JPEG_File.jpeg">
</APPLET>
```

Not all Web browsers can display Java applets. Incompatible browsers will instead display the *error-text* portion of the **<APPLET>** tag. This text can inform Web surfers that they won't be able to view the entire page and should upgrade to a Java-enabled browser.

Java On Windows

On December 7, 1995, Microsoft licensed Java from Sun Microsystems. This agreement allows Microsoft to sell Java development tools—such as Visual J++—and to provide Java applet support in their Internet Explorer Web browser. But the license also gives Microsoft an advantage that the industry press hasn't talked about much: permission to integrate Java with Windows.

Integration with Windows will jump-start Java faster than any browser ever could. When the language is a central part of the operating system, as it will be when Microsoft releases the "Nashville" update for Windows, Java will become universal (to the Windows universe, that is). Any program, even such traditional desktop applications as spreadsheets and word processors, will be able to incorporate Java code (see Figure 2.5). Furthermore, applets will no longer be restricted to Web browsers. The operating system will treat them as programs, and you'll even be able to convert them into true executable files (EXEs).

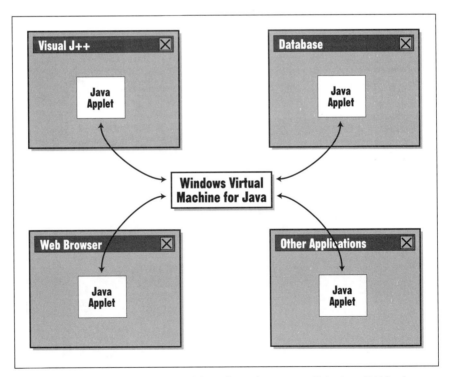

Figure 2.5 In the future, Java will be directly accessible to all Windows applications.

These capabilities, along with the Web browser support that exists today, will elevate the power of Java substantially. The language will become more ubiquitous than any other in history. (It could destroy Visual Basic; Microsoft may not realize that.)

The Windows VM Today

In the meantime, many of these features are already available through Microsoft's current support for Java. The Windows virtual machine, as it exists today, is accessible from most applications (but not directly through the operating system). Developers wanting to encapsulate Java in their programs must support the ActiveX architecture (see Chapter 4). This support is required because the Windows VM is actually just an ActiveX control which understands and executes Java code. It also provides a bridge between Java applets and ActiveX applications (see Figure 2.6).

Microsoft's VM also provides Java integration in the reverse direction—that is, your applets can talk to non-Java programs. This intriguing feature allows you to import code from third-party tools and incor-

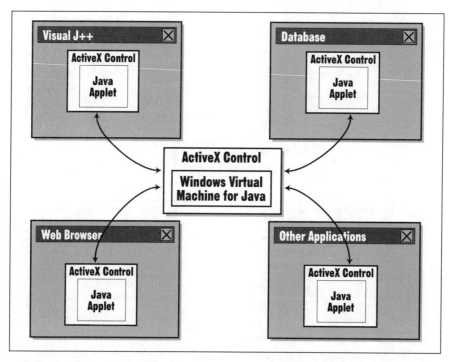

Figure 2.6 In the current Windows VM, Java is still accessible to all applications, as long as they support ActiveX controls.

porate them in your Java projects. These tools don't even have to be designed for Java; they just need to support the ActiveX controls architecture.

Taking advantage of ActiveX controls reduces the time and effort you spend on your Java projects. You can also step beyond Java's security and file-access restrictions (see Chapter 7). With the Windows VM, you can even convert your Java applets into ActiveX controls and use them in non-Java development tools such as Visual Basic (see Chapter 8). Figure 2.7 shows how you can start with a simple Java applet and end with powerful ActiveX control..

The Feature Set

Microsoft has stuffed the Windows VM with several tasty features:

- *High performance*—Microsoft's VM includes an optimized JIT compiler that provides fast execution of Java code. But Microsoft's JIT offers a unique feature: It's modular. Tool vendors can replace Microsoft's JIT with their own version. In most cases, however, this won't be necessary. Microsoft's JIT is plenty fast; it uses a special stack model and optimizes byte order within function calls for a speed increase of up to 4,000 percent.

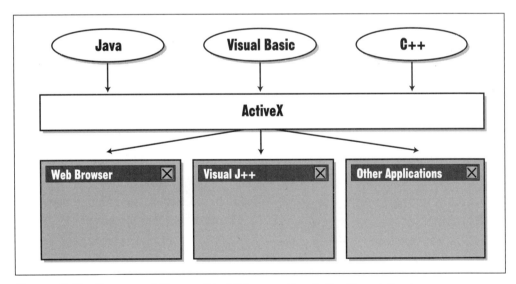

Figure 2.7 Because Microsoft's VM uses the ActiveX architecture, you can insert Java code—or code from Visual Basic, C++, and other languages—into Windows applications.

- *ActiveX integration*—Microsoft has combined the simplicity of Java with the strength of ActiveX. As a result, their Windows VM creates a development environment that is more powerful than either technology alone.

- *Multimedia features*—Because the ActiveX architecture provides such multimedia enhancements as full-screen video, your Java applets can offer multimedia features, too. You even have direct access (that is, directly through the ActiveX layer) of advanced hardware features, such as 3D video.

- *Distributed network support*—Microsoft recently put the code freeze on the Distributed COM protocol, or DCOM (see Chapter 11). Since DCOM is available to ActiveX controls, the protocol is also accessible from Java. It allows you to divide your code into multiple parts and run them on separate computer systems for increased speed.

The strength of these features prompted Sun Microsystems to license Microsoft's VM as a reference implementation for Java on Windows.

Advanced Graphics

Programming in Java can be like the smell of cold corn pone on a warm summer day—refreshing, relaxing, and relieving. Sometimes, though, your Java code could use a little sweetening. Handling graphics, for instance, can be tedious and cumbersome. This section presents three graphics tricks that will make your programming tasks a little easier to swallow.

Double-buffering

Despite JIT compilers and other optimizations, Java code can run slowly, especially when drawing to the screen. A technique known as *double-buffering* can make your graphics operations seem faster than they really are.

Double-buffering combines all graphics calls into a single line of code. The trick is to create an invisible, off-screen **Graphics** object that exists only in memory. Then, rather than draw directly to the screen, you send all graphics calls to the off-screen object. When you're done, you can blast the entire image to the screen, creating the illusion of faster graphics even though the painting process is actually a few hundred milliseconds slower.

Double-buffering also eliminates flicker when painting to the applet window. For example, if you draw a square and then immediately draw an overlapping circle, you'll see the entire square before the circle covers it up a split-second later. This split-second delay creates an annoying flicker that you can prevent through double-buffering.

Figure 2.8 illustrates the basic steps in the double-buffering process. In Step 1, the square is drawn to the off-screen image while the physical screen remains blank. In Step 2, the circle is drawn, and the applet window is still empty. (Note that without double-buffering, the drawing is already complete at this point.) And in Step 3, the shapes are transferred to the screen in a single step, giving the illusion of faster graphics while also preventing flicker.

By adding just a few lines of code to the **paint**() function, you can incorporate double-buffering in your Java applets. An example is given

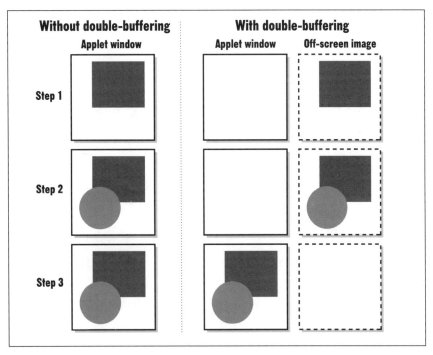

Figure 2.8 Double-buffering prevents flickering and gives the illusion of faster graphics.

in Listing 2.1. (For an increase in speed, you should move the buffer creation out of the **paint**() function and into your applet's **init**() function, as demonstrated in the Magnifying Glass example in Chapter 3.)

LISTING 2.1 A PAINT() FUNCTION ENABLED FOR DOUBLE-BUFFERING.

```
public void paint(Graphics g)
{
   Dimension d = size();   // Get the size of the window

   // Create the buffer...
   Image imgBuffer = createImage(d.width, d.height);
   Graphics gcBuffer = imgBuffer.getGraphics();

   // Draw to the buffer instead of the actual screen.
   // This is simply a matter of replacing all instances
   // of "g" with "gcBuffer".
   gcBuffer.setColor(Color.red);
   gcBuffer.fillRect(d.width / 3,
                     10,
                     d.width * 2 / 3 - 10,
                     d.height * 2 / 3);
   gcBuffer.setColor(Color.blue);
   gcBuffer.fillOval(10,
                     d.height / 3,
                     d.width * 2 / 3 - 10,
                     d.height * 2 / 3 - 10);

   // Now, blast the buffer onto the screen.
   // Notice that this line is the only physical drawing
   // operation.
   g.drawImage(imgBuffer, 0, 0, this);
}
```

Palette-based Images

In Java, graphics images come in two flavors (see Figure 2.9):

- *True-color*—These images, also called RGB images, can contain up to 16.7 million unique colors. Each pixel in the image is mapped to a 32-bit integer that contains the red, blue, green, and alpha (amount of blend with the background color) components.

- *Palette-based*—True-color images are slow and require large amounts of memory. As an alternative, Java offers palette-based

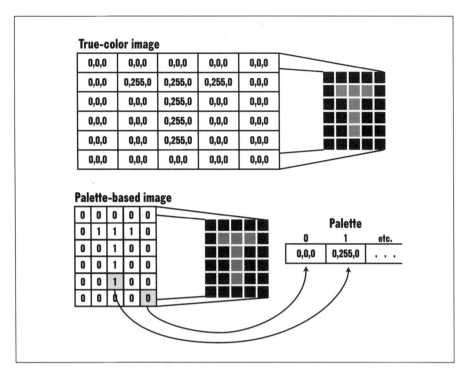

Figure 2.9 The structure of Java images.

images, also known as Index images, which contain 8-bit bytes instead of integers. Each byte is an index into the palette.

Palette-based images are important because they allow you to manipulate pixels quickly. As a simple example, let's say you wanted to change every red pixel in an image to green. With true-color images, this hypothetical algorithm would require iterating through each pixel, checking to see if it's red, and, if so, changing it to green. With palette-based images, you could simply find the red pixel in the palette, change it to green, and save a magnitude of time.

Despite these advantages, Java has an apparent bias against palette-based images. Images loaded with the **getImage()** function are automatically converted to true-color, even if the original file contains a palette. I've checked the documentation, the FAQs, and the forums looking for a way around this problem. I've also left messages on CompuServe in the hope that some Java guru would know how to retain an image's palette. No dice.

Ultimately, I decided the only way around the problem was to solve it myself. I wasn't allowed to change the **getImage()** function, of course, so I had to write an algorithm that re-creates the palette from scratch. It uses a simplistic brute-force technique that constructs a palette from the true-color image's data. It's terribly slow, but it's certainly better than nothing.

The key to this algorithm is a Java class called **IndexColorModel**. It specifies how the pixels in the image correspond to a table of colors. In other words, this class is essentially the image's palette. The algorithm creates an instance of **IndexColorModel**, filling it with the proper palette information, and then passes it to the **createImage**() function. The return value of this function is a palette-based image that replaces the original true-color version.

Listing 2.2 contains the code listing for my palette-creation algorithm. Note: Before applying this code to an image, you must ensure that it contains 256 colors or fewer. (GIF images contain a maximum of 256 colors, so you're always safe with them.)

LISTING 2.2 A BRUTE-FORCE ALGORITHM FOR LOADING PALETTE-BASED IMAGES.

```
import java.awt.image.*;

void getIndexColorData(Image img, byte[] byPixels, byte[]
   byReds, byte[] byGreens, byte[] byBlues)
{
   int nWidth         = img.getWidth(this);
   int nHeight        = img.getHeight(this);
   int nPaletteIndex  = 0;
   int[] nPixels      = new int[nWidth * nHeight];
   int[] nPalette     = new int[256];

   // The PixelGrabber transfers pixel data from the image to
   // an array.
   PixelGrabber pg    = new PixelGrabber(img, 0, 0, nWidth,
   nHeight, nPixels, 0, nWidth);

   try
   {
      pg.grabPixels();
   }
   catch (InterruptedException e)
   {
      // Handle the exception...
   }
```

```java
// Loop through each pixel in the image...
for (int y = 0; y < nHeight; y++)
{
   // Tell the user why it's taking so long...
   showStatus("Converting image (" + (y + 1) + "/" + nHeight
      + "). Please wait...");

   for (int x = 0; x < nWidth; x++)
   {
      int nIndex = -1;

      // Search for the palette index of the current pixel's
      // color...
      for (int i = 0; i <= nPaletteIndex; i++)
      {
         if ( nPalette[i] == nPixels[y * nWidth + x] )
         {
            nIndex = i;
            break;
         }
      }

      // If the current pixel's color is not in the palette,
      // add it to the palette.
      if ( nIndex == -1 )
      {
         nPalette[nPaletteIndex] = nPixels[y * nWidth + x];
         nIndex = nPaletteIndex;
         nPaletteIndex++;
      }

      // Change the pixel from a color value to an index
      // value.
      byPixels[y * nWidth + x] = (byte) nIndex;
   }
}

for (int i = 0; i < 256; i++)
{
   int r = (nPalette[i] >> 16) & 0xff;
   int g = (nPalette[i] >> 8 ) & 0xff;
   int b = (nPalette[i]      ) & 0xff;

   byReds[i]   = (byte)r;
   byGreens[i] = (byte)g;
   byBlues[i]  = (byte)b;
}
}
```

```
// Load the image from disk.
Image image = getImage(getDocumentBase(), "MyImage.gif");

// Wait for the image to be read...
MediaTracker tracker = new MediaTracker(this);
tracker.addImage(image, 0);

try
{
   tracker.waitForAll();
}
catch (InterruptedException e)
{
   // Handle the exception...
}

// Obtain the dimensions of the image...
int nWidth = image.getWidth(this);
int nHeight = image.getHeight(this);

// Allocate palette data...
byte[] byReds = new byte[256];
byte[] byGreens = new byte[256];
byte[] byBlues = new byte[256];

// Allocate pixel data...
byte[] byPixels = new byte[nWidth * nHeight];

// Get the palette data from the true-color image.
getIndexColorData(image, byPixels, byReds, byGreens, byBlues);

// Create the palette from the data.
IndexColorModel cmPalette = new IndexColorModel(8, 256, byReds,
byGreens, byBlues);

// Finally, create the palette-based image.
image = createImage( new MemoryImageSource(nWidth,
                                           nHeight,
                                           cmPalette,
                                           byPixels,
                                           0,
                                           nWidth) );
```

Direct Image Manipulation

Once you've converted an image from true-color to palette-based, you'll have a much easier time manipulating it. You can, as I mentioned earlier, change colors in its palette. You can also alter the image's pixel data directly.

Listing 2.3 illustrates direct image manipulation. It assumes that the code in Listing 2.2 from the previous section has already been run, which means that the **byPixels** array contains the pixel data and that the **byReds**, **byBlues**, and **byGreens** arrays contain the palette information. The code runs through a simple algorithm that draws the letter *T* in the image and changes all of its colors to a shade of blue. It then re-creates the altered image, which can later be drawn to the screen. Figure 2.10 provides a comparison between the original bitmap and its appearance after direct manipulation.

LISTING 2.3 DIRECT IMAGE MANIPULATION USING PALETTES.

```
// Draw the letter "T" directly into the image....

for (int x = 0; x < nWidth; x++)
{
   for (int y = 0; y < 5; y++)
   {
      byPixels[y * nWidth + x] = 0;
   }
}

for (int x = m_nWidth / 2 - 5; x < m_nWidth / 2 + 5; x++)
{
   for (int y = 0; y < m_nHeight; y++)
   {
      byPixels[y * m_nWidth + x] = 0;
   }
}

// Give the image a blue hue. To do this, simply set to
// zero the values of each red and green entry in
// the palette. Assume that the image contains 256 colors.
for (int i = 0; i < 256; i++)
{
   byReds[i] = 0;
   byGreens[i] = 0;
}

// Now, re-create the image using the new pixel and palette
// arrays...

cmPalette = new IndexColorModel(8, 256, byReds, byGreens,
byBlues);
```

Learn More Java Now

```
image = createImage( new MemoryImageSource(nWidth,
                                           nHeight,
                                           cmPalette,
                                           byPixels,
                                           0,
                                           nWidth) );
```

News You Can Use

*Internet newsgroups are a great place to get help with writing Java code. The most popular group is **comp.lang.java**, where you'll consistently find several dozen topics on all aspects of Java programming.*

*You should also take a look at Microsoft's public server at **msnews.microsoft.com**. It offers several Java newsgroups, including **microsoft.public.internetexplorer.java** and the **microsoft.public.visualj.*** groups. Microsoft's official statement says that this server is for peer-to-peer support, but you'll find a Microsoftie or two helping out every once in a while.*

Continuing On

For more Java tips and techniques, point your browser to Gamelan, a directory created by EarthWeb, LLC. of more than 3,000 cool applets (see Figure 2.11). This Web site includes some helpful Java source code

Figure 2.10 The before and after shots of an image going through direct manipulation.

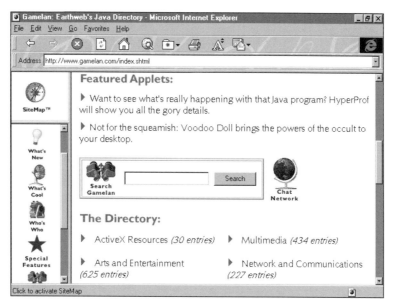

Figure 2.11 Gamelan (pronounced *GAM-uh-lahn*) is an excellent resource for Java programmers.

as well as information on JavaScript and ActiveX. You can find it at **www.gamelan.com**.

Now that you've got a perspective on Java and a few graphics tricks up your sleeve, it's time to apply the skills you've learned. Turn to the next chapter to discover the inner workings of Microsoft's first Java development tool: Visual J++. You'll also find a comparison of Visual J++ with its competitors, along with a couple of sample applets to get you started.

Chapter 3

- **Visual J++ highlights**
- **Building Java projects**
- **Importing resources**
- **Debugging**
- **Visual J++ sample code**

Visual J++

Through all my years of school, I played hooky just once. Three of my best friends desperately wanted to see their first R-rated movie, so, of course, I had to go along. We rode our BMX bikes to the dollar theater one Friday afternoon, and each of us bought a ticket. To avoid suspicion, we asked to see *Star Wars: Return of the Jedi* instead of the verboten film.

Once inside, we casually took our seats in the back row of the *Star Wars* theater. Then, as soon as the coast was clear, we sneaked next door into our first taste of adult entertainment: a mushy movie with a lot of talking and kissing. I got bored real fast.

"Uh, guys," I whispered. "I'm gonna get some popcorn." I tiptoed out to the lobby, but instead of heading to the snack bar, I wandered back to the screen showing *Star Wars*. I knew my friends would laugh if they caught me, so I slouched down as low as I could get in the middle of the third row.

Up on the screen, a big brown blob was laughing at a mysterious figure. "Young Skywalker," grumbled the blob. "Jedi tricks won't work on me. Your powers are useless." I smiled to myself and, cloaked in the safety of darkness, prepared to enjoy an awesome movie.

Today, I'm watching *Star Wars* all over again. This time, Microsoft is the Jedi Knight battling a different sort of enemy: Java the Hut. Java has the strength to cripple the Jedi Knight and render its magical powers—the Windows operating system—useless.

Microsoft, even with help from the Force, can't overpower Java the Hut. Their only recourse has been to join forces with Java's creators, Sun Microsystems, and embrace the language, truly fulfilling the age-old cliché, "If you can't beat 'em, join 'em." Not only has Microsoft licensed Java for Internet Explorer, but they've also created a top-notch Java development environment called Visual J++.

Visual J++ Profile

In the first year of Java's existence, development tools consisted of nothing more than graphical front ends (see Figure 3.1). These applications were simple shells that encapsulated Java's command-line compiler and debugger. As Java became staggeringly popular, programmers grew desperate for better tools. They wanted heavy-duty debuggers and assistance with handling Java's 150-plus classes.

Microsoft heard the call for help (and the eventual ringing of cash registers) and created Visual J++. This chapter takes you on a tour of Microsoft's Java development environment and shows how it can create powerful applications for intranets and the World Wide Web.

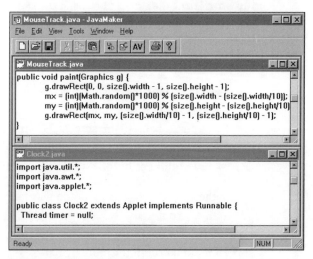

Figure 3.1 JavaMaker by Heechang Choi was a popular front end during Java's early existence.

Highlights

Visual J++ offers a number of handy features and several improvements over the typical Java front end. Here are the highlights:

- *Fully Java-compatible*—Anything you can do with Java, you can do with Visual J++. It's fully compatible with the Java standard, and the class files it produces can run on any Java-compatible platform. (Visual J++ itself runs only under Windows, however.)

- *Intuitive interface*—Visual J++ combines the edit-build-debug cycle into a single environment (see Figure 3.2). Everything you need to create Java applications is available from one intuitive interface, so you never have to switch to the command line. Plus, if you're familiar with other Microsoft development tools (such as Visual C++), you can easily learn Visual J++, because they all share a standard interface.

- *Wizards*—Wizards transform complex tasks into automated, step-by-step guides. Visual J++ includes three wizards: the Java Applet Wizard for creating project skeletons, the Java Resource Wizard

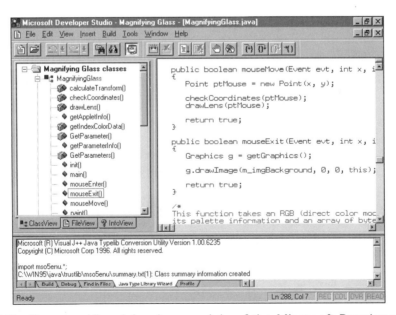

Figure 3.2 Because Visual J++ is a module of the Microsoft Developer Studio, it provides an easy-to-use interface.

for importing resource templates, and the Java Type Library Wizard for importing ActiveX controls.

- *Fast compiler*—Visual J++ compiles Java source code at lightning speed (more than 1 million lines per minute, according to Microsoft), so you can spend more time creating and less time waiting. The compiler also optimizes your code for faster execution without sacrificing cross-platform compatibility.

- *Visual debugger*—Microsoft has built one of the first visual debuggers for Java and integrated it into Visual J++. The debugger gives you multiple windows for viewing watches, bytecodes, and the call stack. It can also set breakpoints, manage threads, and handle exceptions.

further developments

JIT Happens

Most reviews and press releases on Visual J++ refer to Microsoft's Just-in-Time compiler as if it were a part of the product. It's not. The Microsoft JIT is a separate entity that ships with Internet Explorer; it allows Java applets and applications—whether compiled by Visual J++ or any other tool—to run significantly faster. So, although the JIT compiler is an important Java component, it is not a part of Visual J++.

ActiveX Integration

Currently, Visual J++ is the only Java tool that offers ActiveX support. (See Chapter 4 for an overview of ActiveX technologies.) This support allows you to do the following:

- *Import commercial code*—With ActiveX, you don't have to write all of your code from scratch. You can buy ActiveX controls from third-party companies and import their code directly into your Java projects.

- *Retain investments in legacy code*—Many companies have poured thousands of dollars into C++, Visual Basic, and OLE projects. They can't afford to convert all of their code to Java. With the ActiveX support in Visual J++, these companies can retain their previous investments by hooking external code into Java applications.

- *Expand Java functionality*—ActiveX controls offer advanced functions, such as the ability to play videos and compressed audio files. With ActiveX integration, you can include these functions in your Visual J++ projects by adding a single line of code (see Chapter 7).

- *Access databases*—ActiveX can link Java code to a database, including remote databases anywhere on the Internet. See Chapter 11 to learn how.

- *Automate applications*—Certain end-user software, such as the desktop applications in Microsoft Office, can be automated and controlled through Java programs. See Chapter 10 for more information.

Missing Features

A popular adage in the software industry is: "Microsoft never finishes a product until Version 3.0." Witness Microsoft's success with Windows and Excel. Both products were failures until each had gone through two major overhauls.

Unfortunately for users of Visual J++, Microsoft seems to be following tradition. Don't expect to see a killer Java development environment until Microsoft brings us Version 3.0 of this product. The current release is missing several important features, such as:

- *Full ActiveX support*—Visual J++ provides limited support for ActiveX controls. You can't incorporate visual controls into your Java projects (unless you use HTML scripts—see Chapter 9), and you can neither fire nor catch ActiveX events. These restrictions also apply to the ActiveX controls you create with Visual J++. As a result, most commercial ActiveX controls are off-limits in Visual J++. Other development tools, such as Visual C++ and Visual Basic, offer much better integration with ActiveX.

- *JDBC support*—JDBC stands for Java Database Connectivity. It's a protocol and set of drivers that allow Java code to access any database, regardless of the vendor. Visual J++ includes no built-in support for JDBC; it relies instead on ODBC (Microsoft's Open Database Connectivity protocol) and the Database Access Objects, or DAO (see Chapter 11). JDBC was brand new when Visual J++ was in its final stages, so this lack of support is forgivable. Still, Microsoft naturally wants to limit developers to the company's own database standards and may never officially acknowledge JDBC.

- *ClassWizard*—Visual C++ includes an excellent time-saver called the ClassWizard. This tool allows you to add, modify, and delete code with the click of a button. It also shields you from such complicated tasks as adding ActiveX interfaces to C++ projects. Although a Java version of the ClassWizard was expected for the first release of Visual J++, it won't be available until the next major revision.

- *Component Gallery*—In Visual C++, the Component Gallery is a storehouse for ActiveX controls and C++ classes. You can insert this code into a project simply by double-clicking its icon. Surprisingly, Visual J++ omits support for this valuable feature.

- *Integrated resource editor*—Adding dialog box and menu resources to a Visual J++ project is needlessly complex. You must first create the resource using the Visual J++ resource editor, save the file as a resource template, and then import this template into your project. Java development tools, such as Borland Latté and Symantec Visual Café (see the section on competitors near the end of this chapter), offer much better support for integrating resources with Java code.

The Grand Tour

Let me take you on a tour of Visual J++ and each of its three main rooms: Project Workspace, Text Editor, and Output Window. Afterward, we'll peek into the garage where we keep the tools.

Project Workspace

To begin the tour, open any Visual J++ workspace by selecting File|Open Workspace. The Project Workspace is home base for all of your Java projects. You can display it by pressing Alt+0, and you can hide it by right-clicking on the workspace and selecting Hide. It contains three tabs: ClassView, FileView, and InfoView.

CLASSVIEW

The ClassView tab provides a hierarchical list of all classes in your project (see Figure 3.3). Because the list shows logical, not physical, relationships, each class is listed separately—even if it resides in the same file as another class.

You can view the members of a class by clicking the + symbol on its left-hand side (or by highlighting the class and pressing the Right Arrow key). Next to each member is an icon that indicates its type. Table 3.1 explains the meaning of each.

CLASSVIEW'S CONTEXT MENU

With ClassView, you can quickly add functions or variables, create new classes, and set breakpoints. Simply right-click on an item in the list, then choose the proper option from the menu.

Table 3.1 ClassView icons.

Icon	Meaning
	A class header.
	A function accessible from any class in any package (declared as public).
	A function accessible from its own class, its subclasses, or classes in the same package (declared without any modifiers).
	A function accessible from its own class or its subclasses (declared as protected).
	A function accessible only from its own class (declared as private).
	A variable accessible from any class in any package (declared as public).
	A variable accessible from its own class, its subclasses, or classes in the same package (declared without any modifiers).
	A variable accessible from its own class or its subclasses (declared as protected).
	A variable accessible only from its own class (declared as private).

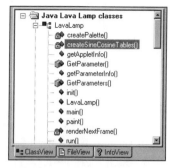

Figure 3.3 The ClassView tab shows all of the classes in your project.

FILEVIEW

The FileView tab lists the Java source code attached to your project (see Figure 3.4). It may also include an HTML source file for testing purposes.

You can add files to the FileView list by choosing Insert|Files into Project. To remove them, select a file and press the Delete key.

INFOVIEW

The InfoView tab displays the contents of the current information title (see Figure 3.5). For Visual J++, the default title is the Visual J++ Books Online.

You can browse InfoView's hierarchical list of help topics in the same manner as ClassView. When you find a topic you wish to view, double-click it (or select it and press Enter). To search for a specific topic or keyword, choose Search from the Visual J++ Help menu.

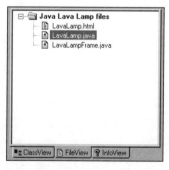

Figure 3.4 The FileView pane shows all of the files in your project.

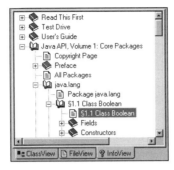

Figure 3.5 The InfoView pane displays the Visual J++ online help.

JUMPING TO HIGHLIGHTS

Searching for keywords in Visual J++'s online help can sometimes be difficult. Although InfoViewer will find topics containing a keyword, it won't show you where that word lies in the text—but only by default. InfoViewer can find the keyword for you if you select the Jump to first highlight box in the InfoViewer tab of Tools|Options.

For more tips on searching Visual J++'s online help, read the Chapter 5 sidebar regarding InfoViewer.

Text Editor

The Text Editor appears (by default) to the right of the Project Workspace. It allows you to create, edit, and print Java source code (see Figure 3.6). You can customize the editor by selecting Tools|Options and viewing the Editor, Tabs, Compatibility, and Format tabs. For example, simplify source code editing by going to the Compatibility tab and checking the Enable virtual space box.

Figure 3.6 The Text Editor highlights source code according to its syntax.

Visual J++ **55**

By right-clicking in the Text Editor, you can access the clipboard, enable breakpoints, and open files. Right-clicking on an import statement, for instance, allows you to open a package's source file.

INDENTING BLOCKS OF CODE

Like most word processors, the Visual J++ Text Editor can change the indentation level of multiple lines. This feature comes in handy when you add, rearrange, or delete blocks of code. First, use the mouse (or hold down the Shift key) to select the lines you want to change. Then, press Tab to move all lines right or Shift+Tab to move them all left.

For more tips on the Microsoft Developer Studio interface, see Chapter 5.

Output Window

The Output Window shows the results of most Visual J++ actions, such as building source code, debugging a project, and finding files (see Figure 3.7). You can view it by pressing Alt+2 or hide it by right-clicking anywhere on the window and selecting Hide.

The Output Window can also display the console of external applications, as explained in the following section.

QUICK HELP FOR COMPILE ERRORS

After building a source-code file, you may run into an error that you don't understand. If so, Visual J++ can quickly give you help directly from the Output Window. Just click on the error number (such as "J0012") and press F1.

Tools

Visual J++ offers several methods for customizing your environment. You can change the layout and appearance of windows from the

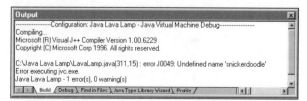

Figure 3.7 The Output Window shows the results of most Visual J++ actions.

Tools|Options dialog box, and you can configure toolbars and shortcut keys by selecting Tools|Customize. The Customize dialog box also contains a tab for adding external applications to the Tools menu.

EXTERNAL TOOLS

When Visual J++ installs itself, it adds several items to its Tools menu, such as the Resource Wizard and Type Library Wizard. You can add your own tools to this menu by opening the Customize dialog box and switching to the Tools tab (see Figure 3.8).

If you add a DOS-based program to the Tools menu, Visual J++ will automatically detect it and enable the Redirect to Output Window box. Checking this box creates a separate tab in the Output Window that displays the results of running your program. If you leave this box unchecked, Visual J++ will run the program in its own console window.

KEEP YOUR TOOLBOX TIDY

If Visual J++ and Visual C++ are both installed on your system, the Tools menu will contain several utilities from each program. Because it's not always clear which item belongs to which program, you could accidentally run the wrong utility. To fix this problem, you can separate the menu items into two distinct sections. Go to the Tools tab in Tools|Customize and arrange the items using the Move Up and Move Down

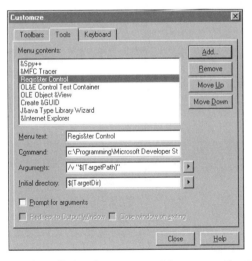

Figure 3.8 The Customize dialog box can add any application to the Tools menu.

Visual J++ **57**

buttons, segregating the Java programs from the C++ programs. You may also want to divide the sections by adding a dummy menu item between them, containing the string "————".

MACROS

The Tools menu includes another convenient feature called Record Keystrokes. As the name implies, it allows you to store a sequence of key presses and play them back. It's not a full-fledged macro utility, and it can hold only one set of keystrokes at a time. But it's still useful and can save you countless minutes. To record a key sequence, position the cursor in the Text Editor and select Tools|Record Keystrokes. A toolbar will appear, allowing you to stop or pause the recording. Click the Stop button when you're finished typing, then press Ctrl+Shift+Q to repeat the keystroke sequence you just recorded.

Starting From Scratch

Now that you're familiar with the Visual J++ environment, you're ready to build a Java application. You have three options for completing this task:

- Create an empty project.

- Import code from an outside project.

- Let the Visual J++ Applet Wizard create the foundation of a project for you.

Creating A Java Workspace

To create a new, empty project, select File|New, click the Project Workspace item, and then click the OK button. Visual J++ will present a dialog box with an icon labeled "Java Workspace" (see Figure 3.9). Make sure this icon is highlighted, then type a name for the project and select its location. Notice that Visual J++ appends the project name to the directory location as you type.

After you click the Create button, Visual J++ builds the empty project, saves it to disk, and brings up the Project Workspace. You may then add code to the project by selecting Insert|New Java Class (see Figure 3.10).

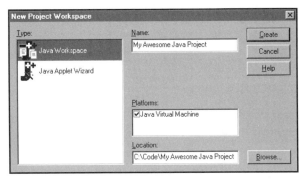

Figure 3.9 You can create Visual J++ projects with the New Project Workspace dialog box.

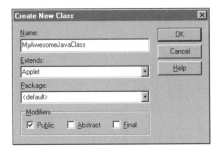

Figure 3.10 The Create New Class dialog box inserts class headers into your project.

If you would rather add code manually, click the New Source File button in the Standard toolbar. This button places a new document in the Visual J++ Text Editor. After typing code in the document, save it as a file, then insert the file into your workspace by selecting Insert|Files into Project.

Importing A Java Workspace

Occasionally, you may want to import code from previous projects into Visual J++, or you may want to transfer projects from another company's Java development tool to Microsoft's. Visual J++ makes short work of either scenario. For instance, if the code lies in a single Java file, you don't even need to create a new workspace. Just open the file and press F7. Visual J++ will create a default project workspace for you and build it immediately.

Importing multiple files is almost as easy. For example, to transfer a project from Symantec Visual Café to Microsoft Visual J++, follow these steps:

1. Create a new project workspace by selecting File|New and choosing the Project Workspace item.

2. Select Insert|Files into Project.

3. Locate the directory containing the Visual Café source files (*.java).

4. Select the files you wish to add by clicking on them while holding down the Ctrl key. You can also select them with the Arrow keys while holding down the Shift key.

5. Click the OK button. Visual J++ will add the files to your project and update ClassView with the new data.

> **TRANSLATING WINDOWS FONTS**
>
> *Creating fonts in Java requires a **Font** object, whose constructor takes the name of the font you wish to create. Even if your Java programs are running under Windows, passing a Windows-style font name won't work. For instance, instead of Arial, you should use Helvetica; TimesRoman instead of Times New Roman; and Courier instead of Courier New. The following code will obtain the names of the remaining fonts:*
>
> ```
> String[] fonts = getToolkit().getFontList();
> ```

The Java Applet Wizard

All Java programs require the same basic framework: either a class derived from **Applet** or an entry function called **main()**. Adding this foundation to every new program can become tedious. For relief, Visual J++ offers a tool called the Java Applet Wizard. It asks you a few simple questions, then generates a complete Java program in seconds.

STEP 1

To start the Applet Wizard, select File|New and create a new project workspace. Type the name and location of the new project, then select the Java Applet Wizard icon. After you click OK, the dialog box shown in Figure 3.11 appears.

By default, the Applet Wizard creates a program that runs only on the Web. It can't access files or run outside of a Web browser. To change this setting, select the As an applet and as an application checkbox. Applet Wizard will attach a special **Frame**-derived class to your

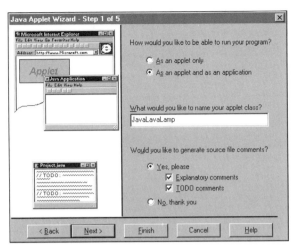

Figure 3.11 In Step 1 of the Applet Wizard you can configure source file comments.

program, allowing it to run as either an applet or a standalone application automatically.

The Applet Wizard can insert comments into the code it builds. These comments may include explanatory hints, such as what your **init()** function should contain, or TODO statements that remind you where to add some muscle to the skeleton program. To insert these comments, simply leave the Step 1 settings as they stand.

STEP 2

In Step 2 (see Figure 3.12), the Applet Wizard asks to generate a sample HTML file for testing your program. It also verifies that the applet window's default height and width (320×240) are acceptable. If you change these dimensions later, be sure to update them in the sample HTML file as well as in the source code.

STEP 3

In the next step (see Figure 3.13), you can decide whether your applet should contain threads, allowing it to perform multiple tasks concurrently. Think very carefully about your selection. Retrofitting an applet for threads can be time-consuming.

If you spring for multithreading, you must also decide whether the Applet Wizard should add simple animation to the skeleton project. Enable this option only if your program will display continuous animation from start to finish.

Visual J++ **61**

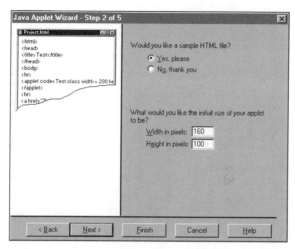

Figure 3.12 In Step 2 of the Applet Wizard you can change the initial size of applet window.

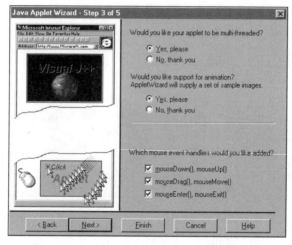

Figure 3.13 In Step 3 of the Applet Wizard you add multithreading support to your program.

In the final section of Step 3, you can add mouse support to your program. Don't worry too much about your choices. Adding mouse support later on is a simple matter of adding a new mouse function, such as **mouseDown()**.

REMEMBER MEMBER MNEMONICS

When the Applet Wizard creates a code skeleton, it begins each variable name with "m_", which stands for member. You should follow this same convention in your own code because it allows you to recognize member variables instantly.

62 *Chapter 3*

> *It also simplifies set functions, as in the following code:*
>
> ```
> public void setPoint(int x, int y)
> { m_x = x;  m_y = y; }
> ```
>
> *Without the "m_" prefix, you would have to use more complicated parameter names, such as "nInitX". This deceptively simple convention saves time in the long run.*

STEP 4

In Step 4 you can add parameters to your program (see Figure 3.14). These parameters are specified in the **<APPLET>** tag for applets and on the command line for applications.

The first column in Step 4 contains the external name of each parameter. It is used by the **getParameter()** function to obtain a parameter's value. The second and third columns contain the internal name and data type of the parameters. Your source code will use these names directly. The Def-Value column contains the initial value of the parameters; these will be used if a value is not specified in the **<APPLET>** tag or the command line. The last column contains a description of the parameter, returned by the **getParameterInfo()** function.

STEP 5

In the Applet Wizard's final step (see Figure 3.15), you can take credit for your work. The applet name and your name are already there, but you

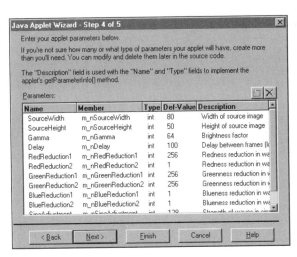

Figure 3.14 In Step 4 of the Applet Wizard you can enter applet parameters.

Visual J++   **63**

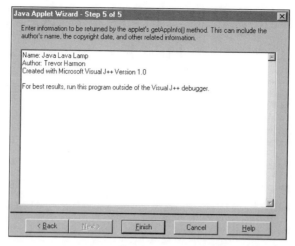

Figure 3.15 In Step 5 of the Applet Wizard you can enter applet information, such as the author name and copyright date.

should type extra information, such as the copyright date and notes on running the applet. This text is returned by the **getAppletInfo()** function.

Where Did All These Files Come From?

Visual J++ requires several intermediate files to keep track of your projects. Some are created by the Applet Wizard; others are created when you build the source code. The following list provides a brief explanation of each type of file:

- *Class*—Java Class file. Created when a Java source-code file is compiled.

- *Dep*—Dependency information. Contains the names of files imported by a source-code file.

- *HTML*—Hypertext Markup Language. Serves as a test page for applets.

- *Java*—Java source-code file. The source code that will be compiled into bytecode.

- *Mak*—Makefile. An ASCII file containing project information, such as the names of source files. Used for command-line utilities and third-party applications. Also serves as a backup for MDP files.

- *MDP*—Microsoft Developer Studio project workspace. A binary makefile used only by Visual J++.

- *NCB*—No-compile browser information. A cache for holding class information displayed by ClassView.

Build Settings

Before running any Java project, you should double-check its build settings. These settings tell Visual J++ how to compile and start your program. To change a setting, open a project and select Build|Settings. Visual J++ will present a dialog box containing three tabs: General, Debug, and Java.

General Tab

The General tab configures only two build options (see Figure 3.16). The first setting specifies additional directories that contain class files required for compiling your project. Visual J++ will search these directories only after searching the directories listed in the Directories tab of Tools|Options. Therefore, you rarely need to change this setting.

The second setting tells Visual J++ where to place the class files it creates. The directory in this setting overrides the default output directory, which is simply the location of the main project.

The General tab also furnishes a file-specific setting that appears only if you select files (instead of projects) from the list at the left of the Project Settings dialog box. This checkbox option, called Exclude File From Build, prevents Visual J++ from compiling the selected files.

Debug Tab

The Debug tab has four separate sections. You can move from one to another by clicking on the Category list box. The first section, General,

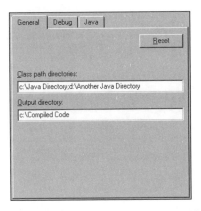

Figure 3.16 The General tab configures project-specific directory settings.

defines the Java class to debug. If you leave this setting blank, Visual J++ will prompt you for a class each time you begin a debugging session.

The General section also tells Visual J++ whether to run your program as a browser-hosted applet or as a standalone application. To switch between these two options, just click on the appropriate radio button.

The next two sections in the Debug tab are called Browser and Standalone Interpreter. They allow you to specify the Web browser and Java interpreter that will run your program. They can also specify runtime parameters for each environment (see Figure 3.17).

The final section in the Debug tab displays a list called Additional Classes. If you want to debug Java classes that are not part of your project, add them to this list. (Note: Visual J++ enables the Additional Classes list only when you select a *single* project from the Settings For list.)

Java Tab

The Java tab configures how Visual J++ will compile your source code (see Figure 3.18). Use this tab to change the number of warnings you receive. For example, setting the warning level to 1 will allow only the most severe warnings to appear, while setting it to 4 will enable all possible warnings.

You can also use the Java tab to define the format of class files. You can enable the Generate Debug info box, for instance, to create class files that contain line numbers and internal variable names. Enabling the Full Optimization box will rearrange Java bytecodes to increase their

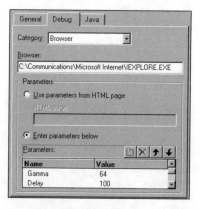

Figure 3.17 The Debug tab specifies runtime parameters for the Java interpreter and the Web browser.

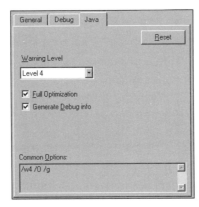

Figure 3.18 The Java tab changes options in the Visual J++ compiler.

execution speed. (Note: To maintain cross-platform compatibility, the full optimization in Visual J++ has little effect.)

LEVEL-HEADED ADVICE ON WARNING LEVELS

The warning levels in Visual J++ are mostly bogus. They're holdovers from Visual C++, which demands precise control over the large number of C++ warnings. In Java, however, warnings are scarce. Most ambiguous and potentially dangerous code generates errors instead of warnings. As a result, increasing or decreasing the Visual J++ warning level makes almost no difference.

I recommend setting the warning level to 4 for all projects. Even at this strict setting, you will see relatively few warnings, and those you do see will be helpful. For example, level 4 will catch such mistakes as defining, but never using, local variables. (Note: In Visual C++, warning level 4 will flag unused function parameters, but in Visual J++ this possible problem is always ignored.)

Resource Wizardry

Although Visual J++ contains an excellent editor for creating dialog-box and menu resources, the integration of this editor with Java is poor. This section explains how to use the Resource Editor and the Resource Wizard, and how to avoid their annoying nuances.

Creating Resources

Microsoft Developer Studio's Resource Editor is one of the best in the industry. It is both powerful and easy to use, providing functions for adding and maintaining all nine types of Windows resources. Unfortunately, the Java version of the Resource Editor supports only dialog boxes, menus, and images.

To create one of these resources, open your project and select Insert|Resource. (You may also create resources by selecting File|New and double-clicking the Resource Template item.) Visual J++ will display a dialog box allowing you to choose the type of resource. Several types will appear (see Figure 3.19), but only three of them are valid for Java projects: Dialog, Menu, and Bitmap.

DIALOG BOXES

Select the Dialog item to bring up the Visual J++ Dialog Editor (see Figure 3.20). Attached to the editor is a Controls toolbar from which you can drag

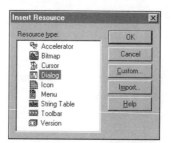

Figure 3.19 Visual J++ can create nine different resources, but your Java projects can use only three.

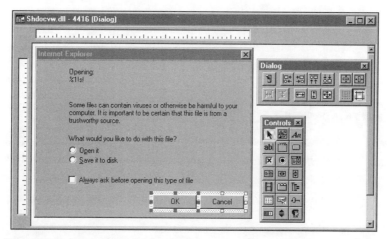

Figure 3.20 The Dialog Editor can align controls vertically or horizontally.

Table 3.2 Dialog box controls supported by Visual J++.

Control	Icon	Windows Name	Java Class Equivalent
Mail:	Aa	Static Text	Label
Whiggle In Line	abl	Edit Box	TextField (or TextArea for multiline edit controls)
Publishers...	▢	Button	Button
☑ Enable Java programs	☒	Check Box	CheckBox
○ Medium	⦿	Radio Button	CheckBox (Visual J++ will generate a CheckboxGroup class)
Hard disk / Keyboard		List Box	List
Start Page / Start Page / Search Page		Combo Box	Choice
◀□▶	◀▶	Horizontal Scroll Bar	Scrollbar (Visual J++ will set the HORIZONTAL property)
		Vertical Scroll Bar	Scrollbar (Visual J++ will set the VERTICAL property)

icons onto a dialog box. Note that only Java-compatible controls—those that have an Abstract Window Toolkit (AWT) equivalent—are valid. Table 3.2 lists all available controls and their AWT counterparts.

Once you have added controls to a dialog box, you can position them using the Layout menu. First, select multiple controls by clicking on them while holding down the Ctrl key. Then choose one of the Layout commands, such as Make Same Size. You can test your changes by pressing Ctrl+T.

Menus

Menus are another Java-compatible resource that Visual J++ supports. To create one, choose Insert|Resource and select the Menu item. The Menu Editor will appear (see Figure 3.21).

To add a cascading menu, click on the dotted new item box and type a caption for the menu. Follow the same process for adding menu items.

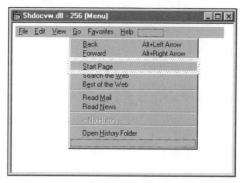

Figure 3.21 The Menu Editor can create standard menu bars.

To rearrange items, simply drag them with your mouse.

IMPORTING RESOURCES FROM PREVIOUS PROJECTS

Instead of creating all resources in Visual J++, you can import them from previous projects. When porting a Visual C++ program to Java, for example, you can load its resources directly into Visual J++ just by selecting File|Open and locating its resource script file (*.rc). This trick works with any Windows-compatible resource script (such as those created by Borland C++), as well as binary files (*.exe, *.dll, *.ocx) that contain resources.

IMAGES

The third and final Java resource available in Visual J++ is the image. To create an image, choose Insert|Resource and select the Bitmap item. The Image Editor window will appear, along with the Graphics and Colors toolbars (see Figure 3.22).

The Visual J++ Image Editor is similar to most graphics programs, allowing you to add shapes, lines, and text. You can draw these objects on either of the two image panes: standard or zoomed. See the Visual J++ online help topic "Using the Graphics Editor" for more information.

ALL I WANNA DO IS A ZOOM-ZOOM-ZOOM

*By default, the Image Editor's zoomed pane is six times larger than the standard pane. The only way to change the default zoom level is to edit the Windows System Registry. To do so, run regedit.exe and find the HKEY_CURRENT_*

Figure 3.22 The Image Editor can create, import, and edit GIF and JPEG images.

*USER\Software\Microsoft\Developer\Graphics Editor key. Next, add a DWORD value called **DefaultZoom** and set it to any number between 2 and 10. Finally, close the Registry Editor and restart Visual J++ for the new default zoom level to take effect.*

Importing Resources

Now comes the hard part. After creating your project's resources, save them as a single file by selecting File|Save. Do *not* save the file as a resource script (*.rc), even though Visual J++ prompts you to do so. Instead, save it as a resource template (*.rct) or a 32-bit resource file (*.res). Once you have saved the resources, you can import them into a Java project using the Resource Wizard.

Running The Resource Wizard

1. To import dialog box and menu resources into a project, select Tools|Java Resource Wizard. Step 1 of this wizard asks you for the location of the resource template you just saved (see Figure 3.23). Type its name or search for it with the Browse button, then continue with the next step.

2. In Step 2, the Resource Wizard lists the dialog boxes and menus in the file you selected. It will import these resources into your project as soon as you click the Finish button. Before doing so, however, you should give each resource an easy-to-read class name. For

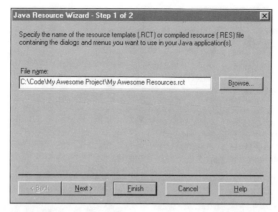

Figure 3.23 In Step 1 of the Resource Wizard enter the file name of a resource template.

example, as shown in Figure 3.24, I renamed **IDD_MYDIALOG** to **MyDialog** by clicking on the item's Class Name column.

After changing the class names, you can kiss the Resource Wizard goodbye. It provides only two steps and refuses to help out the rest of the way. No problem—I'll pick up where the Resource Wizard leaves off. Here are the steps it forgot:

3. The Resource Wizard generated several Java source-code files, one for each imported resource, and placed them in your project's directory. Add these files to your project by selecting Insert|Files into Project. (Note: Do not edit the wizard-generated files. If you need to modify a resource, make your changes using the Visual J++

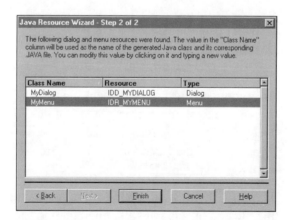

Figure 3.24 In Step 2 of the Resource Wizard you can edit the class names of imported resources.

Resource Editor, then save the template and run the Resource Wizard on it again.)

4. Import the source-code files into your program using the **import** statement. For example, to import a file called MyDialog.java, add the following line to the beginning of your main program:

```
import MyDialog;
```

5. Add code to your program that creates each resource. To create a dialog box resource, for example, insert the following code into your applet's **init()** function:

```
MyDialog dlg = new MyDialog();
dlg.CreateControls();
```

6. To create a menu resource, insert the following code into your application's **main()** function (after the call to **frame.resize()**):

```
MyMenu menu = new MyMenu(frame);
menu.CreateMenu();
```

When you have finished adding code, recompile your program and run it. The dialog boxes and menus will appear exactly as you drew them in the Resource Editor.

IMPORTING IMAGE RESOURCES

The Resource Wizard cannot handle image resources, so you'll have to import them manually. Here are the steps to follow:

1. Create a bitmap using the Visual J++ Image Editor. You may save the bitmap inside a resource template or as a separate file. (Note: Because Visual J++ cannot handle true-color, 24-bit images, you should use another graphics program for creating bitmaps in the JPEG format.)

2. If you have stored the bitmap in a resource template, export it to a separate file by right-clicking the bitmap ID and selecting Export. Be sure to save the image in GIF or JPEG format only.

3. Add code to your program that loads the image resource. For example, to load a GIF image that lies in the same directory as your applet, insert the following lines into your **init()** function:

```
image img = getImage(getDocumentBase(), "My Exported
  Image.gif");
```

After performing these steps, you can manipulate the image as usual. (See "Advanced Graphics Techniques" in Chapter 2 for details.)

Debugging With Visual J++

Until recently, Java programmers have had to cope with Sun's command-line debugger (jdb.exe), simply because it was the only Java debugger in existence. Today, Visual J++ and other Java development environments offer fully graphical debuggers. These integrated, visual debuggers do away with the tedium of switching to a console and fooling around with command-line parameters (see Figure 3.25).

The Visual J++ debugger offers such traditional features as a watch window, call stack, and breakpoints. It also borrows a few innovations from Visual C++, such as DataTips, thread management, and debugging of exceptions. A closer look at each of these features follows.

Setting Breakpoints

To begin a debugging session in Visual J++, set a breakpoint anywhere in your code. You can toggle breakpoints on and off in several ways:

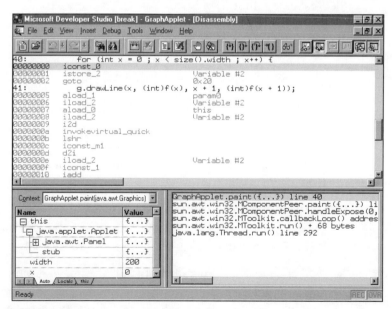

Figure 3.25 Visual J++ includes one of the first integrated, visual debuggers for Java.

You can press F9; you can right-click and select Insert Breakpoint from the menu; or you can open the Breakpoints dialog box by selecting Edit|Breakpoints (see Figure 3.26).

The Breakpoints dialog box lists all of the breakpoints in your project. You can disable them using the checkbox to the left of each item, and you can remove them by clicking the Remove button. To add a breakpoint, click on the pop-up menu button to the right of the Break at edit box.

For advanced control over a breakpoint, select it from the list and click on the Condition button. A dialog box called Breakpoint Condition will appear (see Figure 3.27); it allows you to specify when the break should occur.

Even though this dialog box has two fields, you actually have four options for breakpoint conditions:

- *Changed expression*—To stop on a breakpoint when an expression changes, type the expression in the first edit box. For example, to stop only when the variable **bProcessComplete** changes, simply type "bProcessComplete" in the edit box.

- *True expression*—To stop on a breakpoint when an expression becomes true, type the expression in the first edit box. For example, to stop only when the variable **strUserResponse** is equal to "ready", just type "strUserResponse==″ready″" in the first edit box.

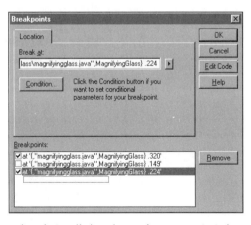

Figure 3.26 The Breakpoints dialog box gives you total control over breakpoints.

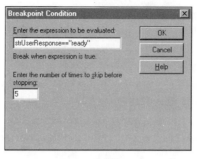

Figure 3.27 The Breakpoint Condition dialog box attaches a condition to a breakpoint.

- *Skip breakpoint*—To stop on a breakpoint only after a certain number of passes, type the number in the second edit box.

- *Skip true expression*—You can combine the conditions of "true expression" with "skip breakpoint". Simply type an expression in the first edit box and a number in the second edit box. Note: You cannot combine breakpoint skips with changed expressions.

Controlling Program Flow

After setting a breakpoint, you can run the Visual J++ debugger by pressing F5. Your program will execute normally until it hits one of the breakpoints you set. The debugger will halt the program and locate the code containing the breakpoint. You can then look at variables, add more breakpoints, and perform other debugging tricks.

When you're ready to continue the program, you have five alternatives:

- *Go*—Pressing F5 will continue the program until it hits another breakpoint.

- *Step Into*—Pressing F11 continues to the next statement. If the current statement is a function, the first line of this function will be the next statement.

- *Step Over*—Pressing F10 continues to the next statement. If the current statement is a function, the debugger steps over it and continues with the next line.

- *Step Out*—Pressing Shift+F11 runs your program until it reaches the end of the current function. The debugger will then exit the function and position the cursor inside the calling function.

- *Run to Cursor*—Pressing Ctrl+F10 is like setting a temporary breakpoint. Your program will run until it reaches the line containing the cursor.

STEPPING INTO STANDARD CLASSES

Visual J++ can trace into standard Java classes, but only if it can find the source code. This code may already be available if you performed a custom installation of Visual J++ and checked the Java Class Library Source Code box. If not, you can install the source code manually by running javasrc.exe, located in Java\Classes under your Windows directory. The parameter "classes.zip" will extract the source code, and "-classes.zip" will delete it.

The Call Stack Window

In the German city of Stuttgart, a street map is posted on nearly every corner. You can locate your position in the city just by finding a little red circle next to the words "Sie Sind Hier." Visual J++ includes a Java-style "You Are Here" indicator called the Call Stack window. It lists the functions that brought you to wherever you are in the source code (see Figure 3.28).

To change the display format of the Call Stack window, such as whether to include parameter values, right-click on the window and select the appropriate item from the menu. You can also jump to any function in the call stack by double-clicking on it.

The Variables Window

The Variables window lists the variables in the current function (see Figure 3.29). It has four tabs:

- *Context list*—The Context list box is a shortcut to the call stack. Just like the Call Stack window, it displays the functions in the

Figure 3.28 The Call Stack window lists the function calls of the current context.

Figure 3.29 If a variable changes as you step through the source code, the Variables window highlights its value in red.

current context and allows you to switch between them. The Variables window updates its display when you move to a new function.

- *Auto tab*—The Auto tab displays variables that are accessed in the current and previous statements. It also displays return values when you step over or out of a function.

- *Locals tab*—The Locals tab lists all local variables in the current function.

- *This tab*—The This tab displays the object referenced by the **this** keyword. It automatically expands to show all members of the object.

In addition to checking the value of variables, the Variables window allows you to change the values. Simply click on a value in the Value column and type new data. The Variables window will display the new value in red to show that it has been changed.

DataTips
To check the value of a variable, you don't have to find it in the Variables window. Just position your mouse over the variable name in the source code. A DataTip will pop up and display the variable's contents.

The Watch Window

In the Variables window, you can't choose which variables to display, and you can't rearrange their order. The Watch window can get you around these limitations. Located to the right of the Variables window (by default), the Watch window contains four tabs: Watch1, Watch2,

Watch3, and Watch4 (see Figure 3.30). The tabs allow you to separate variables into groups for better organization. When you are debugging multiple functions, for instance, you can give each function its own watch tab instead of dumping all the variables into a single column.

To add a variable to the Watch window, click on the new item box and type the name of the variable. To change a variable's value, click on its Value column and type the new data.

AUTO-SIZING COLUMNS

The columns in the Watch and Variables windows are sometimes not wide enough to show all of their data. To fix this problem, double-click on the divider bar between the Name and Value columns. This will auto-size the columns.

Debugging Exceptions

At first glance, Visual J++ offers powerful support for Java exceptions. You can select Debug|Exceptions to display the elaborate dialog box shown in Figure 3.31.

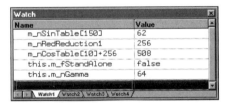

Figure 3.30 The Watch window is a customized version of the Variables window.

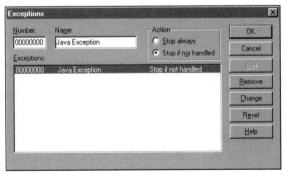

Figure 3.31 The Exceptions dialog box tells the debugger how to handle exceptions.

Visual J++ **79**

The Visual J++ online help contains several paragraphs about this dialog box. Here is an excerpt:

> The Exceptions list box in the Exceptions dialog box contains Java Exception—currently the only system exception available. You can remove the Java Exception or add exceptions of your own. This information is saved in the project.MDP file, which persists with the project.

These statements are false. You cannot add exceptions, and the Visual J++ debugger treats all exceptions identically. You can, however, use this dialog box to configure how the debugger handles exceptions. For instance, to prevent Visual J++ from stopping your program when an exception is thrown but not caught, simply remove the Java Exception item from the list. Conversely, to stop your program when it throws any exception—caught or uncaught—click the Stop Always radio button. Apart from these options, the Exceptions dialog box is useless.

Debugging Advice For C++ Programmers

further developments

I started programming in C++ several years ago, and I've gotten used to the glitches and gotchas of the language. For instance, accessing an out-of-bounds element in a C++ array can crash the program, and a stray pointer can lock up the entire system.

My job got a little easier when I moved to Windows 95, where 32-bit protected-mode debuggers caught errors before they did any damage, and just-in-time exception handling gave me the power to squash just about any bug.

In Java, debugging is somewhat different. The absence of pointers greatly reduces the number of potential bugs, and you still have access to exception handling. If you're a C++ programmer, however, you may find Java bugs harder to track down. For example, accessing an out-of-bounds array element won't halt your program and point you to the offending code (which is what would happen under a 32-bit C++ debugger). Instead, the runtime system will simply throw an exception and continue on its merry way. Unless you explicitly catch the exception or use some other debugging trick, you'll never know what happened.

This approach to Java debugging can make life tough. You may find yourself scratching your head, wondering why your multithreaded applet suddenly stopped for no reason. Usually, the obstacle is an exception that halted the main thread. If this ever happens, check your code to make sure it's not accessing out-of-bounds memory or uninitialized objects. Also, check the Visual J++ Output Window for any warning messages that might clue you in to the problem.

Debugging Threads

When debugging a multithreaded Java class, Visual J++ automatically detects it and enables the Threads item in the Debug menu. Selecting this item brings up the Threads dialog box, which provides a list of all running threads (see Figure 3.32).

The only really useful element in the Threads dialog box is the Suspend button. Clicking this button will increment the selected thread's suspend count, causing it to stop. The ability to suspend multiple threads allows you to concentrate your debugging efforts on a single thread.

> **DEBUGGING WITHOUT THE DEBUGGER**
>
> *The Visual J++ debugger places significant overhead on Java code, causing it to slow down noticeably. As a faster (but dirtier) alternative to the debugger, you can call the **System.out.print**() function. This function takes a string, such as "value of MyVar in init(): " + MyVar, and passes it to the Java virtual machine.*
>
> *The virtual machine handles these strings differently depending on whether your program is running under the standalone interpreter (javaview.exe) or the Web browser (Internet Explorer). The interpreter will display the string in its console, but only if you append it with the newline character ('\n'). Microsoft's Web browser, on the other hand, will never display the string. It merely dumps the text to a file called javalog.txt located in c:\Windows\Java. Note that this occurs only if the Enable Java Logging box, located in Internet Explorer's Advanced options tab, has been checked.*

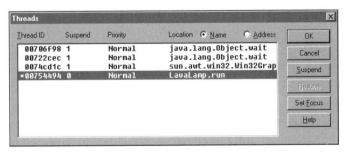

Figure 3.32 The Threads dialog box allows you to suspend any running thread.

Visual J++ **81**

Disassembly

If Visual J++ cannot find the source file of the Java program you're debugging, it will disassemble the code and display its internal bytecodes (see Figure 3.33).

Even if Visual J++ can find the source file, it can still display a program's bytecodes along with source-code annotation. Just right-click in the Text Editor while debugging and select Go To Disassembly (or press Alt+8). The bytecodes will appear, giving you insight into how Visual J++ optimizes your code.

Disassembly allows you to debug any applet, even those that you find on the Web. To debug an applet across the Internet, follow these steps:

1. Create a new Java Workspace by selecting File|New.

2. Open the HTML source of the Web page containing the applet you want to debug. Find the **<APPLET>** tag and make a note of the class file name.

3. Go to the Debug tab of Build|Settings. In the General category, type the name of the class file.

4. In the same tab, switch to the Browser category. Select the Use parameters from HTML page radio button, then type the complete URL (including **http://**) of the Web page containing the applet.

5. Press F11 to step into the first line of the disassembled applet. Answer No when Visual J++ asks you to build.

TAKE CHARGE OF DATA EXPANSION

Visual J++ automatically expands items in the Variables window, the Watch window, and in DataTips to show their most important elements. You can change the predefined rules for this expansion, or you can add rules for your own data types. See the JAutoExp.dat text file, located in Visual J++'s bin directory, for more information.

Sample Code

To help get you started writing Java applets in Visual J++, I've created two sample projects. You can use them as study guides, or you can insert them directly into your own Web pages. The CD-ROM included with this book contains the complete source code to each project.

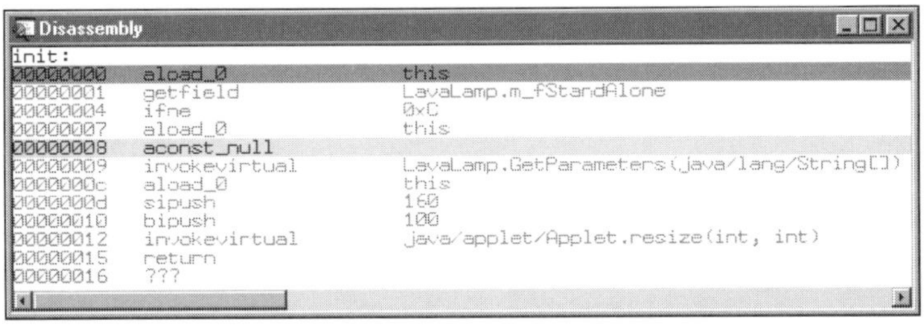

Figure 3.33 Visual J++ displays a program's bytecodes when it cannot find the source file.

Java Lava Lamp

Remember the Seventies? That golden era of disco clubs, bean bag chairs, and "Y.M.C.A"? Me neither. When John Travolta was teaching us how to catch a fever on Saturday night, I was teaching myself how to walk. Because I'm too young to have ever seen an authentic lava lamp—the ultimate symbol of the Seventies—I decided to create one in its honor. I call it the Java Lava Lamp (see Figure 3.34).

This Java applet animates sine waves in vivid colors, giving the illusion of a lava lamp. You can alter the colors, trigonometry, and speed of the waves in two ways: You can either open the sample HTML file and enter numbers into its form, or you can edit the HTML file and add parameters to the **<APPLET>** tag. Table 3.3 lists and describes each parameter.

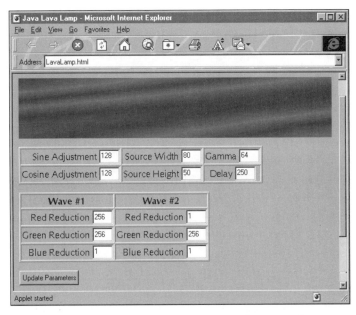

Figure 3.34 The Java Lava Lamp turns your Web browser into eye candy.

Visual J++ **83**

Table 3.3 The Java Lava Lamp parameters.

Name	Description
RedReduction1	Redness reduction in the palette of the first wave (1 = maximum red).
RedReduction2	Redness reduction in the palette of the second wave (1 = maximum red).
GreenReduction1	Greenness reduction in the palette of the first wave (1 = maximum green).
GreenReduction2	Greenness reduction in the palette of the second wave (1 = maximum green).
BlueReduction1	Blueness reduction in the palette of the first wave (1 = maximum blue).
BlueReduction2	Blueness reduction in the palette of the second wave (1 = maximum blue).
SineAdjustment	Amount of wave motion in the sine direction (1 = motionless).
CosineAdjustment	Amount of wave motion in the cosine direction (1 = motionless).
Gamma	Brightness of palette (1 = dark; 256 = bright).
Delay	Number of milliseconds to pause between frames (low delay = fast animation).
SourceWidth	Width of the source bitmap (greater width = higher resolution).
SourceHeight	Height of the source bitmap (greater height = higher resolution).

Listing 3.1 contains an abridged version of the source code to the Java Lava Lamp.

LISTING 3.1 THE JAVA LAVA LAMP SOURCE CODE.

```
import java.applet.*;
import java.awt.*;
import java.awt.image.*;

public class LavaLamp extends Applet implements Runnable
{
    // THREAD SUPPORT:
    // m_LavaLamp is the Thread object for the applet
    // ─────────────────────────────
    Thread    m_LavaLamp = null;

    // Private member variables
    private int m_nSourceWidth = 80;
    private int m_nSourceHeight = 50;
    private int m_nGamma = 64;
```

```java
    private int m_nDelay = 100;
    private int m_nRedReduction1 = 256;
    private int m_nRedReduction2 = 1;
    private int m_nGreenReduction1 = 256;
    private int m_nGreenReduction2 = 256;
    private int m_nBlueReduction1 = 1;
    private int m_nBlueReduction2 = 1;
    private int m_nSineAdjustment = 128;
    private int m_nCosineAdjustment = 128;

    private int[] m_nSinTable, m_nCosTable;
    private byte[] m_byBits;
    private IndexColorModel m_cmPalette;
    private Image m_imgLava;
    private int m_i, m_j;

    // LavaLamp Class Constructor
    //-----------------------------------------
    public LavaLamp()
    {
        m_i = 0;
        m_j = 0;

        createTrigTables();
        createPalette();
        createImage();
    }

    // APPLET INFO SUPPORT:
    // The getAppletInfo() method returns a string describing
    // the applet's author, copyright date, or miscellaneous
    // information.
    //-----------------------------------------
    public String getAppletInfo()
    {
        return "Name: Java Lava Lamp\r\n" +
               "Author: Trevor Harmon\r\n" +
               "Created with Microsoft Visual J++ Version 1.0";
    }

    public void init()
    {
        resize(160, 100);
    }

    // LavaLamp Update Handler
    //-----------------------------------------
    public void update(Graphics g)
    {
```

```
      paint(g);
   }

   // LavaLamp Paint Handler
   //--------------------------------------------------
   public void paint(Graphics g)
   {
      Dimension d = size();

      g.drawImage(m_imgLava, 0, 0, d.width, d.height, this);
   }

   // The start() method is called when the page containing the
   // applet first appears on the screen. The AppletWizard's
   // initial implementation of this method starts execution of
   // the applet's thread.
   //--------------------------------------------------
   public void start()
   {
      if (m_LavaLamp == null)
      {
         m_LavaLamp = new Thread(this);
         m_LavaLamp.start();
      }
   }

   // The stop() method is called when the page containing the
   // applet is no longer on the screen. The AppletWizard's
   // initial implementation of this method stops execution of
   // the applet's thread.
   //--------------------------------------------------
   public void stop()
   {
      if (m_LavaLamp != null)
      {
         m_LavaLamp.stop();
         m_LavaLamp = null;
      }
   }

   // THREAD SUPPORT
   // The run() method is called when the applet's thread is
   // started. If your applet performs any ongoing activities
   // without waiting for user input, the code for implementing
   // that behavior typically goes here. For example, for an
   // applet that performs animation, the run() method controls
   // the display of images.
   //--------------------------------------------------
   public void run()
```

```
{
   while (true)
   {
      repaint();
      renderNextFrame();

      try
      {
         Thread.sleep(m_nDelay);
      }
      catch (InterruptedException e)
      {
         stop();
      }
   }
}

protected void renderNextFrame()
{
   int x, y, r, s;

   for (y = 0; y < m_nSourceHeight; y++)
   {
      r = m_nSinTable[(y + m_i) % 256];
      s = m_nCosTable[m_j % 256];

      for (x = 0; x < m_nSourceWidth; x++)
      {
         m_byBits[y * m_nSourceWidth + x] = (byte)
            ((m_nSinTable[(x + r) % 256] + m_nCosTable[(y +
               s) % 256]) % 256);
      }
   }

   if (m_i == 0)
      m_i = 255;
   else
      m_i--;

   if (m_j == 255)
      m_j = 0;
   else
      m_j++;

   m_imgLava = createImage( new
                     MemoryImageSource(m_nSourceWidth,
                                       m_nSourceHeight,
                                       m_cmPalette,
```

```java
                                          m_byBits,
                                              0,
                                          m_nSourceWidth));
}

protected void createTrigTables()
{
   m_nSinTable = new int[256];
   m_nCosTable = new int[256];

   for (int i = 0; i < 256; i++)
   {
      m_nSinTable[i] = (int) (Math.sin(2 * Math.PI * i /
         256) * m_nSineAdjustment + 128);
      m_nCosTable[i] = (int) (Math.cos(2 * Math.PI * i /
         256) * m_nCosineAdjustment + 128);
   }
}

protected void createPalette()
{
   byte[] byReds   = new byte[256];
   byte[] byGreens = new byte[256];
   byte[] byBlues  = new byte[256];
   int i;

   for (i = 0; i < 64; i++)
   {
      byReds[i]        = (byte)(i / m_nRedReduction1);
      byGreens[i]      = (byte)(i / m_nGreenReduction1);
      byBlues[i]       = (byte)(i / m_nBlueReduction1);

      byReds[127 - i]   = (byte)(i / m_nRedReduction1);
      byGreens[127 - i] = (byte)(i / m_nGreenReduction1);
      byBlues[127 - i]  = (byte)(i / m_nBlueReduction1);

      byReds[127 + i]   = (byte)(i / m_nRedReduction2);
      byGreens[127 + i] = (byte)(i / m_nGreenReduction2);
      byBlues[127 + i]  = (byte)(i / m_nBlueReduction2);

      byReds[254 - i]   = (byte)(i / m_nRedReduction2);
      byGreens[254 - i] = (byte)(i / m_nGreenReduction2);
      byBlues[254 - i]  = (byte)(i / m_nBlueReduction2);
   }

   // Brighten up the palette a bit...

   for (i = 0; i < 256; i++)
   {
```

```
      if (byReds[i] + m_nGamma > 255)
         byReds[i] = (byte)255;
      else
         byReds[i] += (byte)m_nGamma;

      if (byGreens[i] + m_nGamma > 255)
         byGreens[i] = (byte)255;
      else
         byGreens[i] += (byte)m_nGamma;

      if (byBlues[i] + m_nGamma > 255)
         byBlues[i] = (byte)255;
      else
         byBlues[i] += (byte)m_nGamma;
   }

   m_cmPalette = new IndexColorModel(8, 256, byReds, v
      byGreens, byBlues);
}

protected void createImage()
{
   m_byBits = new byte[m_nSourceWidth * m_nSourceHeight];

   m_imgLava = createImage( new
   MemoryImageSource(m_nSourceWidth,
                     m_nSourceHeight,
                     m_cmPalette,
                     m_byBits,
                     0,
                     m_nSourceWidth) );
   }
}
```

Magnifying Glass

The Magnifying Glass is another somewhat useless, but very cool, Java applet. It displays a bitmap of your choice in the Web browser and, as you move the mouse across the image, generates a spherical magnification of the pixels in realtime (see Figure 3.35).

You can specify the magnification, sphere diameter, and bitmap name by supplying parameters, either through the supplied HTML form or directly through the **<APPLET>** tag. Table 3.4 lists each parameter and gives its description.

The Magnifying Glass applet offers an excellent opportunity to see Microsoft's Just-In-Time compiler in action. First, start Internet

Figure 3.35 The Magnifying Glass applet can zoom in on an image's pixels, as shown in this close-up of my guinea pig's nose.

Table 3.4 The Magnifying Glass parameters.

Name	Description
Diameter	Diameter of the magnifying glass in pixels.
Magnification	Power of the magnifying glass. Must be less than half of the diameter.
Background	GIF image to use as the background bitmap. (JPEG images are not supported.)

Explorer and select View|Properties. Go to the Advanced tab, uncheck the Enable Java JIT compiler box, and restart the browser. Next, load the Magnifying Glass applet and take note of how much time is required to convert the bitmap. Finally, recheck the JIT compiler box and load the applet again. You'll find that the bitmap conversion is several times faster with the JIT compiler enabled.

Listing 3.2 contains an abridged version of the source code to the Magnifying Glass.

LISTING 3.2 THE MAGNIFYING GLASS SOURCE CODE.

```
import java.applet.*;
import java.awt.*;
```

```java
import java.awt.image.*;

public class MagnifyingGlass extends Applet
{
   // Private member variables
   Image m_imgBackground, m_imgLens;
   int m_nWidth, m_nHeight, m_nRadius;
   int[] m_nTransform;
   byte[] m_byPixels;
   IndexColorModel m_cmPalette;
   Point m_ptMouse;

   // APPLET INFO SUPPORT:
   // The getAppletInfo() method returns a string describing
   // the applet's author, copyright date, or miscellaneous
   // information.
   // ────────────────────────────────────────
   public String getAppletInfo()
   {
      return "Name: Magnifying Glass\r\n" +
             "Author: Trevor Harmon\r\n" +
             "Created with Microsoft Visual J++ Version 1.0";
   }

   public void init()
   {
      showStatus("Loading image. Please wait...");

      if (m_fStandAlone)
      {
         m_imgBackground =
            getToolkit().getImage(m_strBackground);
      }
      else
      {
         m_imgBackground = getImage(getDocumentBase(),
                        m_strBackground);
      }

      MediaTracker tracker = new MediaTracker(this);
      tracker.addImage(m_imgBackground, 0);

      try
      {
         tracker.waitForAll();
      }
      catch (InterruptedException e)
      {
      }
```

```
    m_nWidth = m_imgBackground.getWidth(this);
    m_nHeight = m_imgBackground.getHeight(this);
    m_nRadius = m_nDiameter / 2;

    if (m_nMagnification > m_nRadius)
       m_nMagnification = 0;
    else
       m_nMagnification = m_nRadius - m_nMagnification;

    if ( m_nDiameter > Math.min(m_nWidth, m_nHeight) )
       m_nDiameter = Math.min(m_nWidth, m_nHeight);

    byte[] byReds = new byte[256];
    byte[] byGreens = new byte[256];
    byte[] byBlues = new byte[256];

    m_byPixels = new byte[m_nWidth * m_nHeight];

    getIndexColorData(m_imgBackground, m_byPixels, byReds,
    byGreens, byBlues);

    m_cmPalette = new IndexColorModel(8, 256, byReds,
    byGreens, byBlues);

    m_imgBackground = createImage( new
                                  MemoryImageSource(m_nWidth,
                                  m_nHeight,
                                  m_cmPalette,
                                  m_byPixels,
                                  0,
                                  m_nWidth) );
    calculateTransform();
}

// MagnifyingGlass Update Handler
// ─────────────────────────────────────
public void update(Graphics g)
{
    // Override the update() function to do nothing.
    // This will prevent flicker.
}

// MagnifyingGlass Paint Handler
// ─────────────────────────────────────
public void paint(Graphics g)
{
    g.drawImage(m_imgBackground, 0, 0, this);
}
```

```java
// The start() method is called when the page containing the
// applet first appears on the screen. The AppletWizard's
// initial implementation of this method starts execution of
// the applet's thread.
// ────────────────────────────
public void start()
{
    resize(m_nWidth, m_nHeight);
}

public boolean mouseEnter(Event evt, int x, int y)
{
    Point ptMouse = new Point(x, y);

    checkCoordinates(ptMouse);
    drawLens(ptMouse);

    return true;
}

public boolean mouseMove(Event evt, int x, int y)
{
    Point ptMouse = new Point(x, y);

    checkCoordinates(ptMouse);
    drawLens(ptMouse);

    return true;
}

public boolean mouseExit(Event evt, int x, int y)
{
    Graphics g = getGraphics();

    g.drawImage(m_imgBackground, 0, 0, this);

    return true;
}

/*
This function takes an RGB (direct color model) image and
obtains its palette information and an array of bytes which
are indexes into the palette. The implementation supports
only 8-bit (256 color)images.
*/
protected void getIndexColorData(Image img, byte[] byPixels,
byte[] byReds, byte[] byGreens, byte[] byBlues)
{
```

```java
        int nWidth          = img.getWidth(this);
        int nHeight         = img.getHeight(this);
        int nPaletteIndex = 0;
        int[] nPixels       = new int[nWidth * nHeight];
        int[] nPalette      = new int[256];
        PixelGrabber pg     = new PixelGrabber(img, 0, 0, nWidth,
    nHeight, nPixels, 0, nWidth);

        try
        {
            pg.grabPixels();
        }
        catch (InterruptedException e)
        {
        }

        // Loop through each pixel in the image...
        for (int y = 0; y < nHeight; y++)
        {
            showStatus("Converting image (" + (y + 1) + "/" +
            nHeight + "). Please wait...");

            for (int x = 0; x < nWidth; x++)
            {
                int nIndex = -1;

                // Search for the palette index of the current
                // pixel's color...
                for (int i = 0; i <= nPaletteIndex; i++)
                {
                    if ( nPalette[i] == nPixels[y * nWidth + x] )
                    {
                        nIndex = i;
                        break;
                    }
                }

                // If the current pixel's color is not in the
                // palette, add it to the palette.
                if ( nIndex == -1 )
                {
                    nPalette[nPaletteIndex] = nPixels[y * nWidth +
                x];
                    nIndex = nPaletteIndex;
                    nPaletteIndex++;
                }
                // Change the pixel from a color value to an index
                // value.
                byPixels[y * nWidth + x] = (byte) nIndex;
```

```java
        }
    }

    for (int i = 0; i < 256; i++)
    {
        int r = (nPalette[i] >> 16) & 0xff;
        int g = (nPalette[i] >> 8  ) & 0xff;
        int b = (nPalette[i]       ) & 0xff;

        byReds[i]   = (byte)r;
        byGreens[i] = (byte)g;
        byBlues[i]  = (byte)b;
    }
}

// This function fills an array that describes how to
// transform a rectangle of pixels into a spherical lens.
protected void calculateTransform()
{
    m_nTransform     = new int[ m_nDiameter * m_nDiameter ];
    double dSphereRay = Math.sqrt( m_nRadius * m_nRadius -
        m_nMagnification * m_nMagnification );
    int x, y, a, b;

    for (y = -m_nRadius; y < -m_nRadius + m_nDiameter; y++)
    {
        for (x = -m_nRadius; x < -m_nRadius + m_nDiameter;
          x++)
        {
            if ( x * x + y * y < dSphereRay * dSphereRay )
            {
                double z = Math.sqrt( m_nRadius * m_nRadius - x
                    * x - y * y );
                a = (int)((double)x * (double)m_nMagnification /
                    z + 0.5);
                b = (int)((double)y * (double)m_nMagnification /
                    z + 0.5);
            }
            else
            {
                a = x;
                b = y;
            }

            m_nTransform[(y + m_nRadius) * m_nDiameter + (x +
                m_nRadius)] = (b + m_nRadius) * m_nDiameter + (a +
                m_nRadius);
        }
    }
}
```

```java
// This function uses the transformation array and a double-
// buffer to draw the lens on the applet window.
protected void drawLens(Point pt)
{
   int x, y;
   byte[] bySrcPixels  = new byte[ m_nDiameter *
   m_nDiameter ];
   byte[] byDestPixels = new byte[ m_nDiameter *
   m_nDiameter ];

   // Grab the pixels from the area to be transformed and
   // put them in a buffer...
   for (x = pt.x - m_nRadius; x < m_nDiameter + pt.x -
   m_nRadius; x++)
   {
      for (y = pt.y - m_nRadius; y < m_nDiameter + pt.y -
      m_nRadius; y++)
      {
         bySrcPixels[(y - (pt.y - m_nRadius)) * m_nDiameter
            + x - (pt.x - m_nRadius)] = m_byPixels[y * m_nWidth
            + x];
      }
   }

   // Transform the pixels...
   for (int i = 0; i < m_nDiameter * m_nDiameter; i++)
   {
      byDestPixels[i] = bySrcPixels[ m_nTransform[i] ];
   }

   m_imgLens = createImage( new
                        MemoryImageSource(m_nDiameter,
                        m_nDiameter,
                        m_cmPalette,
                        byDestPixels,
                        0
                        m_nDiameter)
                     );
   Graphics g = getGraphics();

   // Create a double-buffer...
   Image imgBuffer = createImage(m_nWidth, m_nHeight);
   Graphics gBuffer = imgBuffer.getGraphics();

   gBuffer.drawImage(m_imgBackground, 0, 0, this);
   gBuffer.drawImage(m_imgLens, pt.x - m_nRadius, pt.y -
   m_nRadius, this);
   g.drawImage(imgBuffer, 0, 0, this);
}
```

```
// This function changes the mouse coordinates so that the
// lens lies within the applet window.
protected void checkCoordinates(Point ptMouse)
{
   Dimension sizeWnd = size();

   ptMouse.x = Math.min(ptMouse.x, sizeWnd.width -
     m_nRadius);
   ptMouse.x = Math.max(ptMouse.x, m_nRadius);
   ptMouse.y = Math.min(ptMouse.y, sizeWnd.height -
     m_nRadius);
   ptMouse.y = Math.max(ptMouse.y, m_nRadius);
}
}
```

A Look At The Competition

In the Java arena, Microsoft has two competitors: Borland and Symantec. Each company sells Rapid Application Development (RAD) tools for creating high-performance Java applications. This section includes an overview of Borland's and Symantec's products to see how they compare with Visual J++.

BORLAND LATTÉ

Borland's Java offering is code-named Latté and should be widely available by the time this book is published. Latté's user interface is radically different from Visual J++ (see Figure 3.36). It borrows heavily from Borland Delphi, in that you draw visual components on a form and then glue them together with Java code. It also combines a project manager, class browser, and source code editor into one window for easy navigation.

Borland Latté shares many features with Visual J++, such as an IDE you can customize, a high-performance optimizing compiler, and a visual debugger. It outshines Visual J++ in three areas:

- *Component reuse*—Latté provides a storage area for Java classes, allowing you to recycle code with minimal effort. Support for this code reuse comes from BAJA, a Borland implementation of Sun's Java Beans specification (see Chapter 10). BAJA components are written entirely in Java, so they can run anywhere that Java runs—including Visual J++.

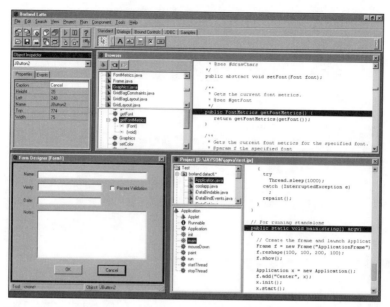

Figure 3.36 The Latté user interface is based on Borland's Delphi visual design environment.

- *Component editing*—Latté includes a visual component editor analogous to the Resource Editor in Visual J++. It inserts components directly into your Java project without the need for an extra import step. As you edit the component source code, your changes are updated automatically in the visual editor.

- *Database support*—Unlike Visual J++, Latté offers out-of-the-box JDBC support. This support comes from InterClient, a Java-based companion to Borland's InterBase RDBMS server. It gives your programs full, distributed access to client/server databases.

Borland Latté does not support ActiveX.

Symantec Visual Café

Like Borland Latté and Microsoft Visual J++, Symantec Visual Café is a full-featured Java project manager with flexible editing and browsing tools. It includes a syntax-highlighted source-code editor, a component builder, and an integrated visual debugger (see Figure 3.37). It also includes wizards for generating application skeletons quickly. Visual Café offers minimal support for database access, however.

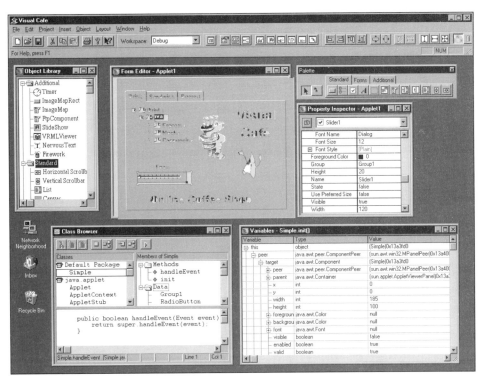

Figure 3.37 Visual Café's class editor provides intuitive access to functions and variables.

Resource editing in Visual Café goes far beyond Visual J++. As you build dialog boxes and menus visually, your creations are instantly converted into Java source code. For example, by drawing a button on a dialog box form, you insert code for creating a **Button** object into your project. If you change the size of the button, Visual Café automatically changes the size parameters in the source code. This labor-saving process is much more intuitive and convenient than the Visual J++ Resource Wizard.

Symantec Visual Café does not support ActiveX.

Summary

Visual J++ is typical of a 1.0 release. It shows a lot of potential, but still has room for improvement. Without ActiveX support and the debugger, Visual J++ would be nothing but a very expensive Java front end. Competing products offer certain advantages, especially in the area of resource editing. Still, Visual J++ is a pleasant development environment that can simplify most Java tasks.

Chapter 4

ActiveX Fundamentals

- What is ActiveX?
- ActiveX controls vs. Java applets
- Controls and the Web browser
- The ActiveX Control Pad

ActiveX is an upside-down umbrella. Just about any new Microsoft technology rains down on the developer community and gets caught in the ActiveX bumbershoot. Today, the word ActiveX embodies nearly a dozen architectures: ActiveX controls, ActiveX scripts, ActiveX documents, and more. Tomorrow, it will include countless others.

Most of these technologies are beyond the scope of this book, and you don't need them to build cool applications with Visual J++. Knowing how to create ActiveX *controls*, however, is very practical. When writing Java applications, controls can save you time and effort through the magic of code reuse.

What Is ActiveX?

Before I delve into the details, I should explain the concept of an ActiveX control. Most definitions of ActiveX contain fancy phrases such as *software component technology*, *dispatch interfaces*, and *Component Object Model*. These definitions are entirely accurate, but they're also entirely confusing.

My ActiveX Analogue

Here's my definition: *ActiveX controls are reusable code in binary form*. That's a simple statement, but it opens up a world of possibilities. Let's look at it in detail.

REUSABLE CODE

Reusable code is commonplace with most modern programming languages. In Java, for example, you can encapsulate code within a class and then extend that class for use in other Java programs. This technique is a huge timesaver, but there's hitch: To use the class, you need full access to the source code.

In the ActiveX realm, you don't need *any* source code. As long as the original code has been converted to an ActiveX control, you can use it in any ActiveX-compatible program (such as the Visual J++ programs you create—see Chapter 7). The downside is that you can't extend ActiveX controls in the same way that you can extend Java classes (see Figure 4.1), unless you resort to esoteric techniques such as aggregation, which I won't cover in this book.

Despite the handicap, ActiveX controls are an excellent approach to code reuse because they're language-independent. Controls allow you to interface C++ code with Java, Java code with Visual Basic, Visual Basic code with C++, and so on.

BINARY REUSE

ActiveX controls can achieve this language independence because their code is tucked away in binary form, not as source code. No matter which development tool you use to create ActiveX controls, you'll produce a standard ActiveX control, readable at the binary level by any ActiveX-compatible program (see Figure 4.2).

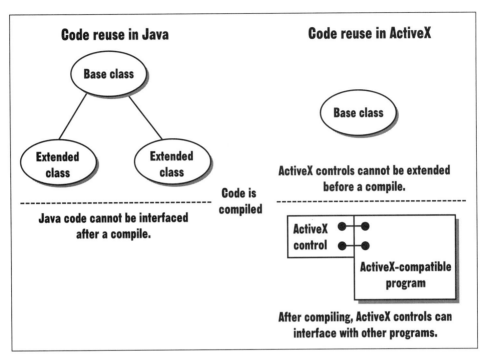

Figure 4.1 Java applets can be extended but not interfaced; ActiveX controls can be interfaced but not extended.

Language independence is not the only benefit of putting reusable code into a binary form. For example, after converting an algorithm to an ActiveX control, you can sell it to other programmers without giving away your valuable source code. Plus, your algorithms are no longer restricted to development tools. Any application that conforms to the ActiveX standard for controls—and that can include end-user software such as spreadsheets and databases—may use your code. Suddenly, the market for your software has exploded! Your nifty algorithms are available to a new realm of users—and their checkbooks.

Hundreds of companies have realized the market potential for ActiveX controls, and they offer everything from simple 3D button controls to full-blown spreadsheets (see Figure 4.3). You can purchase ActiveX controls through mail order, the shareware market, or right off the shelf at the local computer store.

ActiveX Containers

The programs that use ActiveX controls are called *containers*. A control container is an ActiveX-enabled application that serves as the user-

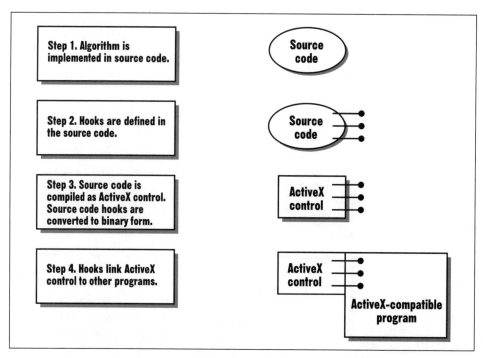

Figure 4.2 The fundamental process of creating an ActiveX control.

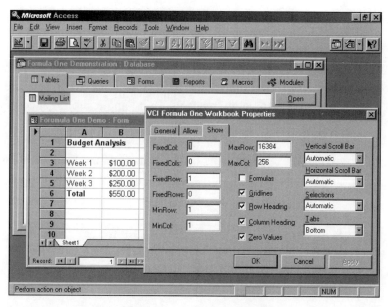

Figure 4.3 Formula One/NET Pro, a commercial ActiveX control from Visual Components, Inc., can run in database programs as well as Web browsers.

interface framework for your control. It may display a button that, when clicked, sends a message to the control. Containers can also respond to *events*, which are special messages sent from the control to its container. Events can indicate a mouse click, the completion of a task, or any other occurrence.

The most important—or at least the most publicized—ActiveX container is the Web browser. A browser can display ActiveX controls on a Web page even when the control is located on a remote computer. For more information, see the section titled "ActiveX Controls And The Web Browser" later in this chapter.

Both controls and containers are necessary to gain the full benefits of the ActiveX architecture. The controls allow you to package source code into a single, reusable object that you can sell to other companies. Those same companies can also sell ActiveX controls back to you, in which case you'll need an ActiveX container to use them.

You can create a container using development tools such as Visual J++, Visual C++, and Visual Basic. Once that's done, inserting an ActiveX control into a container is as easy as clicking a few buttons (see Figure 4.4). In the end, you've saved yourself time and effort by using another company's source code in your own programs.

ActiveX Controls Vs. Java Applets

As I mentioned in the first chapter of this book, the ActiveX architecture cannot be compared with the Java language. ActiveX *controls*, however, can be directly compared with Java *applets*.

But first, a note on terminology: Just as Java classes have functions and variables, ActiveX controls have methods and properties. A *method* is like an ordinary Java *function*; it takes in a certain number of parameters and optionally returns a value. A *property* is simply a *variable* that stores an attribute of your control. In other words, a function is to Java as a method is to ActiveX, and a variable is to Java as a property is to ActiveX. (The root of this difference in terms is Visual Basic, which uses the same screwy naming conventions as ActiveX.)

Similarities

Just like Java applets, ActiveX controls supercharge the Web and give it a fourth dimension. Both can:

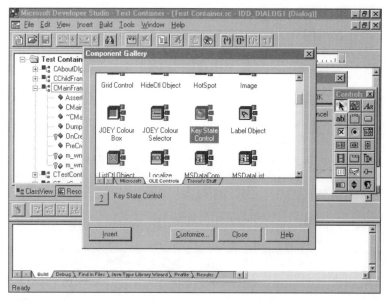

Figure 4.4 With just a few clicks, you can insert ActiveX controls into Visual C++ containers.

- Simplify and automate your Web authoring tasks by displaying "NEW!" images for new items on your site. After a certain date, the images will automatically become invisible.

- Display data in ways other than text and tables, such as a chart or graph at user-selectable angles.

- Add functionality to your pages with timers, animation, and background downloading.

These parallels put ActiveX controls in direct competition with Java applets.

Differences

The similarities between controls and applets are largely external, so most casual Web surfers can't tell them apart. Their differences, however, are mostly internal, so programmers need to be aware of them. Table 4.1 provides an overview of how ActiveX controls differ from Java applets.

Table 4.1 ActiveX controls vs. Java applets.

Feature	ActiveX controls	Java applets
Portable	No (available soon)	Yes
Access to files on client machine	Yes	No
Support for OLE	Yes	No (available soon)
Support for legacy code	Yes	Minimal
Limited to browser or standalone application	No	Yes
Fast compilation	No	Yes
Fast execution	Yes	No

The Portability Problem

Unlike Java applets, ActiveX controls were never designed to be cross-platform. The ActiveX architecture is closely tied to the Microsoft Windows operating system; ActiveX controls cannot run on other platforms. The portability problem, in fact, is even more severe: ActiveX controls are not only platform-dependent, but also *browser-dependent*. With the exception of Microsoft Internet Explorer, browsers must be tricked up in order to support ActiveX.

A ray of hope: Microsoft has formed several corporate partnerships that will bring ActiveX support to the Apple Macintosh and certain Unix platforms. This change, however, does not mean that ActiveX controls will be as portable as Java applets. Developers must compile separate controls for each platform and store all of them on the Web server. The Web browser must then determine which version to download (see Figure 4.5). For example, the upcoming Internet Explorer for Unix would detect and download the version of an ActiveX control compiled for Unix systems. This process is all automatic; it does not interrupt the user.

If you absolutely need platform independence, you may as well forget about ActiveX controls. The architecture's roots are in Windows, so any cross-platform solution, whether from Microsoft, its partners, or third parties, will always be a hack. Java applets will better serve your portability needs.

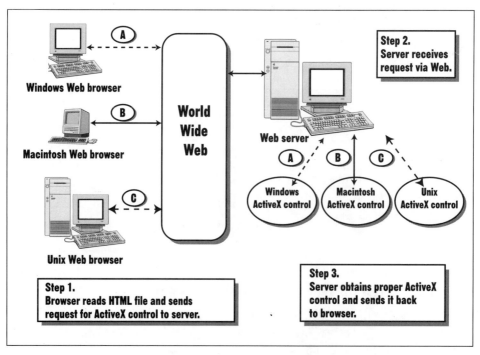

Figure 4.5 In the future, Web browsers will automatically download the ActiveX control designed for their specific platform.

further developments

Microsoft seems to have changed the way in which they operate. Their ActiveX architecture, into which they have poured millions of dollars in development and promotion, was donated to an industry standards council on July 26, 1996. The independent council will consist primarily of consumer representatives who decide the future course of ActiveX technologies. Microsoft will contribute specifications, source code, and all ActiveX trademark rights to the group.

What does this mean for ActiveX users and developers? You can probably expect to see better cross-platform support. Because Microsoft no longer has an exclusive say in the future direction of ActiveX, that direction may turn away from Windows. The exact route is now up to the consumers—people like you and me—who voice their opinions to the standards body.

Microsoft's donation of their ActiveX technologies could well be the most generous act that any software company has ever performed. Then again, maybe not; this move may give ActiveX the advantage over Java that Microsoft has been looking for all along. In the end, Microsoft may destroy Java and once again maintain its dominant position in the industry.

File Access

Unlike Java applets, ActiveX controls can access files on your computer. This valuable ability creates opportunities for ActiveX that Java simply doesn't have. For example, an ActiveX control could save the results of a database query onto a hard disk for future reference, while a Java applet would be forced to reload the query again and again.

Access to files may be handy, but it's also dangerous. Eventually, someone is bound to abuse this feature. Rogue programmers could exploit ActiveX to search your hard disk for credit card numbers and other confidential information. Since controls are installed just like applets—automatically—you would never know what was happening until it was too late.

Fortunately, a solution is available. Before loading any ActiveX control, the Web browser searches the control for an encrypted sequence of bytes. This sequence, or *digital signature*, is created by a process known as *code-signing*. (See Chapter 13 for more details.) If the sequence is found, the browser is able to determine who wrote the code, who distributed it, and, therefore, who is responsible if the control does something malicious. If not, the browser warns the user that the control may be dangerous and gives the option not to load it.

OLE Support

As noted in Chapter 1, ActiveX controls are just OLE controls incognito. Because they are true OLE objects, they provide all the benefits of the OLE architecture. Controls can interact with other OLE objects, embed themselves in documents, respond to a universal drag-and-drop interface, and so on. Support for OLE also means that ActiveX controls can run without modification across distributed, scaleable computer networks.

Java applets, by comparison, do not support OLE, unless those applets are written specifically for Windows using Visual J++ (see Chapter 10). Sun Microsystems acknowledges the need for OLE support in Java and is building a new technology to provide it. Called Java Beans, this technology wraps Java code in an OLE shell to make it look like an OLE object. See Chapter 11 for a discussion of Java Beans.

Legacy Code

If you want to convert your existing code, also called *legacy code*, to Java, you're not required to translate every single line. You can take advantage of Java's native code interface (see Chapter 2). Unfortunately, this interface is far from ideal: It's hard to use, poorly documented, and works only with code written in C.

In contrast, ActiveX controls offer much better support for legacy code. The process of converting your existing programs to ActiveX controls is fairly easy and reasonably documented by Microsoft. And because ActiveX controls are language-independent, it doesn't matter which language you have chosen for your code base.

In addition to your own legacy code, you can reuse legacy *controls*. The hundreds of OLE controls already on the market (remember that ActiveX controls and OLE controls are one and the same) are fully compatible with ActiveX. Consequently, you can continue enhancing your code with the latest ActiveX controls while retaining your previous investments in OLE controls.

Support For Non-Internet Applications

The publicity surrounding ActiveX controls focuses on the World Wide Web. ActiveX controls are certainly great for the Web, but they work just as well in ordinary programs. You can insert ActiveX controls into word processors, spreadsheets, and just about any type of development tool. Unlike Java applets, they're not limited to Web browsers or running as standalone applications.

This friendliness toward non-Internet applications has changed the software market somewhat. In the past, companies would design add-ins for a specific product, such as a multilingual thesaurus for Microsoft Word. Today, by converting their add-ins to ActiveX controls, these companies can take advantage of a larger market for their software.

Compilation

When creating an ActiveX control in Visual C++, you must compile the control into native machine language before testing or debugging it. Visual C++ requires a lot of computer power to translate your C++ source code into native machine language, so you will often spend a good portion of your time sitting around waiting for your code to compile. It must be preprocessed, parsed, translated, optimized, linked, and then, finally, written to disk.

Java code, on the other hand, does not compile in the same way as other computer languages. Visual J++ simply translates Java code into bytecode, which must then be compiled into native machine language by the Web browser. No preprocessing or linking steps are necessary. As a result, "compile" times are much faster for Java applets than for ActiveX controls.

One way to avoid the sluggishness of ActiveX compile times is to develop your controls with Visual J++. You can combine the execution power of ActiveX controls with the compile speed of Java applets. See Chapter 8 for details on how to do this.

Execution

As discussed in Chapter 2, Java applets are not designed for any particular computer. The inside of an applet is just a string of bytecodes that describes how the program would run on a generic, virtual computer. Before actually executing your Java code, the Web browser or a command-line interpreter must translate the bytecodes into native machine language. Even with the most advanced just-in-time compilers, this translation slows the execution speed of a Java applet.

ActiveX controls, on the other hand, run directly on the system for which they were compiled. Thus, your controls will execute faster than applets, even if they contain the same algorithms. In addition, most compilers will optimize your ActiveX code by taking out redundant and unnecessary code.

ActiveX Controls And The Web Browser

To enable a Web page for Java applets, you first create an HTML file that contains the **<APPLET>** tag. This tag allows the Web browser to find, load, and display an applet. Then you simply upload the HTML file and the applet to a directory on the Web server. Any Java-compatible browser will automatically download the applet upon viewing the Web page.

Enabling a Web page for ActiveX controls works the same way; but instead of the **<APPLET>** tag, you use the **<OBJECT>** tag.

The <OBJECT> Tag

The **<OBJECT>** tag is an HTML code that provides information about an ActiveX control. Today, only Microsoft Internet Explorer has integrated support for ActiveX controls via this tag. Netscape Navigator also supports ActiveX controls and the **<OBJECT>** tag, but only with the addition of a plug-in available from NCompass Labs (**www.ncompasslabs.com**).

The format of the **<OBJECT>** tag looks like this:

```
<OBJECT
ALIGN=align-type
BORDER=n
CLASSID=url
CODEBASE=url
DATA=url
DECLARE
HEIGHT=n
HSPACE=n
ID=string
SHAPES
STANDBY=message
USEMAP=url
VSPACE=n
WIDTH=n>
<PARAM NAME="name" VALUE="value">
<PARAM ... >
...
error-text
</OBJECT>
```

The meaning of each line is as follows.

ALIGN sets the alignment for the control. The *align-type* can be one of these values:

- **BASELINE**—The bottom of the control aligns with the baseline of surrounding text.

- **CENTER**—The control is centered between the left and right margins. Subsequent text starts on the next line after the control.

- **LEFT**—The control aligns with the left margin, and subsequent text wraps along the right side of the control.

- **MIDDLE**—The middle of the control aligns with the baseline of the surrounding text.

- **RIGHT**—The control aligns with the right margin, and subsequent text wraps along the left side of the control.

- **TEXTBOTTOM**—The bottom of the control aligns with the bottom of the surrounding text.

- **TEXTMIDDLE**—The middle of the control aligns with the midpoint between the baseline and the x-height of the surrounding text.
- **TEXTTOP**—The top of the control aligns with the top of the surrounding text.

BORDER specifies the width of the border if the control is defined as a hyperlink.

The **CLASSID** parameter is a 16-byte number that uniquely identifies an ActiveX control. Also called a **GUID**, or globally unique identifier, it has no meaning in itself, but is required by the Web browser to find and load the control. **CLASSID** is analogous to the **<APPLET>** tag's **CODE** parameter.

When the browser hits an **<OBJECT>** tag, it reads the **CLASSID** parameter and searches the user's system registry for the **ID**. If the **ID** is found, the ActiveX control has already been installed. The registry contains further information on where to find the control on disk. Otherwise, the browser checks the **CODEBASE** parameter to obtain and install the new ActiveX control.

CODEBASE identifies the URL where the ActiveX control is located.

DATA is an optional parameter that identifies URL where external data can be loaded into the control.

DECLARE declares the control without loading it. Use this when you create cross-references to the control later in the document or when you use the control as a parameter in another control.

HEIGHT specifies the suggested height for the control. This parameter is required.

HSPACE specifies the horizontal gutter—the extra, empty space between the control and any text or images to the left or right of the control.

ID sets the name of the control. This name can be used in scripts and forms as a mnemonic reference to the control.

SHAPES specifies that the control has shaped hyperlinks.

STANDBY sets the message to show while loading the control. The user may then choose to cancel the download. In addition to the **STANDBY** message, the control's digital certificate will be displayed if the control has been digitally signed (see Chapter 11).

USEMAP specifies the image map to use with the control.

VSPACE specifies the vertical gutter—the extra, empty space between the control and any text or images above or below the control.

WIDTH specifies the suggested width for the control. This parameter is required.

The **<PARAM>** parameter allows you to set the properties of the ActiveX control immediately after it is loaded. For example, if you wanted to load an ActiveX timer control and knew beforehand that you wanted the period set at 250 milliseconds, your **<OBJECT>** tag would look something like this:

```
<OBJECT
   ID="Timer"
   WIDTH=39
   HEIGHT=39
   CLASSID="CLSID:59CCB4A0-727D-11CF-AC36-00AA00A47DD2">
   <PARAM NAME="Interval" VALUE="250">
</OBJECT>
```

The **error-text** portion of the **<OBJECT>** tag provides backward compatibility. Older Web browsers will display the *error-text* in place of the control, allowing you to inform the Web surfer that she should upgrade to an ActiveX-compatible browser.

Loading The Control

Unlike Java applets, ActiveX controls are *persistent*. This simply means that the Web browser saves a copy of the control to disk. If the browser encounters the same control in the future, it can quickly reload it directly from the user's system. A Java applet, in contrast, must travel through the network each time the browser encounters it. (Sun Microsystems is rumored to be working on a persistence capability for applets.)

Before actually saving an ActiveX control to disk, the Web browser performs three checks—license, version, and signature—to protect copyrights and ensure security.

LICENSE CHECK

The idea of persistence might make you a little uneasy. Even though you automatically receive a copyright by publishing an ActiveX control on the Web, unscrupulous users would still be able to use your control in their programs.

ActiveX controls include a mechanism to prevent the unlicensed use of controls on Web pages. The licensing mechanism works by allowing controls to be distributed with a *developer license*. With this license, users can insert the control into tools such as Visual Basic, Visual J++, and Visual C++. Without the developer license, users can only view the control within an existing application or Web page; they cannot modify its operation (see Figure 4.6). See Chapter 5 for information on how to create a developer license for your controls.

Supporting the licensing mechanism is entirely up to you. Some control vendors choose not to implement the mechanism, so their controls can be used for development purposes the moment they are installed in your computer. (Microsoft is one of the few companies that does this; they desperately want to turn ActiveX controls into a standard, so they're giving away tons of controls for free.) Other vendors permit royalty-free

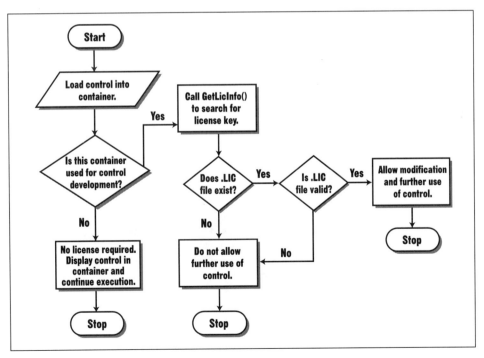

Figure 4.6 How the Web browser searches for an ActiveX control license.

ActiveX Fundamentals

distribution of the runtime version of the control only, while charging for the developer license. Before you use a control in a Web page, read its license agreement so you understand how it can be distributed.

VERSION CHECK

All ActiveX controls can be stamped with a version number, such as 2.01. Before downloading the control, the Web browser reads this number, and if an older control is installed on the user's system, it replaces the old version with the new one.

SIGNATURE CHECK

To ensure that an ActiveX control will not harm your system, the Web browser searches the control for a digital signature before installing it. If the license is found, the browser displays a digital certificate (see Figure 4.7) that informs you of who wrote the control. Otherwise, the browser asks for permission to download the potentially harmful control.

After performing license, version, and signature checks, the browser can safely load and display an ActiveX control on a Web page.

ActiveX Control Pad

When ActiveX controls first came on the scene, inserting them into an HTML file was mighty tedious. First you had to look up the control's

Figure 4.7 When downloading a signed control for the first time, Microsoft Internet Explorer will display its digital certificate.

CLASSID in the system registry, copy the number to the clipboard, type in the **<OBJECT>** tag, paste the **CLASSID** into the tag, and finally save the control to disk. Whew! To make matters worse, a single typo would cause the browser to whine and complain, and you'd have to start all over again.

I decided that the world of ActiveX needed a break from this tedium, so I spent an afternoon creating a Windows 95 program that automates the task of inserting an ActiveX control into a Web page. It finds all the controls in the system registry and displays a list of them for the user to select. With just the click of a button, the program can then copy the appropriate **<OBJECT>** tag to the clipboard, allowing the user to paste the tag directly into an HTML file.

The very next day, Microsoft announced a new product called the ActiveX Control Pad. It was quite similar to the utility I had created 24 hours earlier. "They stole my idea!" I joked to myself.

Seriously, though, the ActiveX Control Pad is much better than anything I could come up with. It's available free from Microsoft's Web page, and it offers these timesaving features:

- You can write and edit HTML files with the HTML Source Editor.

- It can insert **<OBJECT>** tags automatically from a list of available ActiveX controls.

- It allows you to set the parameters of any **<OBJECT>** using standard ActiveX property pages.

- You can use the Script Wizard to handle events and call methods in the controls you just added.

Check out Chapter 9 for a rundown of the Script Wizard and other Control Pad goodies.

Inserting ActiveX Controls

With the ActiveX Control Pad, you can easily put ActiveX controls on a Web page. You can begin with either a brand new HTML file (see Figure 4.8) or an existing one. Simply select New or Open from the Control Pad's File menu.

Once you've got an HTML file open in the Control Pad, you're ready to insert an ActiveX control. I'll use the Microsoft Image Control as an example of how to do this.

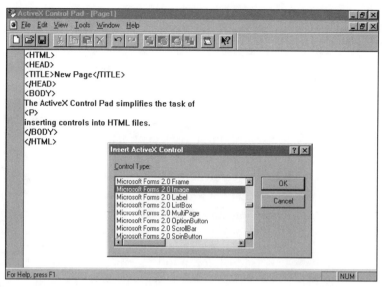

Figure 4.8 The ActiveX Control Pad simplifies the task of inserting controls into HTML files.

SELECT THE CONTROL

First, move the cursor to the position in the HTML file where you want to place the ActiveX control. For this demonstration, you can put it anywhere between the **<BODY>** and **</BODY>** tags.

HTML WYSIWYG ASAP, FWIW

Standard HTML files give you almost no control over the placement of ActiveX controls. To combat this problem, you can use the HTML Layout Editor to specify the exact location, size, and layering of the controls. The Layout Editor is part of the ActiveX Control Pad, located under the Edit menu. For more information, see the Control Pad's online help.

Next, go to the Edit menu and choose Insert ActiveX Control. The Control Pad will present you with a list of all controls installed on your system. Select the Microsoft Forms 2.0 Image item, then click the OK button.

OPEN THE CONTROL EDITOR

After you click OK, the Control Pad will bring up the Control Editor, which consists of two windows:

- *The Form Sheet*—This window allows you to change the size of the control and preview how it will look on the Web page. To change its size, simply drag one of the control's eight handles. As you drag, the control size will conform to the grid settings of the Form Sheet. You can change these settings in the HTML Layout dialog box, which is located in Tools|Options. Note: Some controls, such as timer controls, are not visible when you view them on a Web page. The image you see in the Form Sheet is just a symbolic representation of the control.

- *The Property Sheet*—This window displays a list of each property of the control, such as the background color, caption text, and border style. All properties remain at their defaults unless you explicitly change them. To change a property, select its name from the list, click on the Edit box at the top of the sheet, then type the new value. You must click the Apply button to save your changes.

UNCOVER HIDDEN PROPERTY SHEETS

Many ActiveX controls provide special property sheets that are unique to each control. These sheets allow you to edit certain properties, such as rows and columns of data, that don't fit in the standard Property Sheet window. They also provide a more intuitive view of the properties through their use of tabbed dialog boxes.

In the ActiveX Control Pad, the only time you can view these special property sheets is when the control is displayed in the Form Sheet window. First, right-click on the control; this will bring up a context menu. Next, choose the second item on the menu (the first one is just the normal Property Sheet window). The ActiveX control will display its special property pages—but only if it supports them. If you need an example, check out the Fire Animation control in Chapter 5.

To see the Control Editor in action, change some values in the Image control's Property Sheet. Figure 4.9 shows the result of changing the Image control's Picture property so that it points to a bitmap stored on the hard disk.

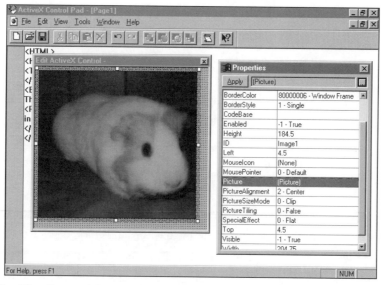

Figure 4.9 The Control Editor allows you to preset a control's properties.

Once you've got the properties the way you want them, you can close the Control Editor windows and see the **<OBJECT>** tag that was instantly created for you by the Control Pad. You'll also see an icon in the left-hand margin of the HTML file (see Figure 4.10). Clicking on this icon brings up the Control Editor windows in case you need to change the control's properties again.

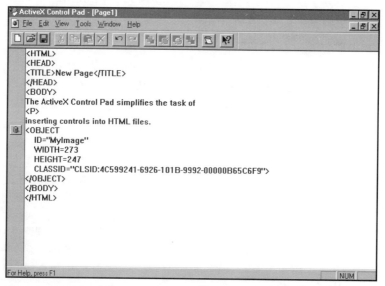

Figure 4.10 The ActiveX Control Pad displays a clickable icon next to each **<OBJECT>** tag.

The Control Editor can't handle all situations. Many times you simply won't know the value of a control's property until the control actually loads onto a Web page. For example, you might want to display a Text control that reads either "Good Morning" or "Good Evening", based on the current time. In this case, you could write an HTML script that checks the time and changes the Text property accordingly. See Chapter 9 for information on how the ActiveX Control Pad can help you write scripts.

Now that you know what ActiveX controls are and how to use them, take a look at Chapter 5 to learn how to create some controls of your own.

Chapter 5

Building ActiveX Controls

- Creating ActiveX controls with Visual C++
- Properties, methods, and events
- Debugging ActiveX controls
- Making your control Java-compatible
- ActiveX sample code

My home town of Kansas City, Kansas, is famous for its infectious jazz, red-hot barbecue sauce, and a massive roller coaster called the Timberwolf. Made entirely of wood, the Timberwolf is 1,400 feet of vicious loops, wicked corkscrews, and other lunch-launching G-forces. One ride will give you a new appreciation for solid ground.

My first trip on the Timberwolf was a lot like my first experience writing ActiveX controls. In the beginning, I was intimidated. The endless connections of bolts and lumber made me suspicious. All I could see was an immense framework looming over me. It was big, powerful, and complex—just like ActiveX. As I climbed into my seat, I crossed my fingers and hoped that the Timberwolf's engineers knew what they were doing.

Moments later, a motorized chain was pulling me carefully up the first slope. I held my breath as the car slowed, almost stopped, and then suddenly rolled over the peak. My stomach stayed behind as the rest of my body plunged down the wooden mountain.

After a few twists and turns, I began to enjoy myself. The Timberwolf wasn't so scary after I learned how to lean into the turns and tighten my grip before each loop. I just wish someone had taught me these basic skills before I started the ride.

I have the same philosophy about learning how to write ActiveX controls. The adventure is much easier if you know the basics before you begin. Once you're past the initial learning curve, you can relax and enjoy the ride. That's exactly how this chapter will help you: It'll pull you over the learning curve without the need for complicated explanations.

Visual C++

Visual J++, while great for writing Java code and integrating it with ActiveX controls, is a poor environment for true ActiveX development. Microsoft offers a better choice for creating ActiveX controls: Visual C++. This program is a sibling of Visual J++, sharing the same interface (see Figure 5.1) and many basic features.

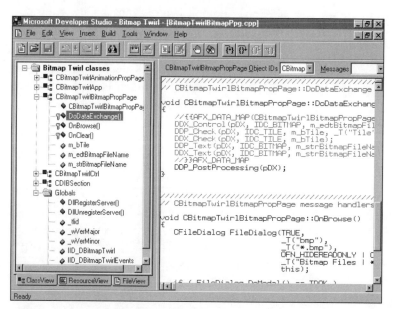

Figure 5.1 Visual C++, a tool for building ActiveX controls, looks similar to Visual J++.

If you don't have Visual C++ 4.x, don't worry. You can still create ActiveX controls with Visual J++. (Chapter 8 shows you how.) But if that's true, then why is Visual C++ necessary? The answer is chronological: Visual C++ is older than Visual J++. The former has been around for half a decade, while the latter was only recently released. Microsoft has had plenty of time to put a new coat of paint and chrome hubcaps on Visual C++, but Visual J++ still carries the factory-installed AM radio. In other words, stick to Visual C++ for any serious ActiveX development.

Visual C++ is obviously a C++ tool, so of course you'll need some knowledge of C++ for this chapter. Experience with the Microsoft Foundation Classes (MFC) would also be helpful, but not mandatory. As long as you can click buttons and know the difference between *public* and *private*, you'll be okay.

further developments

Why Visual C++

As a die-hard fan of Borland's tools, this tutorial on Microsoft's compiler makes me cringe. I don't like to restrict anyone to a single company. But when it comes to writing ActiveX controls, I happen to think that Visual C++ 4.x is a must-have. As you'll discover later in this chapter, it has some nice features that eliminate most of the grunt work in ActiveX development.

As of this writing, Visual C++ is the only tool available that can create ActiveX controls. Competing products from Borland and Symantec can compile OLE controls, but they offer neither a front end as nice as Microsoft's nor the latest ActiveX enhancements. Hopefully, these companies will soon catch up to Microsoft and force Visual C++ to become an even better product.

Building An ActiveX Control

If you've read Chapter 4, then you've learned the basic concepts of an ActiveX control and already have enough information to build one for yourself. Don't fret over the more advanced topics; I'll explain those as I go along. For now, you can use Visual C++ to generate a complete ActiveX control without writing a scrap of code. Simply create a new project with the OLE ControlWizard—remember that ActiveX controls are OLE controls in disguise—leaving all settings at their defaults (see Figure 5.2). After clicking on Finish, you will have written 726 lines of code in less than a minute.

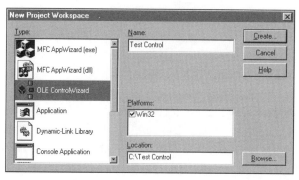

Figure 5.2 The OLE ControlWizard can generate a complete ActiveX control in just a few seconds.

The project you just created is nothing more than a skeleton, but it's still a fully functional ActiveX control. It has three source-code files: **App**, **PropPage**, and **Ctrl**. The **App** module handles such basic housekeeping chores as initializing the control and cleaning up after it. The **PropPage** module provides a dialog-box template that allows users of your ActiveX control to customize its options (in other words, to change its properties). The last module, **Ctrl**, is the meat and potatoes of your ActiveX control (see Figure 5.3). It contains code for drawing the control, sending and receiving Windows messages, and so on.

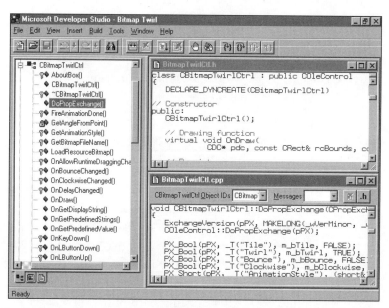

Figure 5.3 In Visual C++, the **Ctrl** module is the heart of an ActiveX control.

126 *Chapter 5*

If you take a closer look at the **Ctrl** module (*Ctl.cpp), you'll notice that your ActiveX control is a class derived from **COleControl**. This MFC class encapsulates the functionality of an ActiveX control and shields you from those funky OLE dispatch interfaces. As you grow more comfortable writing controls, you should take a look at the documentation for **COleControl** to learn more about its advanced features.

further developments

The Invaluable Infoviewer

Microsoft Developer Studio provides a slick interface to its online documentation. This interface, called the InfoViewer, includes a powerful search tool that can adapt to your needs. To access the tool, press Ctrl+F and switch to the Query tab, then type one or more keywords. Pressing Enter will bring up a list of all InfoViewer topics that match those keywords.

Because the InfoViewer's search tool is so comprehensive, you may have a hard time narrowing your query. Here are some simple techniques that will help you find the exact topic you're looking for:

- *Phrases*—To search for a phrase, enclose two or more words in quotes. For example, to find a list of the class members in **COleControl**, type "COleControl class members".

- *AND Operator*—By default, InfoViewer performs an AND search on your keywords. For example, "COleControl class members" typed without quotes will find topics containing the words **COleControl** AND class AND members, in any order.

- *OR Operator*—To expand your search, separate words with the OR operator. Typing "COleControl or COleControlModule", for example, will find topics containing one or both of these words.

- *NOT Operator*—To confine your search, prefix words with the NOT operator. For instance, "COleControl and property not font" will find information on all **COleControl** properties excluding font properties.

- *Parentheses*—You can change the precedence of the AND, OR, and NOT operators using parentheses. For example, a search of "COleControl constructor or destructor" will include *any* topic containing the word *destructor*, whereas "COleControl (constructor or destructor)" will limit the search to **COleControl** topics.

The ClassWizard

At this point, you could jump right in and start developing your newly created control. You could modify the ControlWizard's code or add some of your own. Then, you could simply compile the control and use it directly in your projects.

As a beginner, however, you may find these steps too difficult. You may not always know where to insert new code and how to make it compatible with the ActiveX architecture. A single typo could generate a cryptic and frustrating compiler error.

The ClassWizard can help eliminate these problems (see Figure 5.4). Located under the View menu, this tool can add code with the click of a button. It automates the task of adding, deleting, and modifying code in an ActiveX control.

Although the ClassWizard contains five tabs, only two—OLE Automation and OLE Events—are relevant to this chapter. The OLE Automation tab is more important, so you'll want to check it out first. After switching to this tab, make sure that the Class Name is set to the **Ctrl** module. You'll then see a list of properties and methods under the External Names list box. You will also see several buttons on the right-hand side, as shown in Figure 5.4:

- *Add Property*—This button adds a member variable, also known as a *property*, to your control. (See the following section for details.)

- *Add Method*—This button adds a member function, also known as a *method*, to your control. (See the section titled "Methods" for more information.)

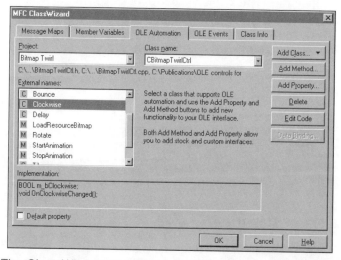

Figure 5.4 The ClassWizard allows you to add code just by clicking buttons.

- *Edit Code*—This button closes the ClassWizard and positions your cursor at the item currently selected in the External Names box. You can then modify the item manually.

- *Delete*—The Delete button allows you to delete code, but it applies only to header files (*Ctl.h). You'll have to remove the implementation from the source file (*Ctl.cpp) manually.

The following sections provide more details on these buttons and the OLE Events tab.

CREATE YOUR OWN SHORTCUT KEYS

Shortcut keys give you instant access to common features. Pressing Ctrl+W, for instance, brings up the ClassWizard. Other handy shortcuts are F7 for Build, F5 for Go, and Alt+F9 for Breakpoints.

Microsoft Developer Studio installs these shortcuts automatically, but you can easily change them or add your own. Choose Tools|Customize, and then select the Keyboard tab. From there, you can choose a command, press the desired key combination, and click on the Assign button to install the shortcut.

*My favorite keyboard shortcut is Ctrl+Q, which toggles between normal and full-screen views. I added this shortcut by choosing the **ViewFullScreen** command from the **View** category. (For proper configuration, I had to add the shortcut twice: once for the Main editor and again for the Text editor.)*

Properties

Most ActiveX controls contain *properties*. A property is like a member variable in C++. It's a data type—such as integer, boolean, or string—that holds some meaningful value. For example, a timer control might contain an integer property that keeps track of elapsed seconds.

In addition to the basic types, properties can hold special data, such as dates, currencies, and colors. ActiveX defines these types; you can't create your own. (You could, however, store user-defined data in memory, then create a property of type **long** that points to that memory.)

Properties come in three flavors:

- *Stock Properties*—Certain properties, such as the background color, the primary font, and the enabled state, are so universal that they're required by even the simplest of controls. Microsoft recognized the need for these properties and put support for them directly into the ActiveX architecture. As a result, stock properties are easy to implement, and the **COleControl** base class provides access to all of them. For instance, to disable your control, you would just call **SetEnabled(FALSE)**.

- *Ambient Properties*—Ambient properties aren't true properties. They're actually property *values* that come directly from a control's container. At any point in your code, you can query a container for the current value of an ambient property. For example, calling **AmbientFont()**, a member function of **COleControl**, will return a handle to the container's primary font.

- *Custom Properties*—Stock properties are convenient, but your control will soon outgrow the built-in variables provided by ActiveX. Eventually, you'll need to add custom properties. These special attributes are nothing more than properties with a user-defined name. A file viewer control, for instance, might contain a custom property called **FileName** of type **CString**.

TRANSLATING OLE_COLOR

OLE_COLOR is a special ActiveX data type for storing color information. All control properties—including stock properties, such as ForeColor and BackColor—must be of this type. Unfortunately, the Windows graphics subsystem can't use OLE_COLOR; it knows only the COLOR_REF data type.

To translate an OLE_COLOR value to a COLOR_REF value, you'll need to call COleControl's TranslateColor() function. As an example, the following code draws text to the screen using the ambient foreground color:

```
CDC* pdc = GetDC();
pdc->SetTextColor( TranslateColor(AmbientForeColor()) );
pdc->TextOut(0, 0, "I can be such a punkin-head sometimes.");
```

HANDLING PROPERTY ACCESS

Normally, ActiveX controls allow complete access to their properties. Containers can read properties directly and can change them to any value; controls are not allowed to intervene.

Controls can, however, create special *notification functions* that are called whenever the value of a property changes. For example, a calendar control might have a notification function tied to its date property. This function would simply repaint the calendar to reflect the new date.

Although you can give notification functions any name, you should label them according to ActiveX etiquette. The naming convention requires that you sandwich the property name between the words "On" and "Changed". For instance, the notification function in the previous example would be called **OnDateChanged**().

THROWING ERRORS

*If your control runs out of memory, can't find a file, or hits some other error, you should notify the user of the problem. To do so, call the **COleControl** member function **ThrowError**(). This function takes two parameters: a status code and a string. The status code signifies the type of error, and the string provides a short description that will appear in a message box for the user. See the documentation of **ThrowError**() for more details, including a complete list of status codes.*

Even with notification functions, properties are utterly naked. Your control and its container can manipulate them freely. This approach simplifies your work, but it also causes problems. Suppose, for example, you want to limit an integer property to values no greater than five. With the default implementation of property access, this scenario would not be possible.

The ActiveX architecture offers a solution: You can shield your property with *Get/Set methods*. The Get method returns the current value of a property, and the Set method changes it to a new value. This technique is helpful if a property must be calculated before it is read, or validated before it is written.

Building ActiveX Controls **131**

Just as notification functions do, Get/Set methods follow a standard naming convention. Simply prefix the property name with "Get" or "Set" accordingly. The ClassWizard can do this work for you, as explained in the next section.

Adding Properties With The ClassWizard

The ClassWizard provides a quick and easy way to add properties to your control. Here is the step-by-step process:

1. Go to the OLE Automation page of ClassWizard.

2. Select the **Ctrl** module from the class name list.

3. Click the Add Property button.

4. Type the name of your property, such as **MyProp**.

5. Select the type of your property, such as **BOOL** for boolean (see Figure 5.5).

After you click OK, the ClassWizard adds the property to your control and provides a member variable for it (such as **m_bMyProp**). You can find the declaration of this variable inside your **Ctrl** module's header file (*Ctl.h), and you can change its value just as you would change any other variable.

Because this member variable is tied to a property, containers automatically have access to it. You need to worry only about special cases, such as redrawing the control when the property changes. (In that case, you would call **InvalidateControl()** inside the **OnMyPropChanged()** notification function.)

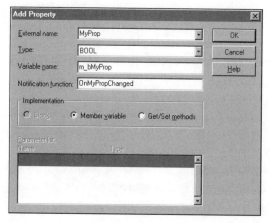

Figure 5.5 With help from the ClassWizard, you can easily add properties to your control.

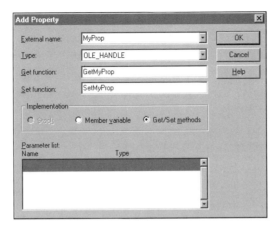

Figure 5.6 Get/Set methods allow you to control property access.

If you don't want containers to have complete access to a property, the ClassWizard can cloak it with Get/Set methods. Simply click on the Get/Set methods radio button when adding the property (see Figure 5.6).

READ-ONLY PROPERTIES
You can make properties read-only. Just make sure that the Set function is blank when adding a property from the ClassWizard.

PROPERTY EXCHANGE FUNCTIONS

After the ClassWizard has added a property, you must initialize it by hand. Don't be tempted to set its value from inside the class constructor, as you would in normal C++ programs. Instead, you should initialize the property in **DoPropExchange()**, a member function of **COleControl** that the OLE ControlWizard added for you automatically.

DoPropExchange() has a dual purpose. First, it sets each property to a default value whenever an instance of the control is created. Second, it allows a container to *serialize* the properties (to save or load them from disk). This feature allows the state of a control to be restored even after the system has shut down.

Each property data type has its own exchange function prefixed with **PX_**. For example, to initialize the **MyProp** property to false, you would insert the following line into the **DoPropExchange()** function:

```
PX_Bool(pPX, _T("MyProp"), m_bMyProp, FALSE);
```

The first parameter points to a **CPropExchange** object provided by **DoPropExchange()**; the second parameter is the external name of the property; the third parameter is a reference to the property's member variable; and the final parameter is the default value of the property. Table 5.1 provides a list of exchange functions for each property type.

ENUMERATED PROPERTIES

C++ provides a keyword called **enum,** which allows you to define a range of values for a given variable. For example, a variable for holding color information may be declared as follows:

```
enum COLOR_TYPE
{ RED, WHITE, BLUE };

COLOR_TYPE clrBackground;
```

The compiler checks **enum** variables to ensure that they always contain proper values. For instance, **clrBackground = BLUE** is a valid

Table 5.1 Property Exchange (PX) functions.

Data Type	Function Declaration
boolean	PX_Bool(CPropExchange*, LPCTSTR, BOOL&, BOOL)
Color	PX_Color(CPropExchange*, LPCTSTR, OLE_COLOR&, OLE_COLOR)
Currency	PX_Currency(CPropExchange*, LPCTSTR, CY&, CY)
double	PX_Double(CPropExchange*, LPCTSTR, double&, double)
float	PX_Float(CPropExchange*, LPCTSTR, float&, float)
Font	PX_Font(CPropExchange*, LPCTSTR, CFontHolder&, const FONTDESC*)
IUnknown	PX_IUnknown(CPropExchange*, LPCTSTR, LPUNKNOWN&, REFIID)
long	PX_Long(CPropExchange*, LPCTSTR, long&, long)
Picture	PX_Picture(CPropExchange*, LPCTSTR, CPictureHolder&, CPictureHolder&)
short	PX_Short(CPropExchange*, LPCTSTR, short&, short)
String	PX_String(CPropExchange*, LPCTSTR, CString&, CString)
ULong	PX_ULong(CPropExchange*, LPCTSTR, ULONG&, long)
UShort	PX_UShort(CPropExchange*, LPCTSTR, USHORT&, USHORT)

statement, while **clrBackground = PURPLE** would generate a compiler error.

In ActiveX controls, the **enum** keyword does not exist. You can still use it for internal C++ code, but you're not allowed to declare properties as **enum**. Luckily, ActiveX does provide an **enum** alternative, but it's a halfhearted solution and a bit of a hack. If you absolutely must create an enumerated property, here are the steps to follow:

1. Use the ClassWizard to create a property of type **short**.

2. Create an **enum** data type that defines a range of possible values for the property (as in the **COLOR_TYPE** example just shown). Insert this declaration into the **Ctrl** module's header file (*Ctl.h).

3. Insert the following lines into the public area of the **Ctrl** module's class declaration (located in the same header file). Don't worry about the purpose of these functions; their meanings are esoteric. Just continue with the remaining steps:

```
BOOL OnGetPredefinedStrings(DISPID dispid, CStringArray*
pStringArray, CDWordArray* pCookieArray);
BOOL OnGetPredefinedValue(DISPID dispid, DWORD dwCookie,
VARIANT FAR* lpvarOut);
BOOL OnGetDisplayString(DISPID dispid, CString& strValue);
```

4. Implement the **OnGetPredefinedStrings()** function inside the **Ctrl** module's source file (*Ctl.cpp). See Listing 5.1 for an example.

LISTING 5.1 THE ONGETPREDEFINEDSTRINGS() EXAMPLE.

```
BOOL CColorCtrl::OnGetPredefinedStrings(DISPID dispid,
                                        CStringArray*
                                        pStringArray,
                                        CDWordArray*
                                        pCookieArray)
{
   BOOL bResult = FALSE;

   switch (dispid)
   {
      case dispidColor: // Replace "Color" with the name of
                       // your property.

      try
      {
         CString Style;
```

```
            Style = "Red";
            pStringArray->Add(Style);
            pCookieArray->Add(0);

            Style = "White";
            pStringArray->Add(Style);
            pCookieArray->Add(1);

            Style = "Blue";
            pStringArray->Add(Style);
            pCookieArray->Add(2);

            bResult = TRUE;
        }

        catch(CException* e)
        {
            pStringArray->RemoveAll();
            pCookieArray->RemoveAll();
            bResult = FALSE;
            e->Delete();
        }

        break;
    }

    if (!bResult)
        return COleControl::OnGetPredefinedStrings(dispid,
                                                    pStringArray,
                                                    pCookieArray);

    return TRUE;
}
```

5. Implement the **OnGetPredefinedValue()** function inside the **Ctrl** module's source file (*Ctl.cpp). See Listing 5.2 for an example.

LISTING 5.2 THE ONGETPREDEFINEDVALUE() EXAMPLE.

```
BOOL CColorCtrl::OnGetPredefinedValue(DISPID dispid,
                                      DWORD dwCookie,
                                      VARIANT FAR* lpvarOut)
{
    switch (dispid)
    {
        case dispidColor: // Replace "Color" with the name of
                          // your property.
```

```
    {
        VariantClear(lpvarOut);
        V_VT(lpvarOut) = VT_I2;
        V_I2(lpvarOut) = (short)dwCookie;
        return TRUE;
    }
}

return COleControl::OnGetPredefinedValue(dispid, dwCookie,
    lpvarOut);
}
```

6. Implement the **OnGetDisplayString()** function inside the **Ctrl** module's source file (*Ctl.cpp). See Listing 5.3 for an example.

LISTING 5.3 THE ONGETDISPLAYSTRINGS() EXAMPLE.

```
BOOL CColorCtrl::OnGetDisplayString(DISPID dispid, CString&
strValue)
{
    switch (dispid)
    {
        case dispidColor: // Replace "Color" with the name of
                          // your property.

            switch (m_Color) // Replace "Color" with the name of
                             // your property.
            {
                case RED:
                    strValue = "Red";
                    break;

                case WHITE:
                    strValue = "White";
                    break;

                case BLUE:
                    strValue = "Blue";
                    break;

                default:
                    return FALSE;
            }

            return TRUE;

        default:
```

```
            return COleControl::OnGetDisplayString(dispid,
        strValue);
    }
}
```

7. Compile the control and insert it into a container. Most containers recognize the enumerated values, and they will display them instead of the integer equivalents.

Methods

Methods in ActiveX controls are similar to C++ member functions. They can take parameters and return a value. Because methods conform to a binary standard, any ActiveX-compatible program can call them without the need for source code.

Adding methods to an ActiveX control is easy. Just bring up the ClassWizard. From there, follow these steps:

1. Switch to the OLE Automation tab.

2. Make sure that the Class Name is set to the **Ctrl** module.

3. Click the Add Method button.

4. Type a name for the method, such as **BeginProcess**, in the External Name box.

5. Skip the Internal Name box, leaving it identical to the External Name.

6. Choose a return type from the Return Type list. (Select **void** if the method does not return a value.)

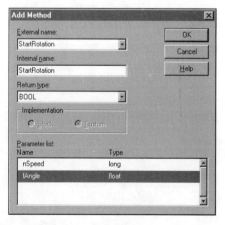

Figure 5.7 The ClassWizard makes adding methods a trivial task.

7. If the method has parameters, add them to the Parameter List by clicking on an empty row (see Figure 5.7).

Casting For Parameters

*ActiveX limits the data types of method parameters and return values to a specific set. This fixed set omits standard Windows types such as **HINSTANCE** and **LPSTR**. You can still use these types, however, by casting them to an ActiveX type. For example, you can cast **HINSTANCE**, **HBITMAP**, and other Windows handles to **OLE_HANDLE**. Likewise, you can cast **LPSTR**, **LPLOGPALETTE**, and any other 32-bit memory pointer to **long**. Remember that ActiveX containers must also cast to these types when calling a control's method.*

Events

A method is an easy way for a container to communicate with an ActiveX control. The conversation, however, can also go in the opposite direction. By sending an *event*, a control can throw information back to its container. Events can notify the container of any occurrence: a key press, the completion of a lengthy process, a timer message, and so on. If necessary, events can hold additional information in the form of parameters. Event parameters are just like method parameters; they can be integers, strings, or any standard ActiveX data type.

To add an event to your control, open the ClassWizard and follow these steps:

1. Click on the OLE Events tab.
2. Click the Add Event button.
3. Type the name of your event, such as **ProcessComplete**.
4. Skip the Internal Name box, allowing ClassWizard to fill it in for you.
5. If your event requires parameters, add them to the Parameter List (see Figure 5.8).

After you click OK, ClassWizard will install the event in the control. You may send it at any point in your code. Simply treat the event's Internal Name as a standard C++ function. The following code, for instance, would send the **ProcessComplete** event shown in Figure 5.8:

Figure 5.8 You can add events quickly when using the ClassWizard.

```
FireProcessComplete(nElapsedTime);
```

After calling this internal function, the event is posted systemwide. Any container that has created an instance of your control will catch the event and respond as necessary.

RECYCLING STANDARD C++ CLASSES

Don't forget to check out the Visual C++ Component Gallery, located under the Insert menu. It's one of those cool tools that makes you say, "Why didn't somebody think of this a long time ago?" Not only can it add ActiveX controls to your project, it can also act as a repository for your standard C++ classes. The Component Gallery can export these classes to a single file, which you can share with your co-workers.

To add a C++ class to the Gallery, go to the ClassView in the Project Workspace, right-click on the class name, and then select Add To Component Gallery. To export a C++ class, open the Component Gallery, click Customize, select the class from the list, click Properties, switch to the Custom tab, and then click Export.

Debugging ActiveX Controls

Debugging an ActiveX control works the same as any other application. You can set breakpoints, add watches, and view the call stack. The only difference is that an ActiveX control requires an ActiveX container. You can debug with an existing container, or you can create one of your own.

Prefabricated Containers

Visual C++ includes an ActiveX testbed called the "OLE Control Test Container" (see Figure 5.9). This program allows you to prototype and debug several controls simultaneously. To set it up, go to the Debug tab of the Visual C++ Build Settings dialog box. Under Executable for debug session, type the complete filespec of tstcon32.exe, found in Visual C++'s bin directory.

You now have the ability to run and debug your control as you would any other Visual C++ application. When the Test Container loads, you can insert the control and view its properties. You can also invoke its methods and catch its events. If these actions cause the control to generate an error or reach a breakpoint, you will automatically bounce back to Visual C++, where you can fix the problem.

Custom Containers

The OLE Control Test Container is quick and easy, but it's brain-damaged. After four revisions, it still contains some minor bugs and doesn't respond properly to certain ActiveX events. As an alternative, you can create your own test container. Just follow these steps:

1. Build your ActiveX control.

Figure 5.9 The OLE Control Test Container can help you test and debug ActiveX controls.

Building ActiveX Controls **141**

2. Create a new project using the MFC AppWizard, making sure that the application is dialog-based and that support for OLE controls is enabled. (See the Visual C++ documentation for enabling this support in an existing project.)

3. Use the Component Gallery, located on the Insert menu, to add your ActiveX control to the test project (see Figure 5.10).

4. In the Project Workspace, switch to the ResourceView and open the main dialog box resource.

5. You will see an icon for your ActiveX control inside the Controls toolbar. Drag this icon onto the dialog box resource.

6. Open the ClassWizard and go to the Member Variables tab. Select the ID of the control you just inserted.

7. Click the Add Variable button, then type a name for the variable (such as **m_MyControl**) and click OK.

When these steps are complete, ClassWizard adds a member variable to your test project. This variable is a wrapper object for your ActiveX control. You can access the control's properties and methods simply by calling the appropriate functions in the wrapper object.

In addition to dialog-based containers, you can also embed controls in Single Document Interface (SDI) or Multiple Document Interface (MDI) applications. But don't count on any help from ClassWizard if you go

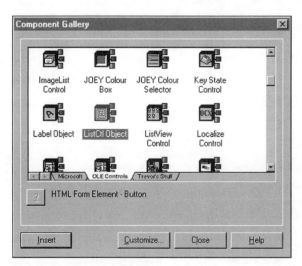

Figure 5.10   With the Component Gallery, you can quickly add ActiveX controls to your projects.

this route. You'll have to do all the coding yourself. See the Bitmap Twirl Container later in this chapter (and found on this book's CD-ROM) for an example.

> **EVENT SINK MAPS**
> *In Visual C++, ActiveX containers must always catch a control's events, even if they plan to ignore them. Otherwise, they will crash violently—a fact that the Visual C++ documentation fails to mention. Catching events requires a cryptic piece of code called an event sink map. In dialog-based applications, event sink maps are virtually invisible because the ClassWizard installs them automatically. In SDI- or MDI-based apps, however, you must insert event sink maps by hand. For more information, see the help topic "event sink maps" in the InfoViewer index, or check out the Bitmap Twirl Container on this book's CD-ROM.*

Just-In-Time Debugging

The Visual C++ debugger places significant overhead on your system. It can slow down the execution speed of ActiveX controls and reduce the amount of memory available to them. Therefore, you may want to test an ActiveX control outside of the Visual C++ environment.

Even when it's not running, Visual C++ can still help you debug ActiveX controls. It includes a handy feature called a *just-in-time debugger*. To enable support for this feature, make sure that a checkmark is placed in the just-in-time debugging box, located under the Debug tab of the Options dialog (see Figure 5.11).

After enabling the just-in-time debugger, you may test any ActiveX control outside of Visual C++. If it tries to access out-of-bounds memory, divide by zero, or perform some other potentially fatal action, the Windows operating system will halt its execution and present you with the dialog box shown in Figure 5.12.

Clicking the Debug button in this dialog box will automatically load Visual C++, open the project settings for your ActiveX control, and display the code that caused the error...just in time! You can then track down the source of the bug and kill it.

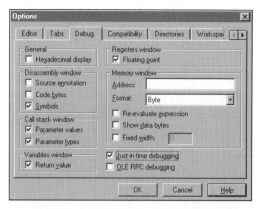

Figure 5.11 When just-in-time debugging is enabled, you can debug ActiveX controls even though Visual C++ is not running.

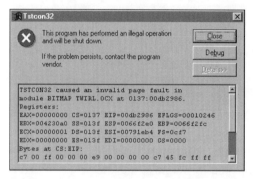

Figure 5.12 Fatal errors in an ActiveX control cause this error message to appear.

GIVE YOURSELF SOME ELBOW ROOM

For more space in the editor window, select Tools|Options, and then go to the Editor tab and uncheck the Selection Margin box.

Preparing Your Control For Visual J++

When Microsoft first announced Visual J++, they glorified the wonders of ActiveX integration. They claimed that your Java code could hook up with any of the hundreds of ActiveX controls already on the market, easily saving you time and money.

As the months passed, the product's features began to solidify. Team J++, in a furious effort to meet their deadline, had to throw out several key innovations of ActiveX controls. The final version of Visual J++ failed to meet the expectations set by Microsoft's press releases.

Feature Limitations

Visual J++ can integrate Java code with ActiveX controls, but only if those controls satisfy the following requirements:

- *Controls must be nonvisual*—Most controls have a visual representation at runtime. They paint themselves whenever their container sends a message to do so. The Java VM, however, does not send ActiveX paint messages, so visual controls cannot integrate with Java code.

- *Controls must not post events*—The Java VM does not catch events thrown by ActiveX controls. Therefore, you should not add event handling to a control if you want to integrate it with Java.

Team J++ will probably remove these restrictions in the next release of their product. Until then, most commercial ActiveX controls cannot integrate directly with your Java code. See Chapter 7 for more information on integrating basic ActiveX controls with Java.

HTML Scripts
HTML scripts allow you to integrate any Java applet with any ActiveX control, including visual controls that post events. See Chapter 9 for details.

Creating Nonvisual Controls

As mentioned in the previous section, ActiveX controls must be nonvisual if you want to integrate them with Java code. To make a control invisible at runtime, follow these steps:

1. Open the **Ctrl** module (*Ctl.cpp).

2. Find the section on Control Type Information, where you should see five **OLEMISC** constants. Replace all of them with the constant **OLEMISC_INVISIBLEATRUNTIME**.

3. Locate the control's constructor (such as **CMyControl::CMyControl**) and add the following line:

```
SetInitialSize(32, 32);
```

4. Locate the control's **OnDraw()** function and replace its contents with these lines:

```
CPictureHolder PictureHolder;
CRect rcIcon(0, 0, 32, 32);

PictureHolder.CreateFromIcon(IDI_ABOUTDLL);
PictureHolder.Render(pdc, rcBounds, rcIcon);
```

5. Go to your project's ResourceView, open the **IDI_ABOUTDLL** icon, and draw a new image that represents your control. (This step is optional.)

Your control is now nonvisual. It will not be seen in runtime programs—such as Web browsers—even if the control has been inserted and is working properly. It will appear only in design-time programs—such as the ActiveX Control Pad—which display your control's **IDI_ABOUTDLL** icon.

Version Stamping

Before using your ActiveX control in Visual J++, you should make sure that it has been stamped with a proper version number. The OLE ControlWizard initialized this number at "1.0", but you should update it with every new version of your control.

Changing The Version Information

To change the version, go to your project's ResourceView and open the **VS_VERSION_INFORMATION** resource. You will see a **FILEVERSION** key containing four numbers. The first and second numbers are the major and minor versions. For example, a major version of 4 and a minor version of 70 would produce a version number of 4.70. The third number is the rarely seen sub-minor version, as in 4.70.13. The last number is the build number, typically used only for large team projects.

After you change the **FILEVERSION** key, Visual C++ will copy it into the **FileVersion** block header, located in the second half of your control's version resource. You should change this header so that it looks like a normal version number. For instance, instead of 4, 70, 13, 0, it should look like 4.70.13. You should also open your control's **IDD_ABOUTBOX** dialog box resource and change its version information to match the **FILEVERSION** key.

INSERTING VERSION INFORMATION INTO THE <OBJECT> TAG

Now that you've added the correct version to a control, your Visual J++ projects can collect their resource information and ensure that they always use the proper version. The secret of this technique is a special string appended to the **CODEBASE** parameter of the **<OBJECT>** tag (see Chapter 4 for information on this tag). The string's format is **#Version=** followed by the control's four version numbers. To illustrate:

```
CODEBASE="http://MyServer.com/MyControl.ocx#Version=4,70,13,0"
```

In this example, the Web browser will download and install MyControl.ocx *only* if the existing control (the one already installed on the user's system) is *older* than the version specified in the **CODEBASE** parameters. For instance, if the previously installed control has a version of 4.60, then the Web browser will download the new control and replace the old one with it.

If, however, the version of the existing control is *identical* to or *more recent* than the specified version, the Web browser assumes that the control already contains the features required by your Java code and does not download it. This assumption eliminates the overhead of downloading unnecessary new versions. (Note: If the version number specified in the **CODEBASE** parameter is -1,-1,-1,-1, then the Web browser will *always* download the latest version of the control.)

VIRTUALLY SPACED OUT
I find that navigating my source code is much easier with virtual spaces enabled. Virtual spaces allow the cursor to move past the end of a line. To use them, select Tools|Options, go to the Compatibility tab, and check the Enable virtual space box.

Sample Code

To help get you started writing ActiveX controls in Visual C++, I've created three sample controls. You can use them as study guides, or you can insert them directly into your own projects. See the CD-ROM included with this book for the complete source code of each control.

Fire Animation

The Fire Animation control has no real purpose. It's just a bit of eye candy that displays some wicked orange flames on a black background.

Figure 5.13 The Fire Animation control displays orange flames on a black background.

It can also overlay a text string on top of the flames (see Figure 5.13). This control would look great in the opening page of a Web site.

The Fire Animation control implements property pages. These pages give users an intuitive way to change the control's properties (see Figure 5.14). To view them, insert the control into an HTML file using the ActiveX Control Pad. Then right-click on the object and select the *second* Properties item from the menu.

Plasma Animation

This control is an ActiveX port of the Java Lava Lamp from Chapter 3. It displays a two-wave plasma field using colors and sine angles that

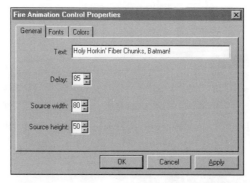

Figure 5.14 Property pages provide a customized view of control properties.

you can customize. (Chapter 3 provides details on these parameters.) Unlike the Java version, this control can overlay a text string of your choice on top of the plasma (see Figure 5.15).

The Plasma Animation control demonstrates the speed advantages that ActiveX has over Java. If you compare this control with its Java sibling, you'll notice that the ActiveX version runs slightly faster with fewer hesitations. (This is mainly because the Java applet uses a software-emulated thread for guiding the animation, while the ActiveX control uses a hardware-based timer.)

Bitmap Twirl

The Bitmap Twirl control can load any 8-bit (256-color) bitmap and display it in a window. With either the mouse or the keyboard, users can rotate the bitmap 360 degrees, zoom in, and zoom out (see Figure 5.16).

Because this control exposes its algorithms as ActiveX methods, you can automate the bitmap rotation by writing just a few lines of code.

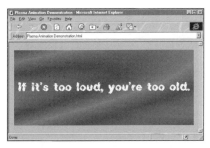

Figure 5.15 The Plasma Animation control is an ActiveX version of the Java Lava Lamp.

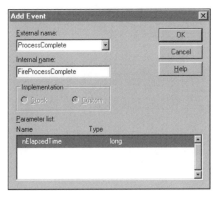

Figure 5.16 The Bitmap Twirl control can tile a bitmap and rotate it 360 degrees.

You can also ask the control to perform some simple animation on the bitmap, zooming the image in and out for a theatrical effect.

To accompany the Bitmap Twirl control, I've written a sample ActiveX container in MFC. It encapsulates the Bitmap Twirl control as an SDI application, providing convenient, customized access to its features. You can find its source code on this book's CD-ROM.

Moving On

Visual C++ is only part of the puzzle. To get the most out of ActiveX controls, you'll need to combine them with the power of Visual J++. Find out how in Part 2 of this book, *Integration*, where you'll learn about linking ActiveX to Java, creating ActiveX controls with Visual J++, and automating visual controls with HTML scripts.

Chapter 6

- What's an interface?
- Interfaces in Java
- Interfaces in ActiveX
- Calling ActiveX interfaces from Java

Interfaces

Ren Hoerk is my favorite cartoon character. Whenever something gets on his nerves, this little Chihuahua screams in a thick Mexican accent, "What *is* it, man!?!" Ren's trademark phrase has apparently rubbed off on me, because almost every book on object-oriented programming (OOP) makes me say to myself, "What *is* it, man!?! Ditch the abstract analogies and get to the point!"

I'm going to take my own advice and avoid abstractions in this chapter. In their place, you'll find some practical tips and several examples. Read on for a concrete tutorial of the most confusing topic in object-oriented programming: the interface.

Interface? What's That?

An interface is nothing special. It's just a function with a vague name. That's right: An interface is just a function—something you already know all about. So what's the big deal?

Uh-oh. Sounds like we're heading for a sea of abstractions. I don't want to break my promise, so I'll lose the general definition for now and move on to something more specific: interfaces in Java.

Java Interfaces

Unless you're into some heavy-duty OOP, interfaces in Java aren't very useful. You can't even define code when you create one. All you can do is declare the interface.

Declaring An Interface

Declaring a new interface is similar to declaring a new class. The format looks like this:

```
InterfaceName
{
    InterfaceBody
}
```

InterfaceName is, of course, the name of your interface. It cannot be a duplicate of any other interface or class in the same package. *InterfaceBody* contains a list of function headers—no function code is allowed. For example, the Java class library includes an interface called **Runnable**, which looks like this:

```
interface Runnable
{
    void run();
}
```

Notice that the function in this interface ends with a semicolon instead of a code block. This semicolon is always required because a Java-style interface function is merely a header, not a true function. You can add as many function headers as you would like, and you can equip them with any legal type of parameters and return values.

At this point, you're probably asking yourself, "If interfaces can't contain code, what's the point of declaring them?" Don't worry—we'll get to that later. For now, just remember that interface declarations are a lot like class declarations, but they can't contain any code.

AVOID THE ABSTRACT

*When Java first came to life, interface declarations required the **abstract** keyword, which tells the compiler not to expect any code inside a function. In later releases of Java, however, all interfaces are implicitly **abstract**, so you should no longer use this keyword within an interface declaration. Also, for interface functions, you cannot use the keywords **transient**, **volatile**, **synchronized**, **static**, **private**, or **protected**.*

CONSTANTS

Like classes, interfaces can contain data members. Interface data, however, are always constant (or *static*, to use Java terminology). For instance, the Java class library includes an interface called **ImageObserver**, which looks like this:

```
interface ImageObserver
{
    int WIDTH = 1;
    int HEIGHT = 2;
    int PROPERTIES = 4;
    int SOMEBITS = 8;
    int FRAMEBITS = 16;
    int ALLBITS = 32;
    int ERROR = 64;
    int ABORT = 128;
}
```

All of the data members in this interface (and in all interfaces) are implicitly **public**, **static**, and **final**, so these keywords are unnecessary. Also, note that a constant value follows each data member. If you leave off this initialization, your interface will generate a compiler error.

MODIFIERS

Interface declarations allow only two modifiers: **public** and **extends**. The **public** keyword makes the interface accessible from any package, and the **extends** keyword inherits data from other interfaces (known as *superinterfaces*). For example, the Java class library includes an interface called **ScrollbarPeer**, which looks like this:

Interfaces **153**

```
      void setLineIncrement(int l);
      void setPageIncrement(int l);
}
```

This interface is available to all classes in all packages, and it contains every function and data member found in the **ComponentPeer** interface.

The **extends** keyword for interfaces is similar to the **extends** keyword in classes. However, while a class can extend only one other class, an interface can extend multiple interfaces, like this:

```
interface MyBasketball extends GameInterface, Bounceable,
  Throwable {}
```

See the section "Why Are They Necessary?" later in this chapter to learn why multiple inheritance in interfaces is a valuable feature.

Using An Interface

After declaring an interface, you're ready to write code that fills in the blanks left by the function headers. You can do this in two ways: either by implementing the interface in a class or using the interface as a data type.

Interface Implementations

Most often, using an interface means writing a class that implements the interface. This requires a keyword called **implements**, as shown here:

```
class LavaLamp extends Applet implements Runnable
{
   void run()
   {
      while (true)
      {
         repaint();
         renderNextFrame();

         try { Thread.sleep(m_nDelay); }
         catch (InterruptedException e) { stop(); }
      }
   }
}
```

In this example, the **implements** keyword indicates that your class will provide a definition for every function in the interface. If the **Runnable** interface declared more than one function, then the **LavaLamp** class would have to define those, as well.

Classes can implement more than one interface. To specify multiple interfaces, just add them to the list:

```
class BasketballGame extends Game implements MyBasketball,
   Referee, Goalpost {}
```

INTERFACES AS DATA TYPES

Classes don't have to implement interfaces to use them. They can also treat interfaces as standard data types, declaring them as variables or method parameters. For example:

```
interface Cell
{
   void paint(Graphics g);
   String toString();
}

class Spreadsheet extends Applet
{
   private Cell[][] grid;

   void drawCellAt(Cell cell, int x, int y)
   {
      Graphics g = getGraphics();
      grid[x][y].paint(g);
   }
}
```

The importance of treating interfaces as primitive data types will become clear in the section "Calling ActiveX Interfaces From Java" later in this chapter.

Why Are They Necessary?

If you're using Java's existing class library, your skills in creating interfaces will go to waste. You almost never need to design interfaces when using someone else's classes. Creating interfaces in pure Java is necessary only when you're building a class library for yourself or for sale. In that situation, interfaces can provide shortcuts around the class hierarchy, emulate multiple inheritance for classes, and offer a Java equivalent of C++ header files.

Interfaces

LOOSEN THE CLASS HIERARCHY

In Java, interfaces exist mainly for just one reason: The language places a huge emphasis on object orientation. Every line of code must be a member of a class, and every class must conform to a rigid structure.

Interfaces can loosen this structure. They can join classes without enforcing a hierarchical relationship, allowing families of classes to have friends. No matter where a class lies in the hierarchy, it can attach to any number of interfaces (see Figure 6.1).

Although interfaces may seem to promote a breakdown in class organization, they actually help to maintain it. Without them, the hierarchy would become far too complex, and classes would pop up where they don't belong. Programmers would have to create objects that don't modify or enhance an existing class—a big-time no-no in the world of OOP.

MULTIPLE INHERITANCE (SORT OF)

Pretend that you want to create a Java applet that plays back a special audio file format. You've already written a class for playing this type of file, so now you want to exploit the power of OOP and simply

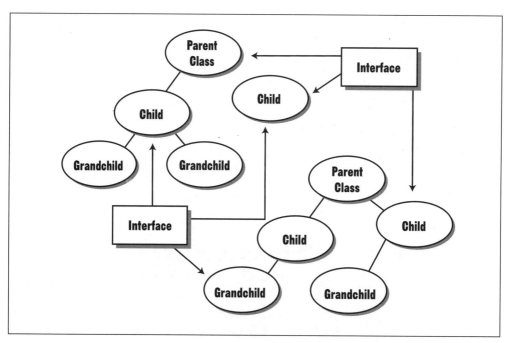

Figure 6.1 Interfaces capture similarities among unrelated classes.

156 *Chapter 6*

inherit from this class, saving truckloads of time and effort. Your applet code might look like this:

```
class AudioPlayback extends Applet, MyAudioFile
{
   ...
}
```

This code fragment will generate a compiler error because Java doesn't allow multiple inheritance—deriving a class from more than one class. But why? C++ allows multiple inheritance, so why not Java?

The Java development team asked themselves the same question. They eventually decided that the problems of multiple inheritance outweigh its benefits. Class hierarchies can grow needlessly complex and oversized with multiple inheritance, making them expensive to update and maintain. The Java makers wanted to avoid these problems, so they threw out the possibility of multiple inheritance.

Sometimes, however, you might really like to derive a class from more than one parent. Interfaces enable you to do this—sort of. They provide a workaround, not a replacement, for multiple inheritance. Because they collect related functions into groups, interfaces encourage the proper organization of multiply-derived classes, but they do not help you reuse them.

A perfect example of this interface workaround comes straight from the Java class library:

```
public interface DataInput
{
   // ... interface declaration omitted
}

public interface DataOutput
{
   // ... interface declaration omitted
}

public class RandomAccessFile implements DataOutput, DataInput
{
   // ... class definition omitted
}
```

Because Java does not support multiple inheritance, the **RandomAccessFile** class cannot reuse code from more than one parent. It can only obtain the data constants and function headers that are defined in the **DataOutput** and **DataInput** interfaces. **RandomAccess File** must then provide definitions for each inherited function (as you can confirm by looking at the source code file RandomAccessFile.java), requiring more development time than is needed with true multiple inheritance.

ANONYMOUS OBJECTS

From a certain perspective, Java interfaces are like C++ header files (*.h). They both reveal an object's member functions without exposing their implementations. Such objects are called *anonymous objects* (even though this term has a different meaning outside of Java). Anonymous objects are helpful only when shipping a package of classes to other developers. In any other circumstance, they can be ignored.

ActiveX Interfaces

Like interfaces in Java, ActiveX interfaces are collections of related functions. The similarities end there. ActiveX interfaces are not designed for OOP, and they have no relation to classes or inheritance.

Binary Functions

So what are ActiveX interfaces? To understand their meaning, try changing the name to this: ActiveX functions. As soon as you start thinking of ActiveX interfaces as functions, you've automatically understood them. They deserve the special name only because ActiveX interfaces live at the binary level.

Normal functions, such as the member functions of a Java class, exist only in source code and are no longer accessible after being compiled. ActiveX interfaces (a.k.a. ActiveX functions) are just the opposite: They can be called only after they are compiled into a binary form.

Once in binary form, ActiveX functions are available systemwide. Any ActiveX-compatible program, no matter how it was created (with C++, Java, Visual Basic, or any other language), can call the binary functions without the need for source code. This unique ability enables a type of software, called *component software,* that provides certain advantages over traditional object-oriented design (see Chapter 4).

Interface IDs

One of the dangers in binary, systemwide functions is the potential for name conflicts. For example, a pair of programmers working independently could create two totally unrelated ActiveX interfaces, both with identical names. When these interfaces are installed on the same system, ActiveX programs wouldn't know which function to call.

To solve this problem, the ActiveX architecture tags every interface with a globally unique identifier. The algorithm used to create these ID numbers *guarantees* that each one is unique. Therefore, as long as an ActiveX program supplies the correct ID, it always calls the correct interface.

Interface IDs also provide a hidden advantage: versioning. A new version of an interface is simply a new ID, not a new version number. Before calling the new interface, ActiveX programs don't have to search for it or make sure it's the proper version. They simply supply the new ID.

Automatic Distributed Functions

Another benefit of turning functions into ActiveX interfaces comes from Microsoft's Distributed COM protocol, or DCOM (see Chapter 10). With this protocol, ActiveX programs can call functions located not just within the system, but anywhere on the network (that is, anywhere on the Internet).

Support for distributed interfaces is achieved through a process called *marshaling*, which was originally designed to pack interface parameters into a portable byte sequence that could pass through the boundaries of system processes. Instead of defining a new communication layer, DCOM simply reroutes these parameters through the network and into another machine.

Why Are You Telling Me All This?

further developments

As a Java programmer, you don't need to know the internal workings of ActiveX, such as DCOM and the **IUnknown** and **IDispatch** interfaces. Visual J++ and the Windows VM shield you from these gritty details. Knowing the internals, however, gives you a background in ActiveX that can help you understand parts of the Visual J++ documentation. It also gives you an appreciation for the ease with which Visual J++ handles ActiveX support.

IUnknown: The Mother Of All Interfaces

Although ActiveX interfaces are not object-oriented, they do conform to a hierarchy similar to class hierarchies in OOP languages. At the root of this hierarchy lies the "mother of all interfaces": **IUnknown**. It's analogous to the **Object** class in Java, and it encapsulates three functions:

- **QueryInterface()**—Before calling an ActiveX interface, programs must first make sure that it is available. They do this by passing the interface's ID to **IUnknown::QueryInterface()**, which asks the ActiveX architecture for a pointer to the interface (see Figure 6.2). If the interface is not available, programs must continue running normally without it.

- **AddRef()**—ActiveX does not support garbage collecting. To keep track of memory, programs must call **IUnknown::AddRef()** each time they use an interface. **AddRef()** increments the interface's reference count, telling the ActiveX architecture to keep it in memory.

- **Release()**—The **Release()** function is a companion of **AddRef()**. It decreases an object's reference count. As soon as the count falls to zero, the ActiveX architecture can remove it from memory.

IDispatch: The Property Provider

Farther down the hierarchy lies an interface called **IDispatch**. This is the most important interface for Visual J++ programmers because it provides access to ActiveX controls and off-the-shelf commercial

Figure 6.2 **IUnknown::QueryInterface()** allows one ActiveX object to ask for a pointer to another ActiveX object.

software. With **IDispatch::Invoke()**, Java programs can call exposed methods in controls and any other ActiveX-compatible programs. (Note: Java programs call **Invoke()** implicitly, not directly. See Chapters 7 and 10 to learn how.)

The **IDispatch** interface also allows ActiveX controls to contain properties. Properties in ActiveX are like class variables in Java. But, like ActiveX functions, properties exist at the binary level, accessible by any program without the need for source code. See Chapter 5 for details on creating ActiveX properties.

Calling ActiveX Interfaces From Java

ActiveX and Java were developed by different companies at different times for different reasons. Each has a separate purpose in mind: Java is a programming language for the Web; ActiveX is a binary standard for program communication. Given these differences, it's surprising how tightly the two technologies integrate. They tend to complement each other and cancel out each other's disadvantages.

Java integrates so well with ActiveX, in fact, that Microsoft has a love-hate relationship with the language. On the one hand, they fear Java's strength and its potential to wipe out Windows. On the other hand, they've discovered that Java is an excellent tool for using ActiveX components. Java gives ActiveX certain advantages that may help it defeat competitors, such as CORBA and OpenDoc.

Advantages Of ActiveX Integration

The key advantage of Java/ActiveX integration is that it makes ActiveX programming easy. In the past, calling an ActiveX interface typically involved several lines of cluttered C++ code. For example, the following code fragment calls an ActiveX interface named **HelloWorld()**:

```
IHelloWorld* pHello;
if ( (HRESULT) CoCreateInstance(CLSID_HelloWorld,
                                NULL, CLSCTX_SERVER,
                                IID_IHelloWorld,
(void**)&pHello) >= 0 )
{
   pHello->HelloWorld();
   pHello->Release();
}
```

Yuck! What a mess. No wonder ActiveX has a reputation for being hard to learn. Now look at the Java version of the same code fragment:

```
IHelloWorld hello = new CHelloWorld();
hello.HelloWorld();
```

Ah...much better. Calling ActiveX interfaces in Java is easier and more straightforward than in C++. You can treat ActiveX interfaces just like Java interfaces, calling them directly without any special functions or communication layers. Plus, with Java's automatic garbage collection, you never have to worry about cleaning up the memory used by an interface.

How Does It Work?

Visual J++ and the Windows VM put the integration of Java with ActiveX behind the scenes. You need never concern yourself with the details of how Java code is translated to ActiveX functions. You may be interested to learn, however, how Microsoft achieved ActiveX integration without adding any keywords or constructs to the Java language.

The secret is the native-code interface (see Chapter 2). When Visual J++ compiles a Java program that uses ActiveX interfaces, it inserts native code into the class file. This native code acts as the ActiveX go-between, allowing Java programs to call ActiveX interfaces directly.

The format of Microsoft's native code is an open, documented standard. Any company can follow the specifications and create a Java compiler that produces ActiveX-compatible class files. Borland, for instance, has announced that the next major release of Latté will include ActiveX support. The integration at the source code level (that is, the format of java files) has not been standardized, however, and may differ among various compilers.

Two caveats come with the ActiveX native-code interface. First, because native code is not secure and can hop out of the Java sandbox, applets must either run locally or contain a security signature (see Chapter 12 for a discussion of sandboxing and code-signing). Second, the native code can translate only those ActiveX calls that can be described by standard Java syntax. Some ActiveX interfaces would require adding special keywords or functions to Java—something Microsoft has pledged not to do.

Just as Java makes ActiveX easier, ActiveX returns the favor and makes Java stronger. It adds powerful features to the language, such as:

- *Inter-process communication*—Most new commercial software for business applications expose their functionality as ActiveX interfaces. Any ActiveX program can call these interfaces for automating and communicating with the software. Java programs, with ActiveX integration, can do the same thing. See Chapter 10 to learn how.

- *Distributed execution*—ActiveX is a distributed architecture. With help from DCOM, ActiveX programs can talk to other ActiveX programs anywhere on the network. They can also run on remote machines automatically. Java programs, as long as they support ActiveX, can exploit distributed execution, as well.

- *Easy access to native code*—Adding native code to Java is relatively tedious. It often requires machine-generated *stubs,* or large class libraries that wrap around existing objects. With ActiveX support, Java programmers can avoid the tedium of the native-code interface and import external code directly, simply by calling ActiveX interfaces.

Calling ActiveX Functions

The first step in calling ActiveX functions from Java is to import the names of those functions into the Java CLASSPATH directories. Otherwise, the Java compiler won't know anything about the function you're calling and will flag it with an error. Visual J++ includes a wizard and a standalone utility that handle the import step for you (see Chapters 7 and 10).

After running either of these programs, you can specify the ActiveX functions in a Java project just as you specify any normal Java class. For example, the Date class from the standard Java class library can be specified in two ways, either with the **import** keyword:

```
import java.util.*;
Date dateToday = new Date();
String strDate = dateToday.toString();
```

or explicitly:

```
java.util.Date dateToday = new java.util.Date();
String strDate = dateToday.toString();
```

Likewise, an ActiveX control named Date may be specified with the **import** keyword:

```
import datectrl.*;
IDateControl dateToday = new CDateControl();
String strDate = dateToday.toString();
```

or explicitly:

```
datectrl.IDateControl dateToday = new datectrl.CDateControl();
String strDate = dateToday.toString();
```

Note that the only significant difference between these examples is the single-letter prefix on the ActiveX names. The *I* indicates that the structure is an interface, and the *C* means that the structure is a class. The interface, as you learned in the previous section, contains only function headers, so the class is necessary to supply the implementation of each function. Visual J++ automatically casts the class to an interface without generating any warning messages.

For more information and examples on calling ActiveX functions from Java, see Chapters 7 and 10.

CALLING JAVA FUNCTIONS FROM ACTIVEX
This section describes how to call ActiveX functions from Java. The opposite is also possible. You can call public Java functions from any ActiveX program. For details, see Chapter 8.

Accessing ActiveX Properties

ActiveX programs can expose their properties as well as their functions (see Chapter 4). Visual J++ provides no built-in support for accessing ActiveX properties; it allows Java to call only ActiveX functions. As a workaround, Visual J++ wraps each ActiveX property with get/put functions. For example, if the **Date** control from the previous section exposed an integer property called **Year**, obtaining its value would involve the following code:

```
import datectrl.*;
IDateControl dateToday = new CDateControl();
int nYear = dateToday.getYear();
```

Changing its value would involve this code:

```
import datectrl.*;
IDateControl dateToday = new CDateControl();
dateToday.putYear(1974);
```

As evidenced by these examples, Java support for ActiveX properties is not as good as it could be. Other languages, such as Visual Basic, offer direct, more intuitive access to properties. Using properties in Java is still fairly easy, however, as long as you remember the get/put convention.

WHAT THE HECK IS COM?

The Visual J++ documentation includes hundreds of references to COM. COM is an acronym for the Component Object Model, which is simply the low-level foundation of ActiveX. When you come across these three letters, don't get confused; just translate them to the word ActiveX.

Handling Errors

If you've read *Learn Java Now*, the printed Java tutorial that ships with Visual J++, you know all about exception handling. To recap, Java exceptions take care of "exceptional" runtime errors without the need for cryptic (and often ignored) error codes.

Exception handling for ActiveX functions works much the same way as for Java functions: with the **try** and **catch** keywords. To use the **Date** control example once again, here is some sample code that catches all runtime errors that might occur from calling the **toString()** interface:

```
import datectrl.*;

try
{
   IDateControl dateToday = new CDateControl();
   String strDate = dateToday.toString();
}

catch (com.ms.com.ComException e)
{
   System.out.println("An error occurred while calling
               toString(): " +
                 e.getMessage());
}
```

In this example, *every* possible exception is caught and dumped to **System.out**. In a real-world situation, however, you'll want to catch specific exceptions and handle them separately. Java provides a means to do this using the exception class hierarchy, as shown in Listing 6.1.

LISTING 6.1   HANDLING EXCEPTIONS FROM FILEINPUTSTREAM.

```
FileInputStream file;
String strFilename = getFilenameFromUser();

try
{
   // Try to open the file for reading.
   file = new FileInputStream(strFilename);
}

catch (FileNotFoundException e)   // A descendant of Throwable
{
   // The file was not found, so open the default file.
   file = new FileInputStream("default.txt");
}

catch (SecurityException e)   // Another descendant of Throwable
{
   // The user does not have permission to read this file.
   displayErrorMessage("You do not have security privileges to
     this file.");
}

catch (Throwable e)   // The root of the exception classes
{
   System.out.println("Some other error occurred.");
}
```

Unfortunately, the ActiveX integration in Visual J++ cannot handle exceptions in this manner. You can catch only one exception—**ComException**—and process the error code it contains. Listing 6.2 provides an example of how you would handle exceptions from a mythical ActiveX object called the ActiveX File Control.

LISTING 6.2   HANDLING EXCEPTIONS FROM AN ACTIVEX CONTROL.

```
IActiveXFileControl file;
String strFile = getFilenameFromUser();

try
{
   // Try to open the file for reading.
   file = new CActiveXFileControl();
   file.OpenFile(strFile);
}
```

```
catch (ComException e)
{
   switch (e.getHResult)   // Obtain the error code (a.k.a.
                           // HRESULT)
   {
      case E_HANDLE:  // Invalid file handle
         file = new CActiveXFileControl();
         file.OpenFile("default.txt");
         break;

      case E_ACCESSDENIED:  // General access denied
         displayErrorMessage("You do not have security +
           "privileges to this file.");
         break;

      default:  // Catch all other errors
         System.out.println("Some other error occurred.");
   }
}
```

The **ComException** class can return a wide range of error codes (**HRESULT**s). Table 6.1 provides a list of the most common system errors.

For error codes returned by a specific ActiveX component, see that component's documentation.

Using Exceptions To Query An Interface

In ActiveX integration, Java exceptions are not just for handling errors. They also provide a Java equivalent of the **IUnknown::QueryInterface**() function. For example, you can switch an ActiveX object to another interface like this:

```
IActiveXPrinter printer = new ActiveXPrinter();
IActiveXPainter painter = new ActiveXPainter();
try
{ printer = (IActiveXPainter) painter; }
catch (ClassCastException e)
{ System.out.println("Error: Interface not supported."); }
```

You can also see whether an object supports an interface by applying Java's **instanceof** keyword:

```
IActiveXPrinter printer = new ActiveXPrinter();
if ( printer instanceof IActiveXPainter )
   printer = (IActiveXPainter);
else
   System.out.println("Error: Interface not supported.");
```

further developments

Interfaces **167**

Table 6.1 Common system error codes returned by ComException.

Name	Value	Description
E_UNEXPECTED	0x8000FFFF	Unexpected failure
E_NOTIMPL	0x80004001	Not implemented
E_OUTOFMEMORY	0x8007000E	Ran out of memory
E_INVALIDARG	0x80070057	One or more arguments are invalid
E_NOINTERFACE	0x80004002	No such interface supported
E_POINTER	0x80004003	Invalid pointer
E_HANDLE	0x80070006	Invalid handle
E_ABORT	0x80004004	Operation aborted
E_FAIL	0x80004005	Unspecified error
E_ACCESSDENIED	0x80070005	General access denied error
DISP_E_UNKNOWNINTERFACE	0x80020001	Unknown interface
DISP_E_MEMBERNOTFOUND	0x80020003	Member not found
DISP_E_PARAMNOTFOUND	0x80020004	Parameter not found
DISP_E_TYPEMISMATCH	0x80020005	Type mismatch
DISP_E_UNKNOWNNAME	0x80020006	Unknown name
DISP_E_NONAMEDARGS	0x80020007	No named arguments
DISP_E_BADVARTYPE	0x80020008	Bad variable type
DISP_E_EXCEPTION	0x80020009	Exception occurred
DISP_E_OVERFLOW	0x8002000A	Out of present range
DISP_E_BADINDEX	0x8002000B	Invalid index
DISP_E_UNKNOWNLCID	0x8002000C	Class ID not found
DISP_E_ARRAYISLOCKED	0x8002000D	Memory is locked
DISP_E_BADPARAMCOUNT	0x8002000E	Invalid number of parameters
DISP_E_PARAMNOTOPTIONAL	0x8002000F	Parameter not optional
DISP_E_BADCALLEE	0x80020010	Invalid callee
DISP_E_NOTACOLLECTION	0x80020011	Does not support a collection

Casting among multiple interfaces is seldom necessary in Visual J++ because most ActiveX components that you would use support only one set of interfaces.

Summary

"So what *is* an interface, man!?!", as Ren might say. It's just a collection of functions pumped up on steroids. In Java, it helps loosen the object hierarchy without resorting to the complexities of multiple inheritance. In ActiveX, it lives in a binary world and can be called by any ActiveX program. This feature allows you to call ActiveX interfaces from Java, and Java interfaces from ActiveX. For examples of how this can help you with your Visual J++ projects, continue on to Chapter 7, where you'll learn how to integrate ActiveX controls with Java applets.

Chapter 7

Activating ActiveX

- ActiveX controls in Visual J++
- The Java Type Library Wizard
- Outside the Java sandbox
- Handling licensed controls
- Example: Taskbar Tray

My encyclopedia says that computers have two parts: hardware and software. My encyclopedia's wrong. Computers actually have a third component known as *vaporware*—an advertised product that is never delivered.

Software companies invented vaporware to stave off competition. They announce a product with such fantastic features that customers will put off buying software from competing companies. The loyal customers wait patiently for release of the mythical software, even setting aside space for it on their hard drives. But as the date draws near, every press release, advertisement, and any other record of the software's existence turns to vapor, vanishing without a trace.

Vaporware also includes software that actually makes it to store shelves, but with fewer features than were originally announced. In this case, the "vapor" in vaporware refers to the hot air coming from a software company's marketing division.

ActiveX Controls In Visual J++

Microsoft's Visual J++ falls into this latter category of vaporware. Even after the product's release, Microsoft's marketeers were spreading misinformation and half-truths in order to drive up sales of the product. For example, the following text was obtained from Microsoft's Web site 10 days after the official release of Visual J++:

> *Visual J++ includes wizards to help developers create ActiveX controls....You can also create more powerful applets quickly by leveraging the huge installed base of existing ActiveX controls. For example, instead of creating an applet using your own tree control, you can write your applet in Java and use an existing ActiveX tree control.*

The first statement is false. Visual J++ contains no wizards that support the creation of ActiveX controls. You have to create each one manually. (See Chapter 8 to learn how.) The second and third statements are misleading. They imply that Visual J++ can handle ActiveX controls in the same way as other ActiveX development tools, such as Borland Delphi or Visual C++. In fact, Visual J++ offers only minimal support for ActiveX controls. Using them in Java programs often requires assistance from external HTML scripts. (See Chapter 9 for details.)

ActiveX Controls Redefined

An explanation for these deceptive claims comes from the new definition of ActiveX controls. Quietly and unofficially, Microsoft expanded ActiveX controls to include not just Internet-enabled OLE controls, but any type of *OLE automation server*. Automation servers are much like traditional ActiveX controls except for two significant differences:

- *They are windowless*—By default, OLE automation servers have no user interface. They can create windows that display information and interact with the user, but these windows cannot be embedded in another application (such as a Web page), as is the case with ActiveX controls.

- *They are eventless*—ActiveX controls can send events to notify their container of an occurrence (such as a mouse click). OLE automation servers cannot send events.

Thanks to this new definition of ActiveX controls, Microsoft can fudge their advertisements of Visual J++. They claim that Visual J++ offers direct support for ActiveX controls, when in reality it supports only OLE automation servers. Your Java code cannot encapsulate true ActiveX controls—a feature that Microsoft originally announced and still insinuates on their Web site.

With Visual J++, Java programs *can* integrate with traditional ActiveX controls, but only indirectly. Java needs help from HTML scripts to catch events and display the control in a browser. For more information, see Chapter 9 and the section titled "Integrating Visual Controls" later in this chapter

Why Integrate?

ActiveX and Java share a common purpose: to help you create Web content that is more beautiful and more interactive than ever before. So why integrate the two? Because they take fundamentally different approaches: Java is simple and elegant; ActiveX is powerful and complex. Combining the technologies cancels out their disadvantages and gains flexibility. You get the programming ease of Java plus the low-level power of ActiveX.

For example, Java applets cannot play video files. Sound files are the only multimedia objects the standard class library recognizes. ActiveX controls, however, can play video files in a variety of formats. If you could find such a control, you could integrate it with a Java applet to give it complete multimedia support. See "Integrating Visual Controls" later in this chapter for a demonstration of exactly that.

The Portability Problem

As discussed in Chapter 4, portability is a serious issue when developing ActiveX controls. When integrating those controls with applets, the issue becomes critical. The moment you have rigged up a Java program to use ActiveX, you have destroyed its greatest advantage—the ability to run on any platform. You have restricted it not just to Microsoft's operating system, but to Microsoft's browser. Internet Explorer is the only Web browser that can handle Java applets that use ActiveX controls. Netscape Navigator, for instance, can't even recognize them.

Although Microsoft has announced that the Macintosh and Unix platforms will soon support ActiveX controls, they have said nothing about how these platforms will handle Java integration. Internet Explorer may be the only compatible browser for quite some time. So, if you're planning to combine a Java applet with an ActiveX control and post it on the Web, beware. It will be visible only to users of Microsoft software.

This portability problem does not affect enterprisewide intranets. Most companies that deploy intranets have a single operating system and a single browser. If their choice happens to be Microsoft, they can bring Java-ActiveX integration to its maximum potential.

The Security Problem

Chapter 6 mentioned that ActiveX integration with Java is made possible by the native code interface. In the name of security, the Java virtual machine places a severe restriction on applets that use this interface: They cannot run directly off the Web; they can only run locally. The VM prevents remote applets from calling native code and gaining direct access to your computer. Thus, applets that are integrated with ActiveX run headfirst into Java's security wall and are prevented from living on the Web.

Microsoft has provided a fix for this problem. It comes in two parts:

- *Code-signing*—Before an ActiveX control can be used on the Web, it must be code-signed, giving the control a digital signature that identifies its author. This signature ensures liability in case the control harms your computer or performs some other malicious act.

- *Cabinet files*—Code-signing of ActiveX controls solves only half the problem. Even if a Java applet integrates with a code-signed control, it is still calling native code and therefore cannot run on the Web. To get around the security barrier, the Java applet can be placed into a *cabinet file*, or CAB file, along with any controls that it uses. This CAB file can be code-signed, allowing Internet Explorer to download it safely, extract its contents, and run the applet (see Figure 7.1).

For complete details on code-signing and CABing your Java applets, see Chapter 12.

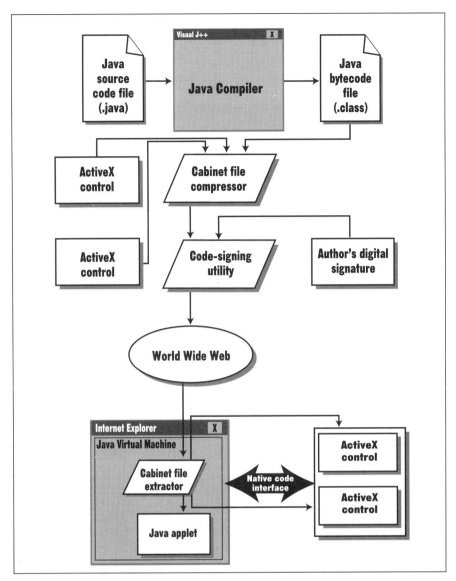

Figure 7.1 Activated applets must be code-signed and CABed before they can run on the Web.

The Java Type Library Wizard

Now that you know the whats and the whys of activating ActiveX, it's time to learn the hows: How do you integrate an ActiveX control with Java? How do you call its methods? How do you change its properties?

The answer is the Java Type Library Wizard, located under the Visual J++ Tools menu. This wizard can read *type libraries*—binary blueprints that describe how to call methods and how to access properties. When you first start the Type Library Wizard, it lists every ActiveX component that it finds on your system (see Figure 7.2).

To integrate one of the listed objects with a Java project, simply click on the checkbox next to its name. You can choose as many as you like. After you click the OK button, you will return to the Visual J++ workspace.

IGNORE THE FUZZY CHECKBOXES
If you run the Type Library Wizard twice in the same project, it will place a fuzzy-state checkbox (also called a three-state checkbox) next to each item that you have previously chosen. You can ignore these indicators because they simply aren't accurate. They don't appear next to objects used in earlier projects, even though those objects are available to all Visual J++ projects, including new ones.

Harnessing The Wizard's Magic

The Java Type Library Wizard's sole function is to translate ActiveX type libraries into Java code. The wizard reads information directly from the object and generates Java classes that wrap the object's methods and properties. It places the code in a separate directory that descends from the Java/Trustlib directory (which descends from your Windows directory).

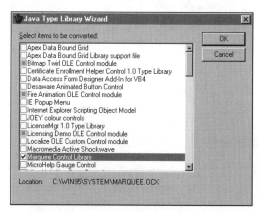

Figure 7.2 The Java Type Library Wizard displays a list box of ActiveX controls and automation servers.

The only time you need to look in the Trustlib directories is when you need to view an ActiveX object's summary information. The summary information is contained in a file called summary.txt, which you can view with any standard text editor (such as the Visual J++ text editor). It describes how to create the object, call its methods, and access its properties.

INSTANT SUMMARY INFORMATION

Instead of searching for an ActiveX object's summary information in the Trustlib directory, you can view it immediately. Just double-click on the line that says "Class summary information created" after running the Type Library Wizard.

Creating The Object

After running the Type Library Wizard on an object, the results are displayed in the Output window (see Figure 7.3).

The first line printed in this window tells you how to import the object into a Java source-code file. For example, to import an ActiveX control called Video Playback, you would insert the following statement at the top of your source-code file:

```
import videoplayback.*;
```

Note that this statement isn't really necessary. You can always reference the control by typing "videoplayback.*identifier*". The **import** keyword simply allows you to reference ActiveX objects by their short names.

Once you have placed the import statement in your source code, you are ready to create the object. First, open the summary.txt file that corresponds to the object you wish to create. In this file, locate the class

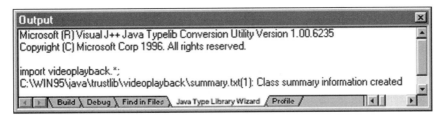

Figure 7.3 The Java Type Library Wizard dumps its results to the Output window.

name and interface name of the object. For example, the Video Playback control's summary.txt file looks like this:

```
public class videoplayback/VideoPlayback
                extends java.lang.Object
{
}
public interface videoplayback/IVideoPlaybackEvents
                extends com.ms.com.IUnknown
{
}
public interface videoplayback/IVideoPlayback
                extends com.ms.com.IUnknown
{
    public abstract void putFitToWindow(boolean);
    public abstract void Stop();
    public abstract boolean getFitToWindow();
    public abstract void putTotalFrames(int);
    public abstract void Pause();
    public abstract int getTotalFrames();
    public abstract void Close();
    public abstract boolean Open(java.lang.String);
    public abstract void Play(boolean);
    public abstract void putCurrentFrame(int);
    public abstract int getCurrentFrame();
}
```

This file indicates that the class name is **VideoPlayback**, and the interface name is **IVideoPlayback**. (You can ignore any event interfaces that you find in a summary.txt file. They are not supported in the current version of Visual J++.)

Next, create a variable for the ActiveX object (use the steps described in Chapter 6). For example, creating a variable for the Video Playback control requires the following code:

```
IVideoPlayback video;
video = new VideoPlayback();
```

Note that the variable declaration must *always* refer to the interface name, and the **new** statement must *always* refer to the class name. Never do this:

```
IVideoPlayback video;
video = new IVideoPlayback();
```

Also, don't be tempted to place the **new** statement in your applet's **init()** function. It won't always work. Instead, put the statement in the **start()** function or some other applet function that will be called after **start()**.

> **USER-FRIENDLY INTERFACE NAMES**
>
> *If you create ActiveX controls in Visual C++ using the OLE ControlWizard (see Chapter 5), your control will end up looking strange when it is imported into Visual J++. For some reason, the ControlWizard places the string "_D" (which stands for dispatch) at the beginning of the interface name. You can change this prefix to give your control a more conventional-looking interface. Simply open the control's ODL file and replace all occurrences of "_D" with "I".*

Calling Its Methods

After creating an ActiveX variable, you can call its methods just as you would call a Java class function. For example, the Video Playback control exposes a method called **Open**. It takes a **String** parameter and returns a boolean value, as evidenced by the summary.txt file from the previous section. The following code demonstrates how you would call this method:

```
if ( video.Open("MyVideo.avi") )
{
   video.Play();
}
else
{
   showStatus("Error: File not found");
}
```

Note that certain ActiveX methods cannot be called from Java. These methods use parameter or return types that do not have a Java equivalent. Most basic data types translate directly into Java, however, and those that do not are handled by Microsoft's com.ms.com package, which is described in Appendix B. Table 7.1 lists the most common Java-compatible data types.

Table 7.1 ActiveX data types available in Java.

ActiveX Data Type	Java Equivalent
BOOL	boolean
char	char
unsigned char	byte
short	short
int	int
long	int
INT64	long
float	float
double	double
BSTR	java.lang.String
VARIANT	com.ms.com.Variant (see "The Variant Class" sidebar)
IUnknown*	com.ms.com.IUnknown
void	void

ACTIVEX EXCEPTION HANDLING

If calling an ActiveX method throws an exception, you can catch it with standard Java exception handling. See the Chapter 6 section titled "Handling Errors" to learn how.

Accessing Its Properties

Java has no notion of ActiveX properties. You can't access a control's properties in Visual J++ as you can in other ActiveX development tools. To fix this problem, the Java Type Library Wizard wraps each ActiveX property with two Java functions: **get***Property* and **put***Property*. For example, the Video Playback control exposes an integer property called **CurrentFrame**. To obtain the value of this property, call:

```
video.getCurrentFrame();
```

And to set its value, call:

```
putCurrentFrame();
```

BUGS IN SPACE
The Java Type Library Wizard in Visual J++ 1.00 contains a bug. It cannot handle ActiveX controls whose file names contain spaces. If you're creating a control for use in the 1.00 release, make sure that the output file name has no spaces. If you're using an ActiveX control that you didn't create, you'll have to reregister it under a new file name before the wizard can import it. For example, if a control is named My Control.ocx, rename it MyControl.ocx, then run regsvr32.exe (located in \Windows\System) on the new name.

The Variant Class

A common ActiveX data type is a structure called **VARIANT**. Controls can use this data type as parameters, properties, and return values. In Java, it allows parameters to be passed *by reference*—that is, any changes made to the parameter will be retained after the function exits.

To allow the **VARIANT** type in Java, Microsoft created a class called **Variant** and placed it in their com.ms.com package. Like the ActiveX data type, the **Variant** class supports many different values, such as integers, objects, and arrays—but it can hold only one type of value at a time.

If you import an ActiveX object that uses the **com.ms.com.Variant** type, don't get confused. It's fairly straightforward and fully documented. Just look in the Visual J++ online help under the topic index of "Variant."

Integrating OLE Automation Servers

Visual J++ offers support for ActiveX controls in two ways: It can either call into a non-visual ActiveX control (a.k.a. OLE automation server) directly, or it can import a true ActiveX control with help from an HTML script. This section deals with the first scenario: OLE automation servers.

To integrate Java with an automation server, you need only to run the Java Type Library Wizard as described in the previous section. The wizard will locate all automation servers and allow you to import their type libraries. You can then write a few lines of Java code that calls their methods and accesses their properties.

COMMAND-LINE SORCERY
If you can't find an ActiveX component in the Type Library Wizard but know the location of its file, you can still

Activating ActiveX

integrate it with Visual J++. Simply run JavaTLB, the command-line version of the wizard, specifying the file name as a parameter.

To illustrate the advantages of OLE automation servers, I've written a sample applet that integrates with an automation server. I call it the Playground Demo because of its ability to hop outside the Java sandbox. The sandbox, which is described in detail in Chapter 12, is a security barrier that prevents applets from:

- Reading or writing files
- Accessing hardware directly
- Launching programs
- Making system calls
- Finding out your name

The Playground Demo applet can do all of the above. When it is loaded into Internet Explorer, it displays various Abstract Window Toolkit (AWT) controls (see Figure 7.4) that expose the features of the automation server with which it has been integrated. (Note: The OLE automation server in the Playground Demo is actually a true ActiveX control posing as an automation server. See the sidebar "MS=Marketing Slime, following Listing 7.1," for more information.) For instance, clicking on the button labeled "Shutdown System" will call the automation server's **ShutdownSystem**() method, which in turn calls the Windows API function **ExitWindowsEx**()—but only after asking your permission.

You may be wondering how the Playground Demo can bypass the Java sandbox. Again, this relates to the security problem of ActiveX integration explained earlier in this chapter. The Playground Demo applet can run locally without any restrictions, but it cannot be distributed through the Web unless it has been code-signed (see Chapter 12). Once code-signed, the applet is considered a "trusted Java class" and can wander freely into your system. (Note: Internet Explorer gives trusted applets the ability to read and write files, so the Read File and Write File features in the Playground Demo are rather moot.)

Listing 7.1 contains an abridged version of the source code to the Playground Demo applet.

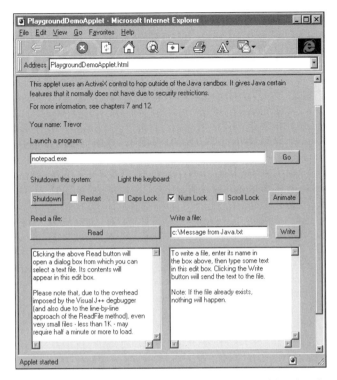

Figure 7.4 The Playground Demo applet can hop outside the Java sandbox.

LISTING 7.1 THE PLAYGROUND DEMO SOURCE CODE.

```
/*
   NOTE: A bug in the 1.00 release of Visual J++ causes all
         BOOL return values and properties to be reversed. In
         other words, Visual J++ makes BOOL properties appear
         FALSE when they're actually TRUE, and TRUE when
         they're actually FALSE. This applet is designed to
         handle this bug, so if you're recompiling it on an
         updated version of Visual J++ (one that has the bug
         fixed), you'll need to change the lines marked with
         "bugbug".
*/

import java.applet.*;
import java.awt.*;
import PlaygroundDemoAppletFrame;
import playgrounddemo.*;

public class PlaygroundDemoApplet extends Applet
{
   MainDialog m_dlgMain;
   IPlaygroundDemo m_playground;
```

Activating ActiveX

```java
      private static String strDefaultLaunch = "notepad.exe";
      private static String strDefaultWrite =
                                    "c:\\Message from Java.txt";
      public void init()
      {
         m_dlgMain = new MainDialog(this);
         m_dlgMain.CreateControls();

         m_dlgMain.IDC_LAUNCHEDIT.setText(strDefaultLaunch);
         m_dlgMain.IDC_WRITEFILENAME.setText(strDefaultWrite);
         m_dlgMain.IDC_READEDIT.setText(strReadMessage);
         m_dlgMain.IDC_WRITEEDIT.setText(strWriteMessage);
      }

      public void paint(Graphics g)
      {
         // No painting is necessary because we use a dialog box
         // template.
      }

      public void start()
      {
         m_playground = new PlaygroundDemo();

         m_dlgMain.IDC_NAME.setText("Your name: " +
                                    m_playground.GetUserName() );

         // bugbug: Designed for BOOL bug (see top of file)
         m_dlgMain.IDC_NUM.setState(!m_playground.getNumLock());
         // bugbug: Designed for BOOL bug (see top of file)
         m_dlgMain.IDC_CAPS.setState(
                                    !m_playground.getCapsLock());
         // bugbug: Designed for BOOL bug (see top of file)
         m_dlgMain.IDC_SCROLL.setState(
                                    !m_playground.getScrollLock());
      }

      public boolean handleEvent(Event evt)
      {
         if (evt.id != Event.ACTION_EVENT)
            return super.handleEvent(evt);

         if (evt.target == m_dlgMain.IDC_LAUNCH)
         {
            m_playground.LaunchProgram(
                           m_dlgMain.IDC_LAUNCHEDIT.getText());
            return true;
         }
         else
```

```
                    {
                        if (evt.target == m_dlgMain.IDC_SHUTDOWN)
                        {
                            // bugbug: Designed for BOOL bug
                            //         (see top of file)
                            m_playground.ShutdownSystem(
                                        !m_dlgMain.IDC_RESTART.getState());
                            return true;
                        }
                        else
                        {
                            if (evt.target == m_dlgMain.IDC_CAPS)
                            {
                                // bugbug: Designed for BOOL bug
                                //         (see top of file)
                                m_playground.putCapsLock(
                                            m_dlgMain.IDC_CAPS.getState());
                                return true;
                            }
                            else
                            {
                                if (evt.target == m_dlgMain.IDC_NUM)
                                {
                                    // bugbug: Designed for BOOL bug
                                    //         (see top of file)
                                    m_playground.putNumLock(
                                                m_dlgMain.IDC_NUM.getState());
                                    return true;
                                }
                                else
                                {
                                    if (evt.target == m_dlgMain.IDC_SCROLL)
                                    {
                                        // bugbug: Designed for BOOL bug
                                        //         (see top of file)
                                        m_playground.putScrollLock(
                                                m_dlgMain.IDC_SCROLL.getState());
                                        return true;
                                    }
                                    else
                                    {
                                        if (evt.target == m_dlgMain.IDC_ANIMATE)
                                        {
                                            if (m_dlgMain.IDC_ANIMATE.getLabel()
                                                                == "Stop")
                                            {
                                                m_dlgMain.IDC_ANIMATE.setLabel(
                                                                "Animate");
                                                m_playground.StopKeyboardAnimation();
```

```
                        }
                        else
                        {
                            m_dlgMain.IDC_ANIMATE.setLabel(
                                                    "Stop");
                            m_playground.StartKeyboardAnimation();
                        }

                        return true;
                    }
                    else
                    {
                        if (evt.target ==
                                    m_dlgMain.IDC_READFILE)
                        {
                            onReadFile();
                            return true;
                        }
                        else
                        {
                            if (evt.target ==
                                        m_dlgMain.IDC_WRITEFILE)
                            {
                                onWriteFile(
                        m_dlgMain.IDC_WRITEFILENAME.getText());
                                return true;
                            }
                        }
                    }
                }
            }
        }
    }

    return super.handleEvent(evt);
}

private void onReadFile()
{
    // bugbug: Designed for BOOL bug (see top of file)
    if ( m_playground.OpenFile("") )
        return;

    StringBuffer str = new StringBuffer();
    String strLine;

    do
    {
```

```java
        strLine = m_playground.ReadFile();

        if ( strLine.equals("{NEWLINE}") )
           str.append("\r\n");
        else
        {
           if ( !strLine.equals("{EOF}") )
              str.append(strLine + "\r\n");
        }
    }
    while ( !strLine.equals("{EOF}") );

    m_dlgMain.IDC_READEDIT.setText(str.toString());

    m_playground.CloseFile();
}

private void onWriteFile(String strFilename)
{
    // bugbug: Designed for BOOL bug (see top of file)
    if ( m_playground.OpenFile(strFilename) )
       return;

    String str = m_dlgMain.IDC_WRITEEDIT.getText();
    int nOffset = 0;
    boolean bDone = false;

    while (!bDone)
    {
       char line[] = new char[256];
       int nEndOffset = str.indexOf("\n", nOffset);

       if (nEndOffset == -1)
          nEndOffset = str.length();

       str.getChars(nOffset, nEndOffset, line, 0);

       nOffset = str.indexOf("\n", nOffset) + 1;

       if (nOffset == 0)
          bDone = true;

       m_playground.WriteFile(new String(line));
    }

    m_playground.CloseFile();
}
}
```

further developments

MS=Marketing Slime

One of my favorite movies is the 1984 hit *Ghostbusters*. Halfway through this flick, a dumpy green ghost barfs all over Bill Murray. Covered head to foot with ectoplasmic goo, the wisecracking Bill sends up a one-liner: "He slimed me!"

Halfway through this book, I got slimed—not by a green ghost, but by Microsoft's marketeers. Their press releases and Web pages misrepresented the features of Visual J++, making the product appear to encapsulate true, event-driven ActiveX controls. When I discovered the truth, I had to rearrange the book's contents completely, throw out a few cool ideas, and do some furious backpedaling just to get the manuscript finished on schedule.

They say that every cloud has a silver lining, and this situation is no different. After I learned that Visual J++ offers direct support only for OLE automation servers—not for true ActiveX controls—I did a little research. I learned of a simple technique that allows traditional controls to masquerade as OLE automation servers. With this trick, you can continue developing ActiveX controls in Visual C++ as you always have (see Chapter 5). You don't need to convert them to automation servers, and you don't have to resort to HTML scripts.

To perform the trick, just add a one-line function to your Visual C++ project:

```
BOOL CMyControl::IsInvokeAllowed(DISPID dispid)
{
    return TRUE;
}
```

This function (which is documented in the Microsoft Knowledge Base article Q146120) allows access to an ActiveX control even when it is not embedded in a container application. Visual J++ does not act as a container, so overriding this function allows Java programs to call a control's methods and to change its properties directly.

For a demonstration of **IsInvokeAllowed**(), see the Playground Demo or Taskbar Tray sample programs included on this book's CD-ROM.

Integrating Visual Controls

Soon before the final release of Visual J++, Microsoft gave it the ability to integrate Java applets with visual ActiveX controls (those that can be contained in a Web page). Unfortunately, this last-minute hack doesn't allow a control to occupy the same screen space as the applet that uses it. The control has to be placed in a separate area on the Web page using the **<OBJECT>** tag (see Chapter 4). Furthermore, ActiveX controls—visual and nonvisual alike—cannot send events directly to a Java applet. Events must be handled by an HTML script and then passed to the applet. (Chapter 9 includes a tutorial on HTML scripts.)

Passing Controls As Parameters

HTML scripts are also required to create the ActiveX control. When the HTML page loads, the script passes a reference to the control using a public function in the applet. The applet saves a copy of this reference and can use it later to call the control's methods and access its properties. (Your Java code cannot create a reference to a visual control using the **new** keyword, as it can with OLE automation servers.)

To illustrate, let's go back to the Video Playback control. Displaying this ActiveX control on a Web page requires the **<OBJECT>** tag, which looks like this:

```
<OBJECT
   ID="VideoPlaybackCtrl"
   WIDTH=300
   HEIGHT=250
   CLASSID="CLSID:D77B7824-1AAA-11D0-8512-0020AFC746E8">
</OBJECT>
```

Likewise, displaying a Java applet that uses this control requires the **<APPLET>** tag, which looks like this:

```
<APPLET
   CODE=VideoPlaybackApplet.class
   NAME=VideoPlaybackApplet
   WIDTH=325
   HEIGHT=125>
</APPLET>
```

When both of these tags have been placed in an HTML file, an HTML script can act as the mediator between them. It can take the ID of the ActiveX control and pass it to the applet, thereby providing the applet with a reference to the control. Here's how the script would look:

```
<SCRIPT LANGUAGE="JavaScript" FOR="window" EVENT="onLoad()">
<!--
 // If this script looks like gibberish, see Chapter 9.
 document.VideoPlaybackApplet.setVideoPlaybackCtrl
   (VideoPlaybackCtrl);
```

Activating ActiveX

```
-->
</SCRIPT>
```

The HTML script in this example assumes that the Video Playback applet contains a public member function called **setVideo_ PlaybackCtrl()**. Here's how that function would look:

```
import videoplayback.*;

public class VideoPlaybackApplet extends Applet
{
   IVideoPlayback m_video;

   .
   .
   .

   public void setVideoPlaybackCtrl(IVideoPlayback
     videoPlaybackCtrl)
   {
      m_video = videoPlaybackCtrl;
   }
}
```

Once the applet has saved a reference to the control, it can use that reference in the same manner as referencing an automation server (i.e., **m_video.Open()**, **m_video.getCurrentFrame()**, and so on).

ONLOAD LOADS LAST

*In HTML scripts, the **window.onLoad** event is sent after all applets and controls on the page have started running. Therefore, you must put any initialization of visual controls inside your applet's **setCtrl()** function, not its **init()** or **start()** functions.*

The Video Playback Control

The Video Playback example cited throughout this chapter is not fictional. I created it to demonstrate the enormous advantages of visual control integration, despite its handicaps. The control can load any standard AVI (Audio Video Interleave) file—the most common format for video in Windows—and display it on a Web page. By calling the control's methods, Java applets can automate the video playback, such as pausing it or stepping through frames (see Figure 7.5).

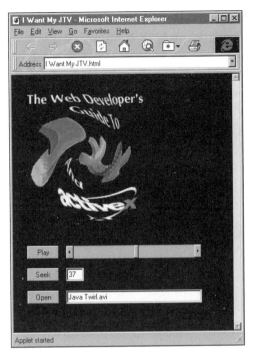

Figure 7.5 The Video Playback applet is the first known applet for playing AVI files.

Although AVI files are highly compressed, most of them are too large for downloading through today's modems. Therefore, the Video Playback control is not intended to be a real-world example of ActiveX integration. Its use, however, may be feasible on local-area intranets, where high-speed hardware is common.

Listing 7.2 contains an abridged version of the source code to the Video Playback applet, and Listing 7.3 contains its HTML file.

LISTING 7.2 THE VIDEO PLAYBACK SOURCE CODE.

```
/*

NOTE: A bug in the 1.00 release of Visual J++ causes all
      BOOL return values and properties to be reversed. In
      other words, Visual J++ makes BOOL properties appear
      FALSE when they're actually TRUE, and TRUE when
      they're actually FALSE. This applet is designed to
      handle this bug, so if you're recompiling it on an
      updated version of Visual J++ (one that has the bug
      fixed), you'll need to change the lines marked
      with "bugbug".
```

```java
*/

import java.applet.*;
import java.awt.*;
import VideoPlaybackAppletFrame;
import videoplayback.*;

public class VideoPlaybackApplet extends Applet
                                 implements Runnable
{
   MainDialog m_dlgMain;
   IVideoPlayback m_video;
   boolean m_bPlaying;

   static String strDefaultFilename = "Java Twirl.avi";

   Thread m_VideoPlaybackApplet = null;

   public void init()
   {
      m_dlgMain = new MainDialog(this);
      m_dlgMain.CreateControls();

      m_dlgMain.IDC_FRAME.setText("0");

      setBackground( Color.black );
   }

   public void paint(Graphics g)
   {
      // No painting is necessary because we use a dialog
      // box template.
   }

   public void start()
   {
      if (m_VideoPlaybackApplet == null)
      {
         m_VideoPlaybackApplet = new Thread(this);
         m_VideoPlaybackApplet.start();

         if ( m_video != null )
         {
           // bugbug: Designed for BOOL bug (see top of file)
           if ( m_video.Open(
                     m_dlgMain.IDC_FILENAME.getText() ) )
              showStatus("Error: AVI file not found");
           else
              m_dlgMain.IDC_SCROLLBAR.setValues(0, 1, 0,
```

```java
                                          m_video.getTotalFrames());
         }
      }
   }

   public void stop()
   {
      m_video.Close();

      if (m_VideoPlaybackApplet != null)
      {
         m_VideoPlaybackApplet.stop();
         m_VideoPlaybackApplet = null;
      }
   }

   public void run()
   {
      while (true)
      {
         try
         {
            Thread.sleep(500);

            if (m_bPlaying)
            {
               int nFrame = m_video.getCurrentFrame();

               if ( nFrame == m_video.getTotalFrames() )
               {
                  m_bPlaying = false;
                  m_dlgMain.IDC_PLAY.setLabel("Play");
               }

               m_dlgMain.IDC_SCROLLBAR.setValue(nFrame);
               m_dlgMain.IDC_FRAME.setText(nFrame + "");
            }
         }
         catch (InterruptedException e)
         {
            stop();
         }
      }
   }

   public boolean handleEvent(Event event)
   {
      if (event.target == m_dlgMain.IDC_SCROLLBAR)
      {
```

Activating ActiveX

```java
            m_video.putCurrentFrame(
                    m_dlgMain.IDC_SCROLLBAR.getValue() );
            m_dlgMain.IDC_FRAME.setText(
                    m_dlgMain.IDC_SCROLLBAR.getValue() + "");

            m_bPlaying = false;
            m_dlgMain.IDC_PLAY.setLabel("Play");

            return true;
        }
        else
        {
            if (event.target == m_dlgMain.IDC_PLAY)
            {
                if (m_bPlaying)
                {
                    m_video.Stop();
                    m_bPlaying = false;
                    m_dlgMain.IDC_PLAY.setLabel("Play");
                }
                else
                {
                    m_video.Play(false);
                    m_bPlaying = true;
                    m_dlgMain.IDC_PLAY.setLabel("Stop");
                }

                return true;
            }
            else
            {
                if (event.target == m_dlgMain.IDC_SEEK)
                {
                    String strFrame = new String(
                                m_dlgMain.IDC_FRAME.getText() );
                    int nFrame =
                            Integer.valueOf(strFrame).intValue();

                    m_video.putCurrentFrame(nFrame);

                    m_dlgMain.IDC_SCROLLBAR.setValue(nFrame);

                    return true;
                }
                else
                {
                    if (event.target == m_dlgMain.IDC_OPEN)
                    {
                        // bugbug: Designed for BOOL bug
```

```
                    // (see top of file)
                    if ( m_video.Open(
                           m_dlgMain.IDC_FILENAME.getText() ) )
                       showStatus("Error: AVI file not found");
                    else
                       showStatus("");

                    m_dlgMain.IDC_FILENAME.setText(
                           m_dlgMain.IDC_FILENAME.getText() );
                    m_dlgMain.IDC_FRAME.setText("0");
                    m_dlgMain.IDC_SCROLLBAR.setValues(0, 1, 0,
                                       m_video.getTotalFrames());

                    return true;
                }
            }
        }
    }

    return super.handleEvent(event);
}

public void setVideoPlaybackCtrl(
                        IVideoPlayback videoPlaybackCtrl,
                        String strCurrentPath)
{
    m_video = videoPlaybackCtrl;

    // bugbug: Designed for BOOL bug (see top of file)
    if ( m_video.Open( strCurrentPath +
                    strDefaultFilename ) )
       showStatus("Error: AVI file not found");
    else
    {
       m_dlgMain.IDC_FILENAME.setText( strCurrentPath +
                                       strDefaultFilename );
       m_dlgMain.IDC_SCROLLBAR.setValues(0, 1, 0,
                                m_video.getTotalFrames());
    }
  }
}
```

LISTING 7.3 THE VIDEO PLAYBACK APPLET'S HTML FILE.

```
<HTML>
<HEAD>

<SCRIPT LANGUAGE="VBScript">
<!--
```

```
' This function obtains the current path so that
' the video can load no matter where the HTML
' file is opened. For a tutorial on HTML scripts,
' see Chapter 9.
Function GetCurrentPath()
   ' Obtain the pathname of this file and
   ' strip the beginning "/"
   Dim path, length
   path = location.pathname
   length = Len(path) - 1
   path = Right(path, length)

   ' Determine the index of the last "\"
   Dim i
   For i = length To 0 Step -1
      If Mid(path, i, 1) = "\" Then
         Exit For
      End If
   Next

   ' Trim everything after the last "\"
   ' (leaving the "\" at the end)
   GetCurrentPath = Left(path, i)
End Function
-->
</SCRIPT>

<SCRIPT LANGUAGE="JavaScript" FOR="window" EVENT="onLoad()">
<!--
   document.VideoPlaybackApplet.setVideoPlaybackCtrl(
                   VideoPlaybackCtrl, GetCurrentPath());
-->
</SCRIPT>

<TITLE>I Want My JTV</TITLE>
</HEAD>
<BODY BGCOLOR="#000000">
<TABLE>
<TR>
<TD>
<OBJECT
   ID="VideoPlaybackCtrl"
   WIDTH=300
   HEIGHT=250
   CLASSID="CLSID:D77B7824-1AAA-11D0-8512-0020AFC746E8">
   <PARAM NAME="_Version" VALUE="65536">
   <PARAM NAME="_ExtentX" VALUE="6265">
   <PARAM NAME="_ExtentY" VALUE="6662">
```

```
   <PARAM NAME="_StockProps" VALUE="0">
</OBJECT>
</TD>
</TR>
<TR>
<TD>
<APPLET
   CODE=VideoPlaybackApplet.class
   CODEBASE="Java applet"
   NAME=VideoPlaybackApplet
   WIDTH=325
   HEIGHT=125>
</APPLET>
</TD>
</TR>
</TABLE>
</BODY>
</HTML>
```

Integrating Licensed Controls

The ActiveX architecture provides copy protection for ActiveX controls in the form of licensing. Licensed controls cannot be used in a design-time environment (such as Visual J++) unless the user provides a valid license key (an unpublished string of characters).

The ILicenseMgr Interface

When integrated with licensed ActiveX controls, Java applets must submit a proper key using the **ILicenseMgr** interface (located in the com.ms.com package). This interface replaces the **new** keyword when creating a reference to the control. For example, assume that a hypothetical ActiveX control called **MyLicensedCtrl** has a class ID value (see Chapter 4) of 391083AF-1234-BC44-AA83-090BA328FE40 and a license key of "Thank you, Thigh Master!". To use this control in a Java applet, you would type the following code:

```
import com.ms.com.*;
import mylicensedctrl.*;
.
.
IMyLicensedCtrl ctrl;
.
.
public void start()
{
```

```
    ILicenseMgr mgr = new LicenseMgr();

    ctrl = (IMyLicensedCtrl) mgr.createWithLic(
        "Thank you, Thigh Master!",              // License key
        "{391083AF-1234-BC44-AA83-090BA328FE40}", // Class ID
        null,                                     // IUnknown* punkOuter
        ComContext.INPROC_SERVER);                // ComContext ctxFlags
}
```

The **createWithLic()** function calls the necessary ActiveX interfaces to provide the control with the license key it needs. Afterward, the function calls **new** to create a reference to the ActiveX control. (Note: Because visual ActiveX controls cannot be instantiated with **new**, the **ILicenseMgr** interface is not compatible with visual controls. You *cannot* use licensed visual controls in Visual J++.)

For more details on the **ILicenseMgr** interface, see the Visual J++ help topic "ILicenseMgr."

The Licensing Demo

The Visual J++ documentation implies that the **ILicenseMgr** interface is required at all times. This is incorrect. You need the interface only if the license key is not available in a license file (which the control looks for by default). To illustrate this little detail, I've created a licensed ActiveX control and a Java applet that uses it (see Figure 7.6). The

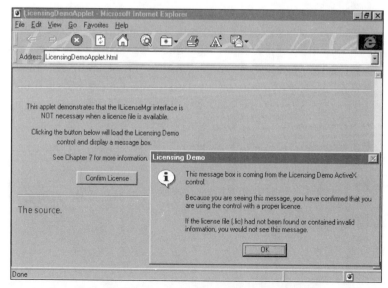

Figure 7.6 The Licensing Demo shows that ILicenseMgr is necessary only when a control's license file is not available.

applet never calls **createWithLic()**, but is still able to call the control's lone method.

Putting It All Together: The Taskbar Tray Example

Up to this point, all examples in this chapter have been demonstrations not intended for the real world. The next example, however, is a practical applet-control combination. It uses the Win32 API to display an icon in the *taskbar tray*, the small area at the bottom-right of your screen (see Figure 7.7). Double-clicking on this icon brings the user to a Web page, such as the home page of the applet's author. Simply resting the mouse cursor on it displays its tip text, which provides a short description or current status of the icon.

Most of the programming techniques in the Taskbar Tray applet are identical to the previous examples, so I won't bore you with the details. The only real difference is that this applet shows a workaround for the lack of event handling in Visual J++. The control can send messages back to the applet, a feat that is normally not possible without the aid of HTML scripts.

The technique isn't fancy. The applet merely sets up a timer that periodically checks the value of the control's **Clicked** property. When the control receives a mouse-click message from the taskbar tray, it sets the **Clicked** property to true, which the applet detects a moment later. In this manner, the control sends a mouse-click event to the applet. You can use the same technique in your own applets for any type of event.

WATCH THAT NAMESPACE
*When you import a control using the Java Type Library Wizard, be sure that you haven't given your applet the same name as the control. I made this mistake when writing the Taskbar Tray applet. I spent 20 minutes pulling my hair out before I realized that the **new** statement was calling the applet's constructor, not the control's constructor.*

Figure 7.7 The taskbar tray provides instant access to a program's features.

Listing 7.4 contains an abridged version of the source code to the Taskbar Tray applet.

LISTING 7.4 THE TASKBAR TRAY SOURCE CODE.

```java
/*
  NOTE: A bug in the 1.00 release of Visual J++ causes all
        BOOL return values and properties to be reversed. In
        other words, Visual J++ makes BOOL properties appear
        FALSE when they're actually TRUE, and TRUE when
        they're actually FALSE. This applet is designed to
        handle this bug, so if you're recompiling it on an
        updated version of Visual J++ (one that has the bug
        fixed), you'll need to change the lines marked with
        "bugbug".
*/

import java.applet.*;
import java.awt.*;
import java.net.*;
import TaskbarTrayAppletFrame;
import taskbartray.*;

public class TaskbarTrayApplet extends Applet
                               implements Runnable
{
   MainDialog m_dlgMain;
   ITaskbarTray m_TaskbarTray;

   private static String strDefaultLocation =
                       "http://TrevorHarmon.com/visualj";
   private static String strDefaultTip =
                                "Book Updates and Info";
   Thread m_TaskbarTrayApplet = null;

   public void init()
   {
      m_dlgMain = new MainDialog(this);
      m_dlgMain.CreateControls();

      m_dlgMain.IDC_LOCATION.setText(strDefaultLocation);
      m_dlgMain.IDC_TIP.setText(strDefaultTip);
   }

   public void destroy()
   {
      m_TaskbarTray.Hide();
   }
```

```java
public void paint(Graphics g)
{
   // No painting is necessary because we use a dialog
   // box template.
}

public void start()
{
   m_TaskbarTray = new TaskbarTray();
   m_TaskbarTray.putLocation(strDefaultLocation);
   m_TaskbarTray.putTip(strDefaultTip);

   if (m_TaskbarTrayApplet == null)
   {
      m_TaskbarTrayApplet = new Thread(this);
      m_TaskbarTrayApplet.start();
   }
}

public void stop()
{
   m_TaskbarTray.Hide();

   if (m_TaskbarTrayApplet != null)
   {
      m_TaskbarTrayApplet.stop();
      m_TaskbarTrayApplet = null;
   }
}

public void run()
{
   while (true)
   {
      try
      {
         Thread.sleep(250);

         // bugbug: Designed for BOOL bug (see top of file)
         if ( !m_TaskbarTray.getClicked() )
         {
            try
            {
               getAppletContext().showDocument(
                   new URL(m_TaskbarTray.getLocation()));
            }
            catch ( MalformedURLException e )
```

```
                    {
                        showStatus("Error: " + e.getMessage() );
                    }
                }
            }
            catch (InterruptedException e)
            {
                stop();
            }
        }
    }

    public boolean action(Event evt, Object arg)
    {
        if (evt.target instanceof Checkbox)
        {
            if ( m_dlgMain.IDC_ENABLE.getState() )
            {
                m_TaskbarTray.Show();
            }
            else
            {
                m_TaskbarTray.Hide();
            }

            return true;
        }
        else
        {
            if (evt.target instanceof Button)
            {
                m_TaskbarTray.putLocation(
                            m_dlgMain.IDC_LOCATION.getText() );
                m_TaskbarTray.putTip(
                            m_dlgMain.IDC_TIP.getText() );

                return true;
            }
        }

        return false;
    }
}
```

Summary

An ActiveX control is an ActiveX control is an ActiveX control...or is it? Remember that Microsoft has expanded the definition of ActiveX controls. They're not what they used to be. You might see them on a Web page handling events, or you might only see them in their altered form, lurking in the background as OLE automation servers.

Although Visual J++ can integrate with both types of ActiveX controls, it needs help from an HTML script to handle the true, event-driven kind. It offers direct support only for OLE automation servers. This support includes not just the ability to connect with servers, but also the ability to create them. Continue on with Chapter 8 to learn how to write automation servers using Visual J++.

Chapter 8

Java Controls

- Java controls vs. ActiveX controls
- Converting a Java class to an automation server
- Calling Java from Visual Basic
- Calling Java from C++
- Example: Lingo Maker

Java is the be-all and end-all of human existence—at least, that's what the hype surrounding this ever-popular computer language would have us believe. More books, magazine articles, and boardroom meetings have been dedicated to Java than to any other language in recent history. One might be surprised that all software in existence has not yet been rewritten in Java.

Java, of course, is not perfect. It has value only in certain environments (such as the World Wide Web). Even if Java were as wonderful as the media says, most source code would remain in its original language, simply because of the expense of translation. This presents a developer's dilemma: All programs must be rewritten in Java before they can take advantage of the features in a Java class.

Visual J++ can help you overcome this problem. With a few source code modifications and some quality time at the command prompt, you can convert your Java class to an OLE automation server. Your code is then available to C++, Visual Basic, and any other language that supports OLE automation. (For a definition of OLE automation servers, see the section "ActiveX Controls Redefined" in Chapter 7.)

What Are Java Controls?

You won't find the term *Java control* anywhere in the Visual J++ documentation. It's a phrase I use throughout this chapter to replace the more accurate (and lengthier) description, "a COM class written in Java and exposed as an OLE automation server." The Visual J++ documentation shortens this phrase to *COM class*, but I prefer my version—not just because it's less cryptic, but because it reflects the similarity of automation servers to ActiveX controls.

Java Controls Vs. ActiveX Controls

As mentioned in Chapter 7, Microsoft has changed the specification of ActiveX controls. It now has two different meanings. An ActiveX control can mean, as it has meant in the past, a miniature program that sits inside another program. But it can also mean simply an OLE automation server with no user interface or event handling.

Don't be fooled by Microsoft's press releases and FAQs on Visual J++. They say that Visual J++ can transform a Java class into an ActiveX control, but they actually mean that it can transform a Java class into an OLE automation server. (The new definition of ActiveX controls keeps everything nice and legal.) Java controls do not support encapsulation nor event handling, as do traditional ActiveX controls. They merely expose their functions and variables through OLE automation (see Figure 8.1).

Still, Java controls are quite similar to true ActiveX controls. Both have methods and properties accessible to all OLE automation controllers in the system. Both can expose their features without exposing their source code. And both can produce a visual user interface (although Java controls cannot display their interface inside another program).

Limitations Of Java Controls

A Java control is neither a true ActiveX control nor a true OLE automation server, but rather a Java class rigged up to look like an automation server. As a result, it carries two significant restrictions:

- *Limited to the Java language*—Java controls are written in Java, of course, so they can do only what the Java language allows them to do. However, because they are installed on your system locally—not through the Weblike applets—they can access files, connect to remote servers, and call native code.

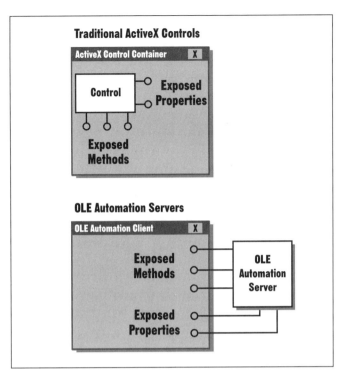

Figure 8.1 Java controls are not true ActiveX controls, but rather OLE automation servers.

- *One-way communication*—Normal OLE automation servers can call into other OLE automation servers. Java controls, because they are limited to Java, know nothing about how to use OLE. They can only expose their functions and properties and sit idly until an automation controller accesses them.

To get around these restrictions, you must rewrite your Java class in another language that supports OLE automation, such as Visual Basic or C++.

How Is Integration Possible?

Since Java was never designed for OLE, and OLE was never designed for Java, you might wonder how integration of the two is possible. The secret is MSJAVA.DLL, a component of Internet Explorer that implements a Java virtual machine in Windows. When an OLE automation controller attempts to access a Java control, the MSJAVA component is automatically loaded by the OLE subsystem. It acts as a shell around the control, passing OLE function calls directly to the Java code.

The MSJAVA.DLL file must be present for any Java control to execute. If you distribute a control, you must either require users to install Internet Explorer or obtain redistribution rights to MSJAVA.DLL and install it along with your control.

Creating Java Controls

Creating a Java control is rather tedious and requires many careful steps. Team J++ reports that an updated version of Visual J++ will provide a wizard to simplify the process, but until then, you'll have to follow the procedure outlined in this section.

Step 1: Write The Java Source Code

You can't convert any old Java class to a Java control. It has to meet a strict guideline set by Visual J++. The two rules of the guideline are:

- *Applets not allowed*—Just as OLE automation servers cannot reside inside a Web browser, neither can Java controls. Deriving your class from **Applet** will cause it to fail. Hence, you shouldn't use the Visual J++ Applet Wizard to create a new project. Just open a new Project Workspace and type the class definition yourself.

- *Public classes not allowed*—For some mysterious reason, Visual J++ does not allow the class of a Java control to be declared **public**. Adding this modifier will break the entire class.

> **FOLLOWING THE CLASS-NAME CONVENTION**
> *You should prefix the class name of your Java control with the letter C. This follows the standard OLE naming convention, where L means library, I means interface, and C means class.*

EXPOSING FUNCTIONS AND VARIABLES

Once your class meets this guideline, you can begin defining functions and variables that you want to expose to users of your Java control. The process for creating these functions is the same as for standard Java class functions. Simply declare a public function and insert its code between two curly braces. The function can take parameters and return a value just as usual.

For variables, the process is a little different. Simply declaring a variable as **public** will not expose it. You must instead wrap the variable, which should be declared **private**, with **get/put** functions. For example, a class that exposes a variable called **MyProperty** would look like this:

```
class CMyJavaControl
{
   private boolean m_bMyProperty = false;

   public boolean getMyProperty()
   { return m_bMyProperty; }

   public void putMyProperty(boolean bMyProperty)
   { m_bMyProperty = bMyProperty; }
}
```

Because the **get/put** functions provide automation controllers with indirect access to the property, you can easily validate its value (for instance, making sure an integer stays within a certain range) just by inserting validation code within the put function.

Data Type Restrictions

*Not all data types can be exposed from Java. Only the primitive types (integers, rationals, char, and boolean), the **String** class, and the **com.ms.com.Variant** class are allowed. This restriction applies to all exposed variables and to the parameters and return values of all exposed functions.*

Handling Errors

In Java, errors are handled by throwing exceptions or returning error codes. In OLE, error codes are universal. The OLE architecture provides a standard error code data type called **HRESULT**. By default, every Java function that you expose returns an **HRESULT** of 0—indicating success—no matter what your function actually returns. (You'll find out how this is possible in the next section, "Create The Object Description.")

To indicate failure, your function must throw the **com.ms.com.ComFailException** exception. Listing 8.1 provides an example of how to throw an HRESULT value called **E_FAIL**, indicating a general failure, defined as 0x80004005. For a list of common HRESULT values, see Table 6.1 in Chapter 6.

Java Controls **209**

LISTING 8.1 RETURNING AN ERROR IN A JAVA CONTROL'S EXPOSED FUNCTION.

```
import com.ms.com.*;

class CMyJavaControl
{
   public int MyExposedFunction() throws ComFailException
   {
      .
      .
      .
      if ( ErrorDetected )
      {
         // An error was detected, so throw an instance
         // of ComFailException. This will return the
         // corresponding HRESULT error code to the calling
         // program.

         throw new ComFailException(0x80004005, // E_FAIL
                                    "An error was detected.");

         // The calling program, if written correctly, detects
         // the HRESULT error code and ignores the actual
         // return value. Therefore, just return a dummy value
         // of zero.
         return 0;
      }
      else
      {
         return SomeMeaningfulValue;
      }
   }
}
```

DEBUGGING JAVA CONTROLS

*Visual J++ cannot debug Java controls. It can, however, debug standalone applications. To convert your control to a standalone application, simply add a **main**() function to the class, and call an exposed function or two. For example:*

```
private static CMyJavaControl ctrl;
public static void main(String args[])
{
   ctrl = new CMyJavaControl();
   ctrl.MyExposedFunction();
}
```

Displaying A User Interface

Because Java controls are not applets, they can't appear inside a Web browser, play sounds, or perform other applet feats. They can, however, reveal a user interface as a standalone window, which can hold graphics, text, and any **Component** class (see Figure 8.2). This window can't appear when the control loads; it can display itself only when an exposed function is called. As shown in Listing 8.2, the trick is simply to create an instance of the **Frame** class.

LISTING 8.2 DISPLAYING A USER INTERFACE IN A JAVA CONTROL.

```
import java.awt.*;

class CMyJavaControl
{
   public void MyExposedFunction()
   {
      .
      .
      .
      // Display a window for the user interface...
      new MyFrame();
      .
      .
      .
   }
}

class MyFrame extends Frame
{
   public MyFrame()
   {
      super("My Frame");

      setLayout( new FlowLayout() );
      resize(225, 220);
      setBackground(Color.lightGray);

      TextArea textStuff = new TextArea(12, 30);
      textStuff.setText("I was in a boxing match once. " +
                        "I came in second.");

      add(textStuff);

      show();
   }

   public boolean handleEvent(Event evt)
   {
```

```
        switch (evt.id)
        {
            // If the user clicks the close box,
            // shut down the window.
            case Event.WINDOW_DESTROY:
                dispose();
                return true;
        }

        return super.handleEvent(evt);
    }
}
```

Changing A Window's Icon
By default, Frame windows have a picture of a coffee cup for an icon. You can change this icon by calling setIconImage().

Step 2: Create The Object Description

Once you've got functions exposed, **get/put** functions installed, and everything debugged, you're ready to convert your Java class to a Java control. The next step is to create an Object Description Language (ODL) file, which defines how your Java class exposes its functions and variables. ODL files are pure text files with three sections:

Figure 8.2 Java controls can display Frame windows that hold a user interface.

212 *Chapter 8*

- *Library*—The library section is simply a container for the interface and coclass sections. By convention, library names begin with the letter *L*.

- *Interface*—The interface section is the guts of the ODL file. It declares your Java class' functions and variables that you want to convert to methods and properties of your Java control. By convention, interface names begin with the letter *I*.

- *Coclass*—The coclass section, which stands for "component object class," declares the sets of interfaces in the library. (You can use this section to declare multiple sets of interfaces, but for simplicity I'll pretend ODL files contain only one set.) The name of the coclass should match the name of your Java class. By convention, coclass names begin with the letter *C*.

DEFINING THE INTERFACES

The library and coclass sections are quite simple. You can learn how to create them just by looking at the sample ODL file at the end of this section. The interface section, on the other hand, requires some explanation. It lists exposed functions and variables in a special format. For example, if your Java class contains a function defined as

```
public void MyExposedFunction() {}
```

then you would list it in the interface section like this:

```
HRESULT MyExposedFunction();
```

Notice that even though the Java function is **void**, its ODL equivalent returns an **HRESULT**. The **HRESULT** allows the function to return an error code (as explained previously in the section "Handling Errors").

ODL interfaces are pretty easy if your Java function takes no parameters. Once you start to add parameters, however, things get weird. For example, an unassuming Java function such as

```
public void MyExposedFunction(int nVar1,
                              String strVar2,
                              boolean bVar3) {}
```

would translate to ODL as:

```
HRESULT MyExposedFunction([in] int nVar1,
                         [in] BSTR strVar2,
                         [in] boolean bVar3);
```

Notice the unusual **[in]**? It indicates that the parameter's value is coming *in* to the function. If the parameter were a single-element array, such as **int[]**, you would use **[in, out]** instead, because any changes to the array would remain when the function exits (hence, the values would go *out*).

Also notice that the **String** parameter was changed to a **BSTR** in the ODL. This is because the OLE automation equivalent of a Java **String** is a **BSTR**, a 32-bit length-prefixed character pointer. See Table 8.1 for a list of the most common conversions of Java data types to ODL data types.

If your Java function returns a value, your ODL interface gets even weirder. Return values go out of the function, so you must specify them with **[out]**. Return values are a special type of out, though, so you must also declare them with **retval**. Furthermore, you must append (*) to the data type as you would for an ODL array. For example,

Table 8.1   ODL equivalents of Java data types.

Java Type	ODL Equivalent
boolean	boolean
char	char
byte	unsigned char
short	short
int	int
long	int64
float	float
double	double
String	BSTR
com.ms.com.Variant	VARIANT
class java.lang.Object	IDispatch*
array of *typename* (i.e., String[])	*typename** (i.e., BSTR*)

```
public boolean MyExposedFunction(char ch,
                                 double[] DoubleArray) {}
```

would convert to this:

```
HRESULT MyExposedFunction([in] char ch,
                          [in, out] double* DoubleArray,
                          [out, retval] boolean* retval);
```

You can have only one **retval** parameter per ODL interface, and it must be listed last.

ODL Comments

Inserting comments into an ODL file can help you—and other programmers—make sense of it down the road. ODL comments are exactly the same as Java comments. Just place two forward slashes (//) at the beginning of each line.

Inserting property declarations into an ODL file is much like inserting methods. The only difference is that you must declare them twice: once for the **get** function and once for the **put** function. For example, a variable declared as

```
private byte m_byMyProperty = 0;

public byte getMyProperty()
{ return m_byMyProperty; }

public void putMyProperty(byte byMyProperty)
{ m_byMyProperty = byMyProperty; }
```

would look like this in the ODL file:

```
[propget]
HRESULT MyProperty([out, retval] unsigned char* retval);

[propput]
HRESULT MyProperty([in] unsigned char byMyProperty);
```

The **[propget]** and **[propput]** keys declare each line of ODL code as either a **get** function or **put** function, respectively.

Generating The UUIDs

Each section in an ODL file—library, interface, and coclass—requires a special identifier called a *universally unique identifier* (UUID). A UUID, also known as a GUID (globally unique identifier), is a 128-bit value that is guaranteed to be unique. Each one is generated by a special algorithm that ensures no two values match, even if two people run the algorithm at the exact same moment.

UUIDs are ideal for OLE automation. By tagging every library, class, and interface with a UUID, the OLE subsystem can always tell them apart. You never have to worry about giving your interfaces unique names.

To generate a trio of UUIDs for your ODL file, run the Create GUID program, located under the Visual J++ Tools menu. It displays the dialog box shown in Figure 8.3.

First, click the fourth radio button to specify that you want the UUID in Registry Format. (ODL files also use this format.) Next, click the Copy button, which will copy the UUID to the Windows clipboard. Finally, open your ODL file and paste the UUID into the appropriate section, as shown in the following sample. (Note: After pasting, you must remove the curly braces that the Create GUID program placed around the text.)

A Sample ODL File

This section presents a sample that should complete your education in writing ODL files. From this code, you will see how the library, interface, and coclass sections relate to each other, as well as where to place the UUIDs. You will also notice a **helpstring** parameter in each

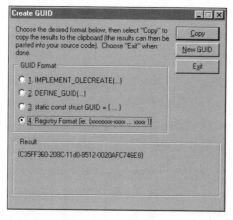

Figure 8.3 The Create GUID program generates unique identifiers for your ODL file.

section. This parameter is merely a description of the library, interface, or class. (Note that the **helpstring** in the library section is the most important because it appears in OLE automation browsers, such as the Java Type Library Wizard and the References dialog box in Visual Basic.)

Listing 8.3 shows the Java class declaration for the sample, and Listing 8.4 shows its ODL representation.

LISTING 8.3   A SAMPLE JAVA CLASS DECLARATION.

```
import java.lang.*;

class CMyJavaControl
{
   private String m_Var1 = "1";
   private int m_Var2 = 2;
   private float m_Var3 = 3;

   public getVar1() { return m_Var1; }
   public putVar1(String Var1) { m_Var1 = Var1; }

   public getVar2() { return m_Var2; }
   public putVar2(int Var1) { m_Var2 = Var2; }

   public getVar3() { return m_Var3; }
   public putVar3(float Var3) { m_Var3 = Var3; }

   public void func1(int param1) {}
   public void func2(String param1, long param2) {}
   public int func3(int[] param1) {}
   public boolean func4(byte param1, short param2) {}
}
```

LISTING 8.4   THE ODL FILE FOR THE SAMPLE JAVA CLASS.

```
// MyJavaControl.odl

[
   uuid (A1ED37A1-208D-11d0-8512-0020AFC746E8),
   version (1.0),
   helpstring("My Java control")
]
library LMyJavaControl
{
   importlib("stdole32.tlb");   // Required for IDispatch

   [
      odl,
      uuid(A1ED37A2-208D-11d0-8512-0020AFC746E8),
      helpstring("IMyJavaControl interfaces"),
```

```
            oleautomation,
            dual
        ]
        interface IMyJavaControl : IDispatch
        {
            // PROPERTY: String Var1
            [propget]
            HRESULT Var1([out, retval] BSTR* retval);
            [propput]
            HRESULT Var1([in] BSTR Var1);

            // PROPERTY: int Var2
            [propget]
            HRESULT Var2([out, retval] int* retval);
            [propput]
            HRESULT Var2([in] int Var2);

            // PROPERTY: float Var3
            [propget]
            HRESULT Var3([out, retval] float* retval);
            [propput]
            HRESULT Var3([in] float Var3);

            // METHOD: void func1(int param1)
            HRESULT func1([in] int param1);

            // METHOD: void func2(String param1, long param2)
            HRESULT func2([in] BSTR param1, [in] int64 param2);

            // METHOD: int func3(int[] param1)
            HRESULT func3([in, out] int* param1,
                    [out, retval] int* retval);

            // METHOD: boolean func4(byte param1, short param2)
            HRESULT func4([in] unsigned char param1,
                    [in] short param2,
                    [out, retval] boolean retval);
        }

        [
            uuid(A1ED37A3-208D-11d0-8512-0020AFC746E8),
            helpstring("CMyJavaControl class"),
            appobject
        ]
        coclass CMyJavaControl
        {
            interface IMyJavaControl;
        }
    }
```

INSTANT ODL

For quick access to an ODL file, insert it into your Visual J++ project by selecting Insert\Files Into Project. You can then double-click the file from the FileView to load it into the Visual J++ Text Editor.

Step 3: Build The Type Library

After you have created an ODL file, you must convert it from its original text form to binary. The binary form of an ODL file is known as a *type library*, or TLB. TLBs are easier for programs to read, and the conversion process checks your ODL file for errors.

THE MKTYPLIB UTILITY

Visual J++ includes a utility called MkTypLib for converting ODL files to TLBs. You can find it in the bin directory. To run this program, just type its name on the command line, specifying your ODL file as a parameter. (Note: If Visual C++ is not installed, you must also specify the /nocpp parameter.) For instance, at the command line you might type

```
"c:\Visual J++\bin\mktyplib" MyJavaControl.odl /nocpp
```

which would produce:

```
Microsoft (R) Type Library Generator   Version 2.03.3027
Copyright (c) Microsoft Corp. 1993-1995.  All rights reserved.

Successfully generated type library 'MyJavaControl.tlb'.
```

FATAL DISTRACTIONS

While developing a Java control, you may occasionally receive the following error from MkTypLib:

```
MyJavaControl.odl : fatal error M0003: Error creating type
   library while processing item 'LMyJavaControl':
   Access denied.
```

This error indicates that a running program, most likely Visual Basic, has a stranglehold on the existing TLB file. Find the program, shut it down, then restart MkTypLib.

THE JAVATLB UTILITY

Now you can run the JavaTLB utility on the type library you just created. JavaTLB, which is the command-line version of the Java Type Library Wizard, generates class files from the library description you provide. These files are not the implementation of your Java control, which you will create in Step 4, but rather entry points to the implementation. It places all files in a directory descending from \Windows\Java\TrustLib so MSJAVA.DLL can find them.

A session with JavaTLB might look like this:

```
C:\My Java Control>"c:\Visual J++\bin" MyJavaControl.tlb
Microsoft (R) Visual J++ Java Typelib Conversion Utility
Copyright (C) Microsoft Corp 1996. All rights reserved.

import myjavacontrol.*;
```

Step 4: Rebuild The Java Class

Take note of JavaTLB's output. It's what you need to create the implementation of your Java control. In the earlier sample session, JavaTLB printed "import myjavacontrol.*". This indicates that the **myjavacontrol** library must be imported into your Java class.

Once you have added the **import** statement, you must also implement the interface defined in your ODL file. For example, if you named your interface **IMyJavaControl**, your Java class would look like this:

```
import myjavacontrol.*;

class CMyJavaControl implements IMyJavaControl
{
   // Class definition
}
```

After importing the library and implementing the interface, rebuild your source code.

Step 5: Register The Java Class

Creating your Java control requires one final step: You must register it with the Windows System Registry. Once registered, OLE automation controllers will know how to call your Java control (a.k.a. your OLE automation server).

To register a control, run the JavaReg utility (located in the Visual J++ bin directory) from the command line. This program takes three parameters:

- */register*—Always include this parameter when registering a Java class. (To unregister a class, use the /unregister parameter.)
- */class*—This parameter specifies the name of the primary class in your Java control. Separate the parameter name from the class name with a colon.
- */clsid*—JavaReg requires the UUID from your ODL's coclass section. Use this parameter to specify the UUID, separating the two with a colon. Be sure to place curly braces around the ID. (Hint: Instead of typing out the number, paste it from the clipboard using the DOS prompt's system menu.)

For example, if your Java control was built from a class called **CMyJavaControl** and was given a UUID of 98A34D60-2100-11d0-8512-0020AFC746E8, you might type the following at the command line:

```
"c:\Visual J++\bin\javareg" /register /class:CMyJavaControl
    /clsid:{98A34D60-2100-11d0-8512-0020AFC746E8}
```

Executing this command loads JavaReg, registers the Java control, and displays the message box shown in Figure 8.4. You should then be able to find your class in the Object List pane of the OLE Object Viewer utility (located under the Visual J++ Tools menu).

Note that if your Java control's implementation—the class files you built in Step 4—are not already in a directory on the CLASSPATH (see sidebar), you must move them to the CLASSPATH so the MSJAVA component can find them. Also, note that if you distribute a Java control, your installation program must register it and place its implementation somewhere in the CLASSPATH.

Figure 8.4 JavaReg displays this message box if it registers your class successfully.

further developments

What's The CLASSPATH?

The CLASSPATH is a list of four directories that the MSJAVA component searches when executing a Java class. If a class does not reside in one of these directories, it cannot execute. By default, all directories in the CLASSPATH descend from \Windows\Java.

Each of the four directories is stored in the Windows System Registry under the key HKEY_LOCAL_MACHINE\Software\Microsoft\Java VM. The subkeys, listed in the order in which they are searched, are:

- *Classpath*—Classes available to all applets, including untrusted applets.
- *LibsDirectory*—Libraries available to all applets, including untrusted applets.
- *TrustedClassPath*—Classes available only to trusted applets.
- *TrustedLibsDirectory*—Libraries available only to trusted applets.

By editing these subkeys, you can change how the MSJAVA component searches for your Java control.

Driving Java Controls

By themselves, Java controls are useless. They can only wait in the background until some other program—known as an *OLE controller* or *Java control driver*—calls on them. Drivers can be written in any language that supports OLE automation; the two most popular are Visual Basic and C++. This section demonstrates how to write a Java control driver in either language.

Driving From Visual Basic

Driving Java controls from Visual Basic is wonderfully simple. You need to write no more than three lines of code. Before calling the control, however, you must create a reference to it.

CREATING A REFERENCE

To create a Visual Basic reference to a Java control, follow these steps:

1. Select Tools|References. This will bring up the dialog box shown in Figure 8.5.

2. Find your Java control in the list, and place a checkmark next to its name.

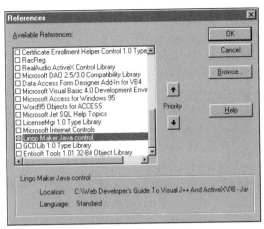

Figure 8.5 The Visual Basic References dialog box defines variables for OLE automation.

3. Select your project's main form from the Project window and click the View Code button.

4. From the Object list, select "(General)", and from the Proc list, select "(declarations)".

5. Define a variable for your Java control's interface using the **Dim** keyword. For example, if your Java control was named My Java Control, you would type:

```
Dim MyJavaControl As IMyJavaControl
```

6. From the Object list, select "Form", and from the Proc list, select "Load".

7. Allocate memory for the interface variable using the **New** keyword. Be sure to allocate it as a class, not an interface. For example:

```
Set MyJavaControl = New CMyJavaControl
```

CALLING METHODS AND ACCESSING PROPERTIES

After you have created a reference to the Java control, you can call its methods and access its properties as you would for any other Visual Basic object. For example, to call a function defined as

```
public void MyExposedFunction() {}
```

you would type:

```
Call MyJavaControl.MyExposedFunction
```

Similarly, to call a function defined as

```
public void AnotherExposedFunction(int param1, String param2)
```

you would type:

```
Call MyJavaControl.AnotherExposedFunction(37,
                 "See? I told you VB was simple.")
```

Accessing a Java control's properties is no more difficult. It works the same as standard Visual Basic properties. A Java variable named **MyProperty** of type boolean would be accessed as:

```
MyJavaControl.MyProperty = True
```

For a complete example of driving a Java control from Visual Basic, see the Lingo Maker Driver program included on this book's CD-ROM.

Driving From C++

Driving a Java control is more difficult from C++ than from Visual Basic. You have to concern yourself with such tedious issues as building a header file, releasing interface handles, and checking for null pointers. I've already worked through these tricky details, however, and can help you avoid the pitfalls. Just follow the steps in this section and you'll be okay.

BUILDING THE HEADER FILE

Before you can write any C++ code that calls a Java control, you have to build a header file so the compiler knows what you're talking about. The MkTypLib utility, discussed in Step 3 of the previous section, can build this header for you when you specify the /h parameter. For example:

```
"c:\Visual C++\bin" MyJavaControl.tlb /h MyJavaControl.h
```

This command will generate a header file similar to the one shown in Listing 8.5. You must "#include" this file, as well as the initguid.h header file that came with your C++ compiler, in your source code.

LISTING 8.5 **THE ODL FILE FOR THE SAMPLE JAVA CLASS.**

```
/* This header file machine-generated by mktyplib.exe */
/* Interface to type library: LMyJavaControl */
```

```c
#ifndef _LMyJavaControl_H_
#define _LMyJavaControl_H_

DEFINE_GUID(LIBID_LMyJavaControl,0x710CA5E1L,0x1F0B,0x11D0,
    0x85,0x12,0x00,0x20,0xAF,0xC7,0x46,0xE8);

DEFINE_GUID(IID_IMyJavaControl,0x710CA5E2L,0x1F0B,0x11D0,0x85,
    0x12,0x00,0x20,0xAF,0xC7,0x46,0xE8);

/* Definition of interface: IMyJavaControl */
#undef INTERFACE
#define INTERFACE IMyJavaControl

DECLARE_INTERFACE_(IMyJavaControl, IDispatch)
{
#ifndef NO_BASEINTERFACE_FUNCS

    /* IUnknown methods */
    STDMETHOD(QueryInterface)(THIS_ REFIID riid,
                              LPVOID FAR* ppvObj) PURE;
    STDMETHOD_(ULONG, AddRef)(THIS) PURE;
    STDMETHOD_(ULONG, Release)(THIS) PURE;

    /* IDispatch methods */
    STDMETHOD(GetTypeInfoCount)(THIS_ UINT FAR* pctinfo) PURE;

    STDMETHOD(GetTypeInfo)(
      THIS_
      UINT itinfo,
      LCID lcid,
      ITypeInfo FAR* FAR* pptinfo) PURE;

    STDMETHOD(GetIDsOfNames)(
      THIS_
      REFIID riid,
      OLECHAR FAR* FAR* rgszNames,
      UINT cNames,
      LCID lcid,
      DISPID FAR* rgdispid) PURE;

    STDMETHOD(Invoke)(
      THIS_
      DISPID dispidMember,
      REFIID riid,
      LCID lcid,
      WORD wFlags,
      DISPPARAMS FAR* pdispparams,
      VARIANT FAR* pvarResult,
      EXCEPINFO FAR* pexcepinfo,
```

```
          UINT FAR* puArgErr) PURE;
#endif

    /* IMyJavaControl methods */
    STDMETHOD(get_MyProp)(THIS_ long FAR* retval) PURE;
    STDMETHOD(put_Prop)(THIS_ long MyProp) PURE;
    STDMETHOD(MyExposedMethod)(THIS) PURE;
    STDMETHOD(AnotherExposedMethod)(THIS_ BSTR str,
          VARIANT_BOOL bShowResults, BSTR FAR* retval) PURE;
};

DEFINE_GUID(CLSID_CMyJavaControl,0x710CA5E3L,0x1F0B,0x11D0,
    0x85,0x12,0x00,0x20,0xAF,0xC7,0x46,0xE8);

#ifdef __cplusplus
class CMyJavaControl;
#endif

#endif
```

CREATING A REFERENCE

Your next step is to create a reference to your Java control by calling **CoCreateInstance()**. This function obtains a pointer to the Java control, which you can use to call methods and access properties. It takes five parameters:

- **REFCLSID rclsid**—Class identifier. This has already been defined for you in MkTypLib's header file (example: **CLSID_CMy JavaControl**).

- **LPUNKNOWN pUnkOuter**—A pointer for aggregate mapping. Specify **NULL** for Java controls.

- **DWORD dwClsContext**—Context for running executable code. Specify **CLSCTX_INPROC_SERVER** for Java controls.

- **REFIID riid**—Interface identifier. This has already been defined for you in MkTypLib's header file (example: **IID_IMy JavaControl**).

- **LPVOID* ppv**—Pointer to storage of interface identifier (see the following example).

Here's an example of how you would create an instance of the Java control from Listing 8.5:

```
IMyJavaControl* iMyCtrl = NULL;

CoCreateInstance(CLSID_CMyJavaControl, NULL,
   CLSCTX_INPROC_SERVER, IID_IMyJavaControl, (void**)&iMyCtrl);

if (iMyCtrl == NULL)
{
   MessageBox(0, "Unable to create instance", "Error", 0);
}
else
{
   // Use iMyCtrl to call methods and access properties.
   // See the following section for an example.
   iMyCtrl->Release();
}
```

Notice that the **iMyCtrl** interface is released when it's no longer needed. This is because OLE keeps track of memory by using reference counting. The **Release()** function decrements the release count on the control. If you forget to call **Release()**, your program will leak memory and could eventually crash the system. (Makes you appreciate Java's garbage collecting, doesn't it?)

SAVING INTERFACE POINTERS

*Instead of calling **CoCreateInstance()** every time you want to use a Java control, you can save a copy of the interface pointer in a global (or member) variable. Saving pointers reduces both execution time and the time you spend coding. Just be sure to release the interface pointer when you're done with it.*

CALLING METHODS

Once you have created an interface, you can use it to call the methods and access the properties of the Java control. Calling methods works just like calling the functions of a C++ class pointer. For example, a Java function defined as

```
public void MyExposedFunction(char param1, float param2) {}
```

would be called in C++ as:

```
iMyCtrl->MyExposedFunction('t', 1.234);
```

Although this syntax is what you're probably used to, note that return values are handled differently. All Java control methods, when called from C++, return an **HRESULT** to indicate success or some type of failure (see Table 6.1 in Chapter 6). To get the actual return value, you must specify a pointer as the last parameter, as indicated in MkTypLib's header file. For example, a Java function defined as

```
public String MyExposedFunction(boolean param1) {}
```

would be called in C++ like this:

```
int nRetVal;
iMyCtrl->MyExposedFunction(TRUE, &nRetVal);
```

Always remember to pass a valid pointer as the return value reference. If you try to cut corners and pass **NULL**, your program will crash.

Managing BSTRs In C++

As indicated in Table 8.1, the ODL equivalent of a Java **String** is a **BSTR**, the string data type used by OLE. Because OLE is based heavily on C++, the C++ equivalent of a Java **String** is also a **BSTR**. As you might expect, managing a **BSTR** variable takes more effort than its Java counterpart. You can't use standard C++ string functions; you must use special OLE-defined functions that handle **BSTR**s. The three most important of these functions are:

- **SysAllocString(OLECHAR*)**—Allocates a **BSTR** from an **OLECHAR** string. (Hint: You can convert a standard C++ string to **OLECHAR** using the **T2OLE** macro.)

- **SysStringLen(BSTR)**—Determines the length of a **BSTR**.

- **SysFreeString(BSTR)**—Frees a previously allocated **BSTR**. Don't forget to call this function when you're finished with the string.

See the OLE SDK documentation for a complete list of **BSTR** functions. Also, if you're creating a C++ driver with the Microsoft Foundation Classes (MFC), see the documentation of **CString** to learn about its built-in support for **BSTR**s.

ACCESSING PROPERTIES

Accessing a Java control's properties from C++ isn't as easy as it could be. The MkTypLib header file wraps each property with **get/put** functions, and you must call these functions every time you access a property value. To illustrate, a control property called **MyProperty** would be accessed in this way:

```
// Get the integer property value...
int i;
iMyCtrl->get_MyProperty(&i)
i++;
// Set it back...
iMyCtrl->put_MyProperty(i);
```

Putting It All Together: The Lingo Maker Example

For my sample code, I've combined all the topics of this chapter into a single Java control called the Lingo Maker. It can translate English text into any of three "lingoes": pig latin, Elmer Fudd talk, or Morse code. Table 8.2 lists the variable and the two functions exposed by the Lingo Maker.

You can find the complete source code to the Lingo Maker control, as well as its compiled class files, on the CD-ROM included with this book. (Listings 8.6 and 8.7 are the abridged source code.) Descending from the same directory, you can also find the source code to a Visual Basic and a Visual C++ program that drive the control. Figure 8.7 is a screen shot of the VB version in action.

Table 8.2 Variables and functions exposed by the Lingo Maker.

Variable/Function	Description
int Lingo	Specifies the type of lingo for translation (1=pig latin, 2=Elmer Fudd talk, 3=Morse code).
String Translate(String str, boolean bShowResults)	Translates the provided string into the lingo specified by the Lingo property, then returns the translated string. If bShowResults is true, displays a window containing the translated text.
void TranslateInteractive()	Displays a window containing two text boxes. As the user types into the first box, the translation of the text—as specified by the Lingo property—appears in the second box (see Figure 8.6).

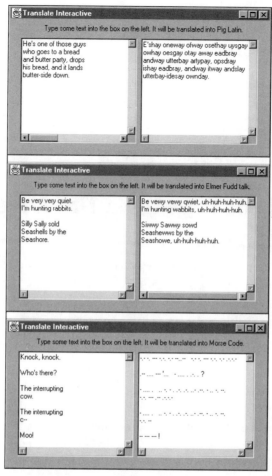

Figure 8.6 The **TranslateInteractive()** function displays a window for instant text translation.

Figure 8.7 Visual Basic programs can drive the Lingo Maker control.

LISTING 8.6 THE LINGO MAKER SOURCE CODE.

```java
import java.awt.*;
import lingomaker.*;

class CLingoMaker implements ILingoMaker
{
   private int m_nLingo = 1;

   // Returns the character in the string at the given offset.
   // Returns 0 if the offset is out of bounds, thereby
   // preventing an exception from being thrown.
   private char getChar(String str, int nOffset)
   {
      if ( nOffset < str.length() )
         return str.charAt(nOffset);
      else
         return '\0';
   }

   private boolean isLetterOrApos(char c)
   {
      return Character.isLetter(c) || c == '\'';
   }

   private boolean isConsonant(String str, int nOffset)
   {
      char c = str.charAt(nOffset);

      if ( !Character.isLetter(c) )
         return false;

      switch ( Character.toUpperCase(c) )
      {
         case 'A':
         case 'E':
         case 'I':
         case 'O':
         case 'U':
            return false;

         case 'Y':

            // If the Y is the first letter in the word...
            if ( nOffset > 0 &&
               Character.isLetter(str.charAt(nOffset - 1)) )
               return false;
            else
               return true;
```

```
            default:
                return true;
        }
    }

    private String toPigLatin(String str)
    {
        StringBuffer strReturn = new StringBuffer();
        char[] strChars;
        int nEnd;

        for (int i = 0; i < str.length(); i++)
        {
            if ( !isLetterOrApos(str.charAt(i)) )
            {
                strReturn.append(str.charAt(i));
            }
            else
            {
                if ( !isConsonant(str, i) )
                {
                    // Determine the index of the end of the word
                    for (nEnd = i;
                         nEnd < str.length() &&
                         isLetterOrApos(str.charAt(nEnd));
                         nEnd++);

                    strChars = new char[nEnd - i];
                    str.getChars(i, nEnd, strChars, 0);

                    strReturn.append(strChars);
                    strReturn.append("way");

                    i = nEnd - 1;
                }
                else
                {
                    int nVowel;

                    // Determine the index of the vowel...
                    for (nVowel = i;
                         nVowel < str.length() &&
                         isConsonant(str, nVowel);
                         nVowel++);

                    // Determine the index of the end of the word
                    for (nEnd = nVowel;
                         nEnd < str.length() &&
```

```java
                        isLetterOrApos(str.charAt(nEnd));
                        nEnd++);

                if (nVowel != nEnd)
                {
                    strChars = new char[nEnd - nVowel];
                    str.getChars(nVowel, nEnd, strChars, 0);

                    if ( Character.isUpperCase(str.charAt(i)) )
                    {
                        strChars[0] =
                                Character.toUpperCase(strChars[0]);
                    }

                    strReturn.append(strChars);

                    strChars = new char[nVowel - i];
                    str.getChars(i, nVowel, strChars, 0);

                    if ( Character.isUpperCase(str.charAt(i)) )
                    {
                        strChars[0] =
                                Character.toLowerCase(strChars[0]);
                    }

                    strReturn.append(strChars);
                    strReturn.append("ay");

                    i = nEnd - 1;
                }
                else
                {
                    strReturn.append(str.charAt(i));
                }
            }
        }
    }

    return strReturn.toString();
}

private String toElmerFudd(String str)
{
    StringBuffer strReturn = new StringBuffer();

    for (int i = 0; i < str.length(); i++)
    {
        switch ( Character.toUpperCase(str.charAt(i)) )
        {
```

```java
            case 'R':
            case 'r':
            case 'L':
            case 'l':
                strReturn.append(
                    Character.isUpperCase(str.charAt(i)) ?
                        'W' : 'w' );
                break;

            case '.':
                strReturn.append(", uh-huh-huh-huh.");
                break;

            case 'Q':
            case 'q':

                if ( getChar(str, i + 1) == 'u' )
                {
                    strReturn.append(str.charAt(i) + "w");
                    i++;
                }

                break;

            default:
                strReturn.append(str.charAt(i));
        }
    }

    return strReturn.toString();
}

private String toMorseCode(String str)
{
    StringBuffer strReturn = new StringBuffer();

    for (int i = 0; i < str.length(); i++)
    {
        switch ( Character.toLowerCase( str.charAt(i) ) )
        {
            case 'a':   strReturn.append(".- ");      break;
            case 'b':   strReturn.append("-... ");    break;
            case 'c':   strReturn.append("-.-. ");    break;
            case 'd':   strReturn.append("-.. ");     break;
            case 'e':   strReturn.append(". ");       break;
            case 'f':   strReturn.append("..-. ");    break;
            case 'g':   strReturn.append("--. ");     break;
            case 'h':   strReturn.append(".... ");    break;
            case 'i':   strReturn.append(".. ");      break;
```

```java
            case 'j':   strReturn.append(".- ");    break;
            case 'k':   strReturn.append("-.- ");   break;
            case 'l':   strReturn.append(".-.. ");  break;
            case 'm':   strReturn.append("- ");     break;
            case 'n':   strReturn.append("-. ");    break;
            case 'o':   strReturn.append("- ");     break;
            case 'p':   strReturn.append(".-. ");   break;
            case 'q':   strReturn.append("-.- ");   break;
            case 'r':   strReturn.append(".-. ");   break;
            case 's':   strReturn.append("... ");   break;
            case 't':   strReturn.append("- ");     break;
            case 'u':   strReturn.append("..- ");   break;
            case 'v':   strReturn.append("...- ");  break;
            case 'w':   strReturn.append(".- ");    break;
            case 'x':   strReturn.append("-..- ");  break;
            case 'y':   strReturn.append("-.- ");   break;
            case 'z':   strReturn.append("-.. ");   break;
            case '0':   strReturn.append("- ");     break;
            case '1':   strReturn.append(".- ");    break;
            case '2':   strReturn.append("..- ");   break;
            case '3':   strReturn.append("...- ");  break;
            case '4':   strReturn.append("....- "); break;
            case '5':   strReturn.append("..... "); break;
            case '6':   strReturn.append("-.... "); break;
            case '7':   strReturn.append("-... ");  break;
            case '8':   strReturn.append("-.. ");   break;
            case '9':   strReturn.append("-. ");    break;
            case ',':   strReturn.append("-..- ");  break;
            case '.':   strReturn.append(".-.-.- "); break;
            case ' ':   strReturn.append("  ");     break;
            default:    strReturn.append(str.charAt(i));
        }
    }

    return strReturn.toString();
}

public String Translate(String str, boolean bShowResults)
{
    String strReturn;

    switch (m_nLingo)
    {
       case 1:
          strReturn = toPigLatin(str);
          break;

       case 2:
          strReturn = toElmerFudd(str);
```

Java Controls **235**

```
            break;

        case 3:
            strReturn = toMorseCode(str);
            break;

        default:
            strReturn = new String();
    }

    if (bShowResults)
    {
        new TranslateResultsFrame(strReturn);
    }

    return strReturn;
}

public void TranslateInteractive()
{
    new TranslateInteractiveFrame(this);
}

public int getLingo()
{
    return m_nLingo;
}

public void putLingo(int nLingo)
{
    if (nLingo < 1)
        m_nLingo = 1;
    else
    {
        if (nLingo > 3)
            m_nLingo = 3;
        else
            m_nLingo = nLingo;
    }
}

////////////////////////////////
// For debugging purposes:   //
////////////////////////////////

private static CLingoMaker lmDebug;

public static void main(String args[])
{
```

```
      lmDebug = new CLingoMaker();
      lmDebug.TranslateInteractive();
   }
}


class TranslateResultsFrame extends Frame
{
   public TranslateResultsFrame(String str)
   {
      super("Translate Results");

      setLayout( new FlowLayout() );
      resize(225, 220);
      setBackground(Color.lightGray);

      TextArea textResults = new TextArea(12, 30);
      textResults.setText(str);

      add(textResults);

      show();
   }

   public boolean handleEvent(Event evt)
   {
      switch (evt.id)
      {
         case Event.WINDOW_DESTROY:
            dispose();
            return true;
      }

      return super.handleEvent(evt);
   }
}


class TranslateInteractiveFrame extends Frame
{
   TextArea m_textSource, m_textDest;
   CLingoMaker m_lm;

   public TranslateInteractiveFrame(CLingoMaker lm)
   {
      super("Translate Interactive");

      m_lm = lm;
```

```java
        setLayout( new FlowLayout() );
        resize(450, 250);
        setBackground(Color.lightGray);

        String strCaption = "Type some text into the box on " +
                            "the left. It will be translated into ";

        switch ( lm.getLingo() )
        {
           case 1:
              strCaption = strCaption + "Pig Latin.";
              break;

           case 2:
              strCaption = strCaption + "Elmer Fudd talk.";
              break;

           case 3:
              strCaption = strCaption + "Morse Code.";
              break;
        }

        add(new Label(strCaption) );

        m_textSource = new TextArea(12, 30);
        m_textDest = new TextArea(12, 30);

        add(m_textSource);
        add(m_textDest);

        show();
    }

    public boolean handleEvent(Event evt)
    {
        switch (evt.id)
        {
           case Event.WINDOW_DESTROY:
              dispose();
              return true;

           case Event.KEY_RELEASE:
              if (evt.target == m_textSource)
              {
                  m_textDest.setText(
                     m_lm.Translate(m_textSource.getText(),
                                    false) );
              }
              break;
```

```
        }

        return super.handleEvent(evt);
    }
}
```

LISTING 8.7 THE LINGO MAKER ODL FILE.

```
// LingoMaker.odl

[
    uuid (710CA5E1-1F0B-11d0-8512-0020AFC746E8),
    version (1.0),
    helpstring("Lingo Maker Java control")
]
library LLingoMaker
{
    importlib("stdole32.tlb");   // Required for IDispatch

    [
        odl,
        uuid(710CA5E2-1F0B-11d0-8512-0020AFC746E8),
        helpstring("ILingoMaker interfaces"),
        oleautomation,
        dual
    ]
    interface ILingoMaker : IDispatch
    {
        // PROPERTY: int Lingo
        [propget]
        HRESULT Lingo([out, retval] long* retval);
        [propput]
        HRESULT Lingo([in] long nLingo);

        // METHOD: String Translate(String str,
        //                          boolean bShowResults)
        HRESULT Translate([in] BSTR str,
                          [in] boolean bShowResults,
                          [out, retval] BSTR* retval);

        // METHOD: void TranslateInteractive();
        HRESULT TranslateInteractive();
    }

    [
        uuid(710CA5E3-1F0B-11d0-8512-0020AFC746E8),
        helpstring("CLingoMaker class"),
        appobject
    ]
```

```
    coclass CLingoMaker
    {
        interface ILingoMaker;
    }
}
```

Summary

Stay tuned to the official Visual J++ Web site at **http://www.microsoft.com/visualj**. A wizard for creating Java controls may soon appear in the Updates section. Until then, this chapter should suffice. It won't automate the process as a wizard would, but it will save you time and effort in writing Java controls—currently the only Visual J++ feature that allows foreign code to call Java classes.

Chapter 9

- **An introduction to JavaScript and VBScript**
- **The ActiveX Control Pad's ScriptWizard**
- **Scripting ActiveX controls**
- **Scripting Java applets**
- **Example: City Selector**

Scripting

The most fertile soil on earth lies beneath millions of gallons of salt water. Rich in copper, cobalt, nickel, and manganese, the soil is a treasure chest for every industrialized nation in the world. Yet none of these nations can claim the right to mine the valuable soil. Its minerals are locked in legal limbo at the bottom of the seven seas.

Disputes over the oceans' rocky resources led to a 1973 convention of the United Nations General Assembly. The international gathering brought together 160 representatives to discuss the future of deep-sea mining. The business, political, and legal issues were formidable, and dozens of mediators were brought in to help with the negotiations.

Seven years and several conferences later, all 160 nations ratified the *Law of the Sea Treaty*[1], a document that set the stage for a new era in oceanic mining and research. That every nation agreed to the treaty is a tribute to the hard-working mediators.

Like the nations of the world, Java applets and ActiveX controls are in a contest for resources—the resources of the Web browser. In this dispute, *you* are the mediator. Your HTML page must endure the constant bickering between applets and the browser, the browser and the controls, the controls and the applets, and so on.

---
[1] Raiffa, Howard. 1982, *The Art and Science of Negotiation*. Harvard University Press.

Take heart: You're not alone in this task. The Web browser provides a tool, called the *HTML script*, to assist you. The script acts as a go-between for applets and controls, allowing them to communicate with each other and to be controlled by you. Scripts are also useful for validating user input and writing data onto a Web page.

This chapter shows you how to integrate *event-driven* ActiveX controls with Java applets (Chapter 7 described how to integrate *non-event-driven* controls with applets). HTML scripts provide the glue for this integration, allowing you to call methods, access properties, and receive events (see Figure 9.1).

This technique offers a major advantage over direct integration of controls and applets. In addition to support for visual controls, you also gain independence from compilers. No matter what program created them, you can use scripts with any ActiveX control or Java applet. Also, with scripts, you don't need the source code to integrate controls and applets.

The only danger in HTML scripts is that, just like HTML code itself, anyone on the Internet can view the source. Therefore, you should tuck away valuable, proprietary code into the control or the applet, then write just enough script code to glue them together.

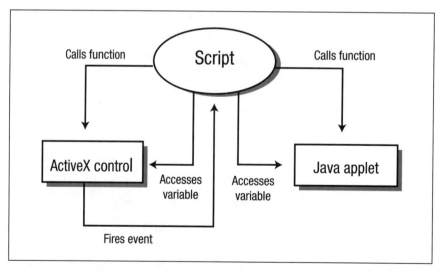

Figure 9.1 The paths of communication among ActiveX controls, HTML scripts, and Java applets.

Back To Script School

To learn how to arbitrate a Web page, you first need some basic knowledge of HTML scripts. The following brief tutorial is no substitute for a true education in HTML scripting, but it includes everything you need for getting the most out of this chapter, even if you've never written a script before. If you already know how to write HTML scripts, you can skip this section.

What's A Script?

A script is like a miniature computer language. Each line of script code tells the computer what to do. And just as with a real computer language, you can call script functions and manipulate script variables. Unlike a traditional computer program, however, a script program exists only within the confines of a Web browser. The source code for a script is inserted directly into an HTML document using the **<SCRIPT>** tag (see Figure 9.2).

The two HTML scripting languages currently available are JavaScript and VBScript. JavaScript was first on the scene; it came to life in revision 2 of Netscape Navigator. VBScript is younger; it's Microsoft's alternative scripting language and first appeared in Internet Explorer 3.0. As their names imply, JavaScript is a derivative of Java, and VBScript is a descendant of Visual Basic.

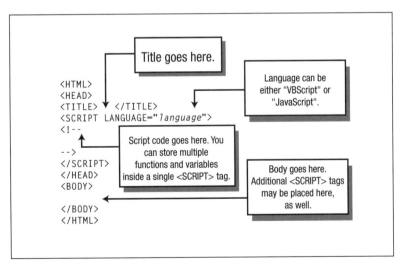

Figure 9.2 The anatomy of the **<SCRIPT>** tag.

further developments

ActiveX Scripting

Don't confuse HTML scripts with ActiveX Scripting. ActiveX Scripting—there's no such thing as ActiveScript—is an architecture based on the Component Object Model (see Chapter 4), and it allows any application to host any scripting language. VBScript, for example, is an ActiveX Scripting engine. It provides Microsoft Internet Explorer—an ActiveX Scripting host—with the ability to read VBScript code. (Internet Explorer also includes an ActiveX Scripting engine for JavaScript, known as JScript.) Expect to see more ActiveX Scripting engines in the future as third-party developers bring REXX, Perl, Python, and other languages to Internet Explorer.

Your choice of a scripting language depends on your audience and experience. If you can somehow ensure that everyone reading your Web page is running Microsoft Internet Explorer (an unlikely proposition), then VBScript is a fine choice. Also, if you're a Visual Basic veteran, you'll feel right at home coding for VBScript.

Microsoft will surely provide the means for running VBScript under Netscape's browser (probably through a Navigator plug-in), but until then, JavaScript is a much better choice. Not only does it provide compatibility with both Internet Explorer and Netscape, it also offers a clean, Java-style syntax.

The Basics

Let's begin the tutorial with a simple script that displays a message box. Here's the JavaScript version of the code:

```
<SCRIPT LANGUAGE="JavaScript">
<!--
alert("Five fourths of Americans have trouble with
  fractions.");
-->
</SCRIPT>
```

Here's the same code written for VBScript:

```
<SCRIPT LANGUAGE="VBScript">
<!--
alert("I'm not spoiled. I just smell that way.")
-->
</SCRIPT>
```

The only difference is syntactical. JavaScript statements take a semicolon at the end (but don't require them), and VBScript forbids them.

Almost all variations between JavaScript and VBScript are equally superficial, and I won't list them explicitly. Instead, I'll provide JavaScript and VBScript versions of every example in this chapter. The differences will be pretty obvious.

COMMENTS

You probably noticed the bizarre comment brackets ("**<!--**" and "**-->**") inside the **<SCRIPT>** tag. Ordinarily, these symbols tell the Web browser to ignore all text within each bracket. But because older Web browsers don't understand the **<SCRIPT>** tag, the brackets prevent error messages from percolating all over the place.

The newer Web browsers are smarter and ignore the comment brackets. If you still want to elucidate your scripts, you'll have to use Java-style comments for JavaScript and Visual Basic-style comments for VBScript. Here's an example:

```
<SCRIPT LANGUAGE="JavaScript">
<!--
// The following line will display a message box.
alert("We were so poor, we had to settle for Hundred Island
   dressing.");
-->
</SCRIPT>

<SCRIPT LANGUAGE="VBScript">
<!--
' The following line will display a message box.
alert("I was born at a very early age.")
-->
</SCRIPT>
```

VARIABLES

Java and Visual Basic require separate keywords for integer, string, and boolean data types. JavaScript and VBScript, on the other hand, combine all three types into a single, generic variable. When parsing the script, the browser automatically determines how to store the data. To illustrate:

```
<SCRIPT LANGUAGE="JavaScript">
<!--
var x = 2, y = "One was assaulted.";
alert(x + " peanuts were walking down the road. " + y);
-->
```

```
</SCRIPT>
<SCRIPT LANGUAGE="VBScript">
<!--
Dim x, y
x = 4
y = "game. How can man with "
alert("Confucius say: Baseball very strange " & y & x & " balls
   walk?")
-->
</SCRIPT>
```

AN AMPERSAND AMPLIFICATION

VBScript provides two string concatenation operators: the plus (+) and the ampersand (&). The plus sign is ambiguous, as shown here:

```
document.write("1+2+" + 3 + 4)
```

Will this print "1+2+3+4" or "1+2+7"? It doesn't matter. VBScript will flag the statement as an error. You'll have to convert the integers to strings to run this code.

A better choice is the unambiguous ampersand operator. Not only will it make your code easier to follow, it will also convert integers to strings automatically.

PROGRAM FLOW

Both JavaScript and Visual Basic provide the usual means for controlling program flow. **While** loops, **do** loops, **for** loops, and **if/then/else** statements are at your disposal. Here's a simple example:

```
<SCRIPT LANGUAGE="JavaScript">
<!--

for (var i = 0; i < 10; i++)
{
   if (i == 5)
      document.write("<B>You're halfway there...</B> ");
   else
      document.write("Counting down... ");
   document.write(i + "<BR>");
}
```

```
while (i < 15)
{
   document.write("<B>Made it!!</B><BR>");
   i++;
}

-->
</SCRIPT>
```

And here's the VBScript version:

```
<SCRIPT LANGUAGE="VBScript">
<!--

Dim i

For i = 0 To 9
   If i = 5 Then
      document.write("<B>You're halfway there...</B> ")
   Else
      document.write("Counting down... ")
   End If
   document.write(i & "<BR>")
Next

Do While i < 15
   document.write("<B>Made it!!<B><BR>")
   i = i + 1
Loop

-->
</SCRIPT>
```

As a Java and C++ programmer, I much prefer JavaScript's curly braces over VBScript's terminating keywords. It's yet another reason to choose JavaScript over VBScript. Still, if you're running Internet Explorer (or an impending VBScript-compatible browser), the choice is up to you.

MENDING YOUR WENDING
*Visual Basic old-timers are familiar with VBScript's **While/Wend** statement. But unless you have a sadistic need for inflexibility, you should use the **Do While/Loop** statement instead. It produces the same result, yet matches the syntax style of the other VBScript loops.*

Scripting

Functions

HTML scripts don't really begin to show their value until you write script functions. Just like functions in any other computer language, script functions can encapsulate algorithms into neat and tidy packages. They can also take parameters and return results.

A JavaScript example:

```
<SCRIPT LANGUAGE="JavaScript">
<!--
function countMississippi(nStart, nEnd)   // A really mundane
                                          // function; sorry
{
   for (var i = nStart; i < nEnd; i++)
   {
      document.write(i + " Mississippi<BR>");
   }

   return nEnd - nStart;
}

document.write("Total count: " + countMississippi(1, 5) +
   " Mississippi's.<BR>");
-->
</SCRIPT>
```

And a VBScript example:

```
<SCRIPT LANGUAGE="VBScript">
<!--
Function countMississippi(nStart, nStop)

   Dim i

   For i = nStart to nStop - 1
      document.write(i & " Mississippi<BR>")
   Next

   countMississippi = nStop - nStart
End Function

document.write("Total count: " & countMississippi(1, 5) &
   " Mississippi's.<BR>")
-->
</SCRIPT>
```

*Note: VBScript draws a distinction between functions that return values and those that do not. In an obvious attempt to make life tough, it requires functions not returning any values to be declared as **Sub**s instead of **Function**s.*

STAKING A STRICT SCRIPT SPOT

Microsoft's VBScript FAQ indicates that the <SCRIPT> tag belongs at the end of the HTML file. Wrong! JavaScript and VBScript functions must be defined before they are used. Therefore, don't place a function at the end of the document; this would render it out-of-scope. A better spot for the <SCRIPT> tag is between the <HEAD> and the </HEAD> tags at the top of the HTML file.

Events

Script events are just as important as script functions. They indicate some sort of occurrence: "the document has been loaded," "a button has been clicked," and others. Events for scripts are similar to those for Java, but script events come in only a few specific types, and they're hardwired into the Web browser. You can't create your own.

To handle one of the predefined events, you simply create a function with the same name as the event. A function called **window_onLoad**, for example, would execute whenever the HTML document is loaded or reloaded. Likewise, to execute a function when a button is clicked, you would name the function as ***button*_onClick**, where ***button*** is the identification value of the button. Listing 9.1 provides an example of handling both of these events.

LISTING 9.1 HANDLING SCRIPT EVENTS.

```
<HTML>
<HEAD>
<TITLE>Lesson 6: Events</TITLE>

<SCRIPT LANGUAGE="JavaScript">
<!--
function window_onLoad()
{
   alert("Mark Twain once said...");
```

```
}
-->
</SCRIPT>

<SCRIPT LANGUAGE="VBScript">
<!--
Sub TwainButton_onClick()
    alert("...and children.")
End Sub
-->
</SCRIPT>

</HEAD>
<BODY>
<INPUT TYPE="button"
       VALUE="Familiarity breeds contempt..."
       NAME="TwainButton">
</BODY>
</HTML>
```

> **DEBUGGING DEBUNKED**
>
> *Scripts are notoriously difficult to debug. Because JavaScript and VBScript are interpreted languages, errors don't pop up until you actually run the script. The simplistic error messages provided by the browser aren't much help, either.*
>
> *About the only weapon in your battle against bugs is a function called **window.status()**. Any string passed to this function—such as "variable i=12 in function onClick"—will appear in the status bar of the Web browser. Beware: Every call to **window.status()** will replace the previous string, so this technique is only for quick-and-dirty debugging.*

The ActiveX Control Pad

Most Webmasters don't know it, but Microsoft has been shipping a secret HTML editor for many years. It's called Notepad. This utility ships free with every copy of Windows—and you get exactly what you pay for. It's just a simple editor, of course, and isn't suited for any real work with HTML. As an alternative, Microsoft offers another piece of free software: the ActiveX Control Pad. Its main purpose, as discussed in Chapter 4, is to simplify the process of inserting ActiveX controls onto a Web page.

The ActiveX Control Pad is also a powerful utility for writing scripts. With help from the Control Pad's Script Wizard, you can easily create and maintain script code. To load the Script Wizard, click on its icon in the toolbar or select Tools|Script Wizard.

Before starting Script Wizard, you must first choose between JavaScript and VBScript. (The Wizard can't handle more than one script language on the same page.) To switch languages, select Tools|Options|Script.

Electing Your Events

Figure 9.3 shows a sample session with the Script Wizard. In the left-hand pane—the Event Pane—is a list of every event available to your script. In the right-hand pane—the Action Pane—is a list of possible actions to take after receiving the event. (These actions are only suggestions. Any script statement is a valid action.)

Sitting beside each item in the Event Pane is a cute little icon. The icons instantly tell you the type of event and whether it is handled by your code. See Table 9.1 for a description of each one.

Code View

Adding an event is simple. Just click on the event of your choice, then double-click on an item in the Action Pane. The Control Pad will insert the

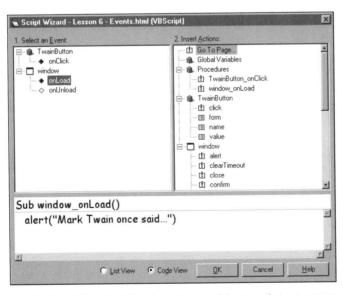

Figure 9.3 The ActiveX Control Pad makes writing scripts a snap.

Scripting **251**

Table 9.1   Event Pane icons.

Icon	Description
🔶	An event sent by an object such as a button, form, hyperlink, and so on
▫	An event sent by the main browser window
◇	Indicates that the event has not been handled
◆	Indicates that the event has been handled

selected action into the bottom pane—the Script Pane. You can add as many actions as you'd like (much easier than typing all that yourself, eh?).

If the action you want isn't listed in the Action Pane, you can add it manually. First, make sure that the Script Pane is set for Code View; this transforms the pane into a text editor. Click on the pane, then simply type your code as you normally would.

LIST VIEW

The Script Pane can also display your event handler in a format called List View. This view enumerates each script statement in an easy-to-read format (see Figure 9.4). Adding, deleting, and reordering the actions is as simple as clicking a button.

LISTLESS LIST VIEW

The List View is strict and cannot recognize all types of actions. It will occasionally cough up this error message:

```
This event is associated with a custom action.
To view or edit this custom action, select
Code View below.
```

List View's simplicity is tempting, but unless you're writing very basic scripts, I recommend letting Code View grow on you. You'll save time in the long run. (To make Code View permanent, click on its radio button in the Script Options dialog box of the Control Pad.)

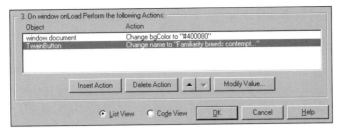

Figure 9.4 The List View provides a clear look at event handlers.

Adding Your Actions

The Action Pane of the Script Wizard lists a variety of activities for your event handler to perform. Each item in the list is matched with an icon that indicates the type of action. See Table 9.2 for descriptions of these icons.

The Action Pane contains too many items to list here, so I'll just highlight the most important ones:

- *Go To Page*—Set this variable to URL string, and the browser will automatically switch to the new URL.

- *Global Variables*—Use these property actions to change one of your script's global variables.

- *Procedures*—All user-defined script functions (*procedures* is a Visual Basic term) are listed under this icon. Double-click a function to call it.

Table 9.2 Action Pane icons.

Icon	Description
	An action relating to a global variable, script procedure, or form object
	An action relating to the main browser window
	An action that calls a function
	An action that sets or changes a property, such as size or color

- *window*—Many handy functions hide under this icon, which symbolizes the browser window.

- *window.document*—The *document* object is located under the *window* icon. It includes functions for writing to the HTML file, properties for changing colors, and more.

- *status (w)*—Changing this string will change the current string in the browser's status bar.

For a list of all actions, check the Developer's Reference section of the ActiveX Control Pad documentation.

further developments

Gloss Over Globals And Remember Those Brackets

As with any computer language, you should avoid global variables in scripts whenever possible. Local variables make your code easier to debug.

Another tip to reduce debugging time: Always surround single-line blocks of JavaScript code with curly braces, even though the browser doesn't require them. Remembering the braces will help you eliminate this type of mistake:

```
if (i == 1)
   alert("I = 1");
   alert("This message appears even when I != 1");
alert("Continuing with the rest of the code...");
```

At first glance, the indentations of this code block seem to indicate that the second **alert()** will occur only if **i** equals 1. Of course, because the braces are missing, it will occur regardless of **i**'s value. Putting braces around the first **alert()** would make the code easier to read and debug, even though they are not required by the JavaScript interpreter.

This doesn't apply to VBScript, which always requires an ending statement, such as **End If** or **Loop,** in code blocks.

Scripting ActiveX Controls

The true power of HTML scripts lies not in what they can do by themselves but in how they integrate with other objects on the Web page. With Internet Explorer, for example, you can write scripts that automate ActiveX controls. You can decide at runtime which ActiveX methods to call, which properties to set, and which events to handle.

Before automating an ActiveX control, you must verify that the control has a name. As discussed in Chapter 4, you can use the ID parameter of the **<OBJECT>** tag to name a control. Here's an example of naming the Microsoft Forms 2.0 ComboBox control:

```
<OBJECT
   ID="MyComboBox"
   WIDTH=96
   HEIGHT=24
   CLASSID="CLSID:8BD21D30-EC42-11CE-9E0D-00AA006002F3">
</OBJECT>
```

After declaring the **ID** parameter, you can refer to the control by its name, instead of its **CLASSID**, in your scripts.

Calling Methods

Calling an ActiveX method from inside a script is much like calling any other script function. The only difference is that you must prefix the call with the name of the control and a period. The ComboBox control, for instance, contains a method called **Paste**, which pastes the contents of the control to the clipboard. A call of this method in either VBScript or JavaScript would look like this:

```
MyComboBox.Paste()
```

Notice that the **Paste** method has no parameters, so the space between the parentheses is empty. If a method does have parameters, you simply type the corresponding values within the parentheses. For example, the ComboBox control has another method called **AddItem**, which adds a string to the list. A VBScript or JavaScript statement that adds "Item #1" to MyComboBox would look like this:

```
MyComboBox.AddItem("Item #1")
```

In addition to constants, of course, you can use variables for parameters.

> ### THE VBSCRIPT CALL KEYWORD
> *The ActiveX Control Pad's Script Wizard, when configured for VBScript, always places the **call** keyword at the beginning of method calls. This keyword is optional. If you use it, however, you must remember to surround method-call parameters with parentheses, which are otherwise not required in VBScript.*

Setting Properties

Setting an ActiveX control's properties is even easier than calling its methods. You treat control properties just as you treat any other field in a script object. In other words, you simply type the name of the ActiveX control, followed by a period and the name of the property you wish to access. For example, the ComboBox has an integer property called **SpecialEffect**, which controls the border style. To change the style to "raised," which corresponds to the integer value 1, you would insert this line into your VBScript or JavaScript code:

```
MyComboBox.SpecialEffect = 1
```

Likewise, you can read the value of an ActiveX control's property, as shown in the following VBScript example:

```
If MyComboBox.SpecialEffect = 1 Then
    alert("The border has been raised.")
End If
```

GENERATING RANDOM NUMBERS

*HTML scripts can generate random numbers. In VBScript, call the **rnd** function, and in JavaScript, call the **Math.random()** function. Both functions return a real number between 0 and 1.*

Handling Events

Calling methods and setting properties allows you to send information to an ActiveX control. But the communication can also go in the opposite direction: Controls can send events back to you for handling in your script. The ComboBox control, to cite just one example, sends an event called **Click** whenever the user clicks on the control with the mouse. You can detect this event in your script and respond accordingly.

VBSCRIPT EVENT HANDLERS

VBScript and JavaScript handle ActiveX events differently. In VBScript, you must create a function whose name indicates the event it handles. For instance, a VBScript function that handles the ComboBox's **Click** event would look like this:

```
Sub MyComboBox_Click()
    alert("The ComboBox was clicked.")
End Sub
```

ActiveX events, as discussed in Chapter 5, can have parameters. To handle these types of events, you would simply type the parameter names between the function's parentheses. Here's an example of the ComboBox's **KeyDown** event, which takes a parameter called **KeyAscii** (see the Control Pad documentation for details):

```
<SCRIPT LANGUAGE="VBScript">
<!--
Sub MyComboBox_KeyPress(KeyAscii)
    alert("The following key was pressed: " & KeyAscii)
End Sub
-->
</SCRIPT>
```

JavaScript Event Handlers

JavaScript event handlers, unlike their VBScript counterparts, are not functions. Rather, they embody an entire <SCRIPT> tag. Each statement in the tag is executed in succession whenever the control sends its event. For the browser to recognize the JavaScript tag as an event handler, you must add two parameters:

- **FOR=**"*ControlName*"—This parameter points to the name of the control, such as "MyComboBox", that sends the event.

- **EVENT=**"*EventName*"—This parameter points to the name of the event that will be handled. Be sure to include the parentheses and any parameter names.

Here's the equivalent JavaScript version of the previous example:

```
<SCRIPT LANGUAGE="JavaScript" FOR="MyComboBox"
  EVENT="KeyPress(KeyAscii)">
<!--
alert("The following key was pressed: " & KeyAscii)
-->
</SCRIPT>
```

Event Assistance From The Control Pad

As indicated in the previous section, the ActiveX Control Pad can save you a lot of typing. It can insert any ActiveX control's event handlers with only a few clicks of the mouse. Just go to the Script Wizard and click on one of the + symbols in the Event Pane. You can then select the event of your choice and add items from the Action Pane or insert your own custom code (see Figure 9.5).

Scripting Java Applets

In HTML scripts, calling applet functions and setting applet variables are pretty much the same as for methods and properties in ActiveX controls. Your scripts have direct access to all publicly defined functions and variables in an applet. The two main differences are:

- *Document object*—The Web browser considers Java applets to be part of the **document** object, rather than the default **window** object. Hence, you must place the word *document* at the beginning of every script statement that calls a function or accesses a variable. (See the examples below.)

- *NAME parameter*—The **NAME** parameter in <APPLET> tags is analogous to the ID parameter in <OBJECT> tags. So, to refer to

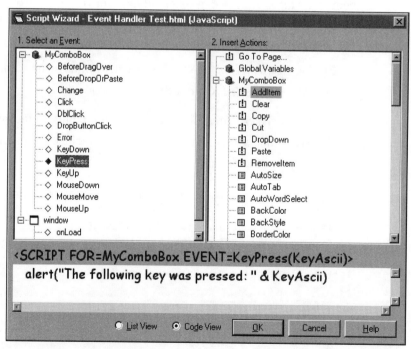

Figure 9.5 The ActiveX Control Pad can quickly add event handlers in either VBScript or JavaScript.

258 *Chapter 9*

an applet in a script, you must first declare the **NAME** parameter inside the tag.

To illustrate, here's how you might define an applet in an HTML file:

```
<APPLET
    NAME=MyApplet
    WIDTH=100
    HEIGHT=56
    CODE=MyApplet.class>
</APPLET>
```

And here's an example of how you would call a public function, defined in the hypothetical applet, named **setValue**:

```
document.MyApplet.setValue(100)
```

Finally, here's an example of how you would set a public integer variable named **nValue** in the applet:

```
document.MyApplet.nValue = 100
```

ACCESSING CLASSES AS VARIABLES

*Only basic Java types, such as **int**, **long**, and **boolean**, can be accessed from HTML scripts as variables. Other objects, such as the AWT class **Button**, cannot be accessed as variables, even if they are declared as public. To reach them, you must wrap each object function with your own applet-derived functions. See **setRotateCheckboxState()** in Listing 9.3 for an example of this technique.*

Handling Events

Watch out for a big-time caveat in scripting applets: You can't handle Java events. In Internet Explorer, an applet has no way to send events or communicate directly with a script. Netscape Navigator, on the other hand, offers a solution in the form of its LiveConnect framework. This framework, along with the Java class **JSObject**, doesn't support events, but it does allow your applet to call script functions and to access script variables. Unfortunately, LiveConnect is not cross-platform and limits your code to Navigator.

Scripting **259**

After thinking about this problem, I came up with a work-around. It's not perfect, but it works with both Internet Explorer and Netscape Navigator. The trick is to take advantage of the browser's **timer** object.

THE TIMER OBJECT

The **timer** object is available to both VBScript and JavaScript. By calling the **setTimeout** function, you can specify a function that the browser will call after a certain number of milliseconds. The format of **setTimeout** looks like this:

```
setTimeout("FunctionName", milliseconds)
```

As an example, Listing 9.2 shows an HTML file with some JavaScript code that calls a function three seconds after it loads (note the parentheses following the function name in the call to **setTimeout**).

LISTING 9.2 DEMONSTRATION OF THE TIMER OBJECT.

```
<HTML>
<HEAD>

<SCRIPT LANGUAGE="JavaScript">
<!--
function displaySillyFact()
{
   alert("Peas and beans are legumes.");
}
-->
</SCRIPT>

<SCRIPT LANGUAGE="JavaScript" FOR="window" EVENT="onLoad()">
<!--
setTimeout("displaySillyFact()", 3000);
-->
</SCRIPT>

</HEAD>
<BODY>
</BODY>
</HTML>
```

POLLING THE APPLET

The **timer** object offers a method for a Java applet to communicate with a script, even though the Web browser provides communication only in the reverse direction. Again, this technique is a hack, but it works just fine (until something better comes along):

1. Define a public variable in your applet's source code that indicates some sort of status. A value of 1, for instance, could mean that the user just clicked on the applet. A value of 2 could indicate mouse motion. A value of 0 could mean that the mouse is outside of the applet window. The choice of values and their meanings is completely up to you.

2. Create a handler for the built-in **onLoad** event. Inside this handler, insert the following code:

```
setTimeout("onTimer()", 5000)
```

3. Create a function in your HTML script called **onTimer** (the name is only a suggestion; any will do). Inside this function, insert the following code:

```
setTimeout("onTimer()", 250)
```

When these steps are complete, you have created a simple message poll. It calls the **onTimer** function every $1/4$ second. You may then add code to this function that checks the "status variable" of the applet. In this manner, the applet can communicate with the script. See Listing 9.3 for an example.

further developments

Timer ID Values

VBScript requires that periodic timers save the return value of every call to **setTimeout**. You'll see this in Listing 9.3, which saves the return value in a variable called **TimerID**. It's a dummy variable in the sample listing, but it can be used to cancel the timer if necessary (by calling **clearTimeout**).

Why does VBScript make this requirement? I haven't the slightest idea.

EVENT ASSISTANCE FROM THE CONTROL PAD

The ActiveX Control Pad offers no support for scripting of Java applets. You'll have to do everything by hand. In the meantime, you can cross your toes and hope that Microsoft adds applet provisions to the Control Pad. (Better yet, you can send them your feature requests directly by posting a message to **news:microsoft.public.activeX_controlpad_HTML_layout_control**.)

Scripting **261**

PICTURE YOUR FRAMES

You can access a control or applet from your script even if it's in a separate HTML frame. Simply prefix the statement with "top.framename", where framename is the identifier of one of your HTML frames. For example:

```
top.MyFrame.MyComboBox.Paste()
```

or

```
top.AnotherFrame.AnotherComboBox.SpecialEffect = 2
```

Putting It All Together: The City Selector Example

To illustrate the concepts presented in this chapter, I've written a sample Java applet, ActiveX control, and HTML script. They combine every technique in applet-to-script-to-control communication (and vice-versa).

I call the applet a City Selector because it gives the user a list of my seven favorite cities. The user can select a city and click on the applet's Go! button, which jumps the browser to a Web page that describes some aspect of the selected community.

The ActiveX control is my Rotating Sphere control. It complements the City Selector with a map of the earth, where each city is highlighted in orange (see Figure 9.6). In realtime, the control runs the image data through an algorithm that transforms the map into a globe (see Figure 9.7). It can also rotate the globe on its polar axis to give the user a view of each city. (By the way, my ActiveX control can work with any 256-color image, not just maps. Try it out with your own pictures and see for yourself.)

Figure 9.6 The original image.

Figure 9.7 The image after being processed by the ActiveX control.

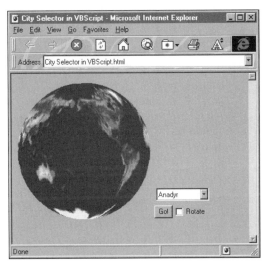

Figure 9.8 The City Selector in action.

The HTML file comes in two versions: one for VBScript (see Figure 9.8) and one for JavaScript. Each file contains the scripting glue that ties the applet and the control together. Listing 9.3 contains the VBScript version, and Listing 9.4 contains the JavaScript version. See this book's CD-ROM for the source code to the Rotating Sphere control.

LISTING 9.3   VBSCRIPT VERSION OF THE CITY SELECTOR.

```
<HTML>
<HEAD>
<SCRIPT LANGUAGE="VBScript">
<!--

Dim TimerID

Function GetCurrentPath()
    ' Obtain the pathname of this file and strip the
    ' beginning "/"
```

```
    Dim path, length
    path = location.pathname
    length = Len(path) - 1
    path = Right(path, length)
    ' Determine the index of the last "\"
    Dim i
    For i = length To 0 Step -1
       If Mid(path, i, 1) = "\" Then
          Exit For
       End If
    Next

    ' Trim everything after the last "\"
    '(leaving the "\" at the end)
    GetCurrentPath = Left(path, i)
End Function

Sub window_onLoad()

    Earth.BitmapFileName = GetCurrentPath() + "City Map.bmp"

    ' Set the Earth position to view the first city
    Earth.Rotation = 4

    ' Start the timer message poll
    TimerID = setTimeout("onTimer()", 1000)

End Sub

Sub onTimer()

    Select Case document.CitySelector.nLastEvent
       Case 1      ' City was changed
          Earth.Stop()
          RotateToCity(
                     document.CitySelector.getSelectedCity() )
          document.CitySelector.setRotateCheckboxState(False)
          document.CitySelector.nLastEvent = 0
       Case 2      ' Rotate checkbox was turned on
          Earth.Start()
          document.CitySelector.nLastEvent = 0
       Case 3      ' Rotate checkbox was turned off
          Earth.Stop()
          document.CitySelector.nLastEvent = 0
    End Select

    ' Keep the message poll running
    TimerID = setTimeout("onTimer()", 250)

End Sub
```

```vbscript
Sub RotateToCity(strCity)
   Select Case strCity
      Case "Anadyr"
         Earth.Rotation = 4
      Case "Kansas City"
         Earth.Rotation = 86
      Case "Fortaleza"
         Earth.Rotation = 142
      Case "Stavanger"
         Earth.Rotation = 186
      Case "Antananarivo"
         Earth.Rotation = 226
      Case "Tashkent"
         Earth.Rotation = 250
      Case "Brisbane"
         Earth.Rotation = 332
   End Select
End Sub

Sub Earth_Rotated(Rotation)
   Select Case Rotation
      Case 4
         document.CitySelector.setSelectedCity("Anadyr")
      Case 86
         document.CitySelector.setSelectedCity("Kansas City")
      Case 142
         document.CitySelector.setSelectedCity("Fortaleza")
      Case 186
         document.CitySelector.setSelectedCity("Stavanger")
      Case 226
         document.CitySelector.setSelectedCity("Antananarivo")
      Case 250
         document.CitySelector.setSelectedCity("Tashkent")
      Case 332
         document.CitySelector.setSelectedCity("Brisbane")
   End Select
End Sub
-->
</SCRIPT>

<TITLE>City Selector in VBScript</TITLE>

</HEAD>

<BODY>
<OBJECT
   ID="Earth"
   WIDTH=227
   HEIGHT=227
```

```
      CLASSID="CLSID:9414F9A3-D728-11CF-850D-0020AFC746E8">
      <PARAM NAME="_Version" VALUE="65536">
      <PARAM NAME="_ExtentX" VALUE="6006">
      <PARAM NAME="_ExtentY" VALUE="6006">
      <PARAM NAME="_StockProps" VALUE="0">
</OBJECT>

<APPLET
   CODE=CitySelector.class
   NAME=CitySelector
   WIDTH=110
   HEIGHT=56>
</APPLET>

</BODY>

</HTML>
```

LISTING 9.4   JAVASCRIPT VERSION OF THE CITY SELECTOR.

```
<HTML>
<HEAD>
<SCRIPT LANGUAGE="JavaScript">
<!--

function GetCurrentPath()
{
   // Obtain the pathname of this file and strip the
   // beginning "/"
   var path, length;
   path = location.pathname;
   length = path.length - 1;
   path = path.substring(1, length);

   // Determine the index of the last "\"
   var i;
   for (i = length; i >= 0; i--)
   {
      if ( path.substring(i, i+1) == "\\" )
         break;
   }

   // Trim everything after the last "\"
   // (leaving the "\" at the end)
   return path.substring(0, i+1);
}

-->
</SCRIPT>
```

```
<SCRIPT LANGUAGE="JavaScript" FOR="window" EVENT="onLoad()">
<!--
   Earth.BitmapFileName = GetCurrentPath() + "City Map.bmp";

   // Set the Earth position to view the first city
   Earth.Rotation = 4;
   // Start the timer message poll
   setTimeout("onTimer()", 1000);
-->
</SCRIPT>

<SCRIPT LANGUAGE="JavaScript">
<!--

function onTimer()
{
   // City was changed
   if ( document.CitySelector.nLastEvent == 1 )
   {
      Earth.Stop();
      RotateToCity( document.CitySelector.getSelectedCity() );
      document.CitySelector.setRotateCheckboxState(false);
      document.CitySelector.nLastEvent = 0;
   }
   else
   {
      // Rotate checkbox was turned on
      if ( document.CitySelector.nLastEvent == 2 )
      {
         Earth.Start();
         document.CitySelector.nLastEvent = 0;
      }
      else
      {
         // Rotate checkbox was turned off
         if ( document.CitySelector.nLastEvent == 3 )
         {
            Earth.Stop();
            document.CitySelector.nLastEvent = 0;
         }
      }
   }

   // Keep the message poll running
   setTimeout("onTimer()", 250);
}

function RotateToCity(strCity)
```

```
         {
            if ( strCity == "Anadyr" )
               Earth.Rotation = 4;
            else
            {
               if ( strCity == "Kansas City" )
                  Earth.Rotation = 86;
               else
               {
                  if ( strCity == "Fortaleza" )
                     Earth.Rotation = 142;
                  else
                  {
                     if ( strCity == "Stavanger" )
                        Earth.Rotation = 186;
                     else
                     {
                        if ( strCity == "Antananarivo" )
                           Earth.Rotation = 226;
                        else
                        {
                           if ( strCity == "Tashkent" )
                              Earth.Rotation = 250;
                           else
                           {
                              if ( strCity == "Brisbane" )
                              {
                                 Earth.Rotation = 332;
                              }
                           }
                        }
                     }
                  }
               }
            }
         }
         -->
         </SCRIPT>

         <SCRIPT LANGUAGE="JavaScript"
                 FOR="Earth"
                 EVENT="Rotated(Rotation)">
         <!--
            if ( Rotation == 4 )
               document.CitySelector.setSelectedCity("Anadyr");
            else
            {
```

```
         if ( Rotation == 86)
            document.CitySelector.setSelectedCity("Kansas City");
         else
         {
            if ( Rotation == 142)
               document.CitySelector.setSelectedCity("Fortaleza");
            else
            {
               if ( Rotation == 186)
                  document.CitySelector.setSelectedCity(
                                                   "Stavanger");
               else
               {
                  if ( Rotation == 226)
                     document.CitySelector.setSelectedCity(
                                                "Antananarivo");
                  else
                  {
                     if ( Rotation == 250)
                        document.CitySelector.setSelectedCity(
                                                   "Tashkent");
                     else
                     {
                        if ( Rotation == 332 )
                        {
                           document.CitySelector.setSelectedCity(
                                                   "Brisbane");
                        }
                     }
                  }
               }
            }
         }
      }
   }
-->
</SCRIPT>

<TITLE>City Selector in JavaScript</TITLE>

</HEAD>

<BODY>

<OBJECT
   ID="Earth"
   WIDTH=227
   HEIGHT=227
   CLASSID="CLSID:9414F9A3-D728-11CF-850D-0020AFC746E8">
   <PARAM NAME="_Version" VALUE="65536">
```

```
      <PARAM NAME="_ExtentX" VALUE="6006">
      <PARAM NAME="_ExtentY" VALUE="6006">
      <PARAM NAME="_StockProps" VALUE="0">
</OBJECT>

<APPLET
   CODE=CitySelector.class
   NAME=CitySelector
   WIDTH=110
   HEIGHT=56>
</APPLET>

</BODY>
</HTML>
```

Summary

HTML scripts aren't the final answer to ActiveX integration with Java. Team J++ reports that they're working furiously on true ActiveX containment—look for it in Visual J++ 2.0. In the meantime, you'll have to cope with scripts. They're quirky and difficult to debug, but at the moment they're the only way to integrate event-driven ActiveX controls with Java applets.

Chapter 10

OLE Automation

- OLE, DCOM, and Java Beans
- Time-saving tricks (with help from OLE)
- Early-binding of automation servers
- Late-binding of automation servers
- ActiveX to the rescue

Writing in Java is sometimes like running in the shallow end of a pool. You know the feeling: Your muscles are straining, you're treading as fast as you possibly can, but you're moving at a snail's pace. You may even slip underwater and wind up with a mouthful of chlorinated water.

If this analogy rings true, take a step back from your Java code and ask yourself these questions: Am I reinventing the wheel? Am I writing code that has been written before? Can some other program do my work for me?

In the object-filled world in which programmers now live, the answer to these questions is often yes. Most software today is built not from scratch, but from prefabricated components, such as C++ classes, function libraries, or simply the previous version of the program. By contrast, most Java programs are built entirely from scratch. The language is so new that many programs are still at version 1.0. Java is also too immature to support an industry for selling Java class libraries (also known as *packages*). Furthermore, support for industry-standard component architectures, such as OLE, CORBA, and OpenDoc, has only recently become available.

The first tool to bring Java component support to life is Visual J++. It can integrate Java programs with ActiveX controls (see Chapter 7), and it allows other programs to integrate with Java (see Chapter 8). It also allows Java code to act as an *OLE automation controller*—a program that harnesses the features of an OLE automation server, reducing development time and effort. (Chapter 7 defined OLE automation servers and how they relate to ActiveX controls.) This chapter will demonstrate how to write OLE automation controllers that help you avoid reinventing the wheel.

OLE Automation In Visual J++

The OLE architecture, which turned eight years old in 1996, has evolved far beyond its original goal of linking and embedding binary objects. Thanks to Microsoft's continual patching, revising, and updating of the bulky and complex architecture (making it even bulkier and more complex), it finally does what it was supposed to do from the beginning: It allows software from completely different vendors to integrate and communicate with each other.

OLE automation—just one of many components in the architecture—enables certain programs, known as *automation servers*, to expose their features through a standard interface, and it provides other programs, known as *automation clients*, with access to those features. Each feature is exposed as either a method (similar to a Java function) or a property (similar to a Java variable). Typically, automation servers organize their methods and properties into sets called *objects*, and the collection of objects in an automation server is known as its *object model*.

Because object models are stored in type libraries—binary descriptions of methods and properties—the Java Type Library Wizard can easily import them into Visual J++. You can then write Java code that calls the methods and accesses the properties in the automation server. The technique for doing this, which is exactly the same as for ActiveX controls, was described in the section "Integrating OLE Automation Servers" of Chapter 7. To recap, here are the steps for controlling an OLE automation server from a Visual J++ program (complete examples come later in this chapter):

1. Run the Java Type Library Wizard (located under the Tools menu). Place a checkmark next to each OLE automation server that you wish to import.

2. Import the server's methods and properties into your Java source code using the **import** statement provided by the Type Library Wizard.

3. Create an instance of one or more automation server objects using the **new** keyword. For example:

```
IMyAutomationServer server = new CMyAutomationServer();
```

4. Call methods and access properties in the server object. For example:

```
server.MyMethod(param1, param2);
int i = server.getMyProperty();
i++;
server.putMyProperty(i);
```

Java On Java

This chapter shows how to create automation controllers in Java, and Chapter 8 shows how to create automation servers in Java. Are you thinking what I'm thinking? That's right: You can control a Java program from another Java program using OLE automation. Just import the Java control (a.k.a. automation server) using the Type Library Wizard and treat it as any other server.

As shown in these steps, accessing the features of an automation server is quite easy. It's so easy, in fact, that you might wonder why any company would choose to expose their valuable code through OLE automation, giving competing companies free access to it. Remember, though, that OLE automation controllers are actually two programs in one: the controller itself and the server it uses. Controllers are not complete unless they can find their server on the same system. Users must purchase both programs. The end result for vendors of automation servers: more profits with less effort.

Late-binding Vs. Early-binding

When an OLE controller accesses an OLE automation server, it *binds* to the automation server. Binding is the process of initializing the functions and function parameters, allowing the controller to call methods in a server. Binding can occur at two instances:

- *Compile time*—With this form of binding, known as *early-binding,* the data types and the number of parameters passed to a function must be known before the compiler translates source code to native code.

- *Runtime*—With this form of binding, known as *late-binding,* the data types and the number of parameters passed to a function are not known until after the program executes. Programs that use late-binding are generally slower than those with early-binding.

Because the data types and number of parameters in Java functions must be known at compile time, Visual J++ cannot create automation controllers that use late-binding. Its compiler can translate functions into bytecode only if it knows exactly how to call them.

Most OLE automation servers support both early-binding and late-binding, so this Java restriction is usually not a problem. Unfortunately, some servers (such as Microsoft Word) offer only late-binding. You cannot control these servers directly from Visual J++.

You can, however, get help from another language that supports late-binding. For instance, you could create a late-binding controller in C++, then integrate that controller with Java through early-binding. The C++ program would act as an interpreter, translating messages between Java and the server. See the section "Creating Late-binding Automation Controllers" later in this chapter for more details and an example.

Stay Tuned: DCOM Is Coming To A Network Near You

further developments

Imagine this: A Java applet that connects to a server at the New York Stock Exchange and pumps the latest market prices to your computer. When you click on a hot ticket, the applet uses OLE automation to open Microsoft Word on your broker's desktop and create a document that says, "Sell! Sell! Sell!"

Impossible? Yes. But not for long, thanks to a relatively new Microsoft protocol called the *Distributed Component Object Model,* or DCOM. DCOM enables OLE automation across networks in a reliable, secure, and efficient manner. Previously called Network OLE, it is designed for multiple network transports, including Internet protocols, such as HTTP. DCOM is based on the Open Software Foundation's remote procedure call (RPC) specification and will work with both Java applets and ActiveX controls.

Until recently, DCOM has been available only on Windows NT, which limited its acceptance. Today, however, it runs on Windows 95 and will soon be available on the Macintosh and Unix platforms.

Visual J++ does not yet offer support for DCOM. Team J++ is working on such support, and it should be available either as an update or in the next major release. When it's ready, be prepared to exploit OLE automation in ways that were not even possible just a few months ago.

The Portability Problem

Java applets that use OLE automation carry some extra baggage: the Microsoft empire. They run only on Microsoft's operating system; they run only under Microsoft's browser; and they can be developed only with Microsoft's Java compiler. Keep this caveat in mind when creating automation controllers in Visual J++.

Also note that simply installing your Java controller on another system, even one that's 100-percent Microsoft-friendly, can get pretty hairy. Your installation program must ensure that the automation server has already been installed, and it must copy the server's interface classes (the ones created by the Type Library Wizard) to the Java\Trustlib directory on the CLASSPATH.

SENDING CODE THROUGH CYBERSPACE

As you dive into the murky depths of Visual J++, you'll eventually run into a problem that you can't solve yourself. You may need to get help in a Usenet newsgroup or by sending code to a co-worker via email. Bear in mind, however, that if your code contains tab characters, it might not appear correctly in someone else's text editor.

Visual J++ can fix this problem by converting tab characters to their space-character equivalents, making your code appear to all recipients exactly as you intend. First, go to the Keyboard tab of Tools|Customize and create two shortcuts: one for TabifySelection and one for UntabifySelection (both are found in the Edit category). Next, switch to the Visual J++ Text Editor and select the code you want to paste into a message. Then press the TabifySelection shortcut key and copy the text to the clipboard. Finally, press the UntabifySelection key to restore all tab characters. You may then paste the text into a message and launch it safely into cyberspace.

The Battle Of The Beans

Microsoft's portability problem may be their Achilles' heel. In May 1996, they gave Sun's engineers a demonstration of their brand new JIT compiler. They showed off its speed and its ability to combine Java applets with ActiveX controls. The very next week, Sun announced Java Beans—a direct competitor to Microsoft's compiler—which links Java to ActiveX, OLE, OpenDoc, and any other component architecture. The initiative received endorsements from IBM, Borland, Netscape, Lotus, Oracle, and Symantec.

Microsoft played down the announcement. "It looks like [Sun] listened closely and took notice [of what we're doing with Java and ActiveX]," said Cornelius Willis, Microsoft's Internet products manager, as reported by Nick Wingfield of C|NET. "It looks like we got their attention."

Sun shot back, maintaining that Java Beans was not vaporware, but simply an alternative to the Microsoft dominion. "The difference between Java Beans and ActiveX is that [Java Beans] is architecture-neutral," said David Spenhoff, director of product marketing at JavaSoft. "There's no lock-in to ActiveX. It's a purely architecture-neutral model."

Regardless of the rhetoric, both companies are obviously listening to the Java community. They're giving developers what they want most: a bridge between the most popular component architectures and Java. Microsoft's compiler and Sun's Java Beans are recognitions of this growing need.

As a Visual J++ programmer, you can stand clear of the Java Beans battle. It doesn't affect you because Visual J++ doesn't support Java Beans—at least, not yet. Java Beans is part of the base Java API, so all licensees (and that includes Microsoft) will have to implement the architecture. Expect to see the company supporting Java Beans in Visual J++ 2.0, but evangelizing ActiveX at Java Beans' expense.

Creating Early-binding Automation Controllers

OLE automation can save you oodles of time. It links your Java code to third-party programs, giving it features you might never have the chance to build on your own. In this section, I present two examples of OLE automation's time-saving tricks: a conversion calculator powered by Entisoft Tools and a mini-database driven by Microsoft Access.

Case Study: Entisoft Tools

Entisoft Tools is a library of more than 800 string-manipulation, text-processing, data-storage, mathematical, and other functions. It exposes these functions as methods in an OLE automation server, so you can call them from Visual Basic, Excel, and, of course, Visual J++. The shareware version of Entisoft Tools is included on this book's CD-ROM (you can order the full version by visiting **home.navisoft.com/entisoft**).

THE OBJECT MODEL

Unlike most automation servers, the Entisoft Tools object model is not hierarchical. The developers sorted its functions into groups, encapsulated the groups as OLE objects, and placed every object at the root level (see Figure 10.1). With this structure, calling Entisoft functions is a pay-as-you-go process: You create objects as you need them, and you don't have to worry about their position in the hierarchy. (For a complete reference to Entisoft Tools' object model, consult its documentation.)

SAMPLE CODE

To demonstrate the power of Entisoft Tools, I've written a Java applet called Conversion Calculator. It creates an instance of the **Units** object, in which lies a method called **ConvertMeasure()**. This method can convert any type of numeric unit, including decimals and fractions, to some other unit. The Conversion Calculator wraps **ConvertMeasure()** in a Web-hosted interface for converting length, time, or temperature measures (see Figure 10.2).

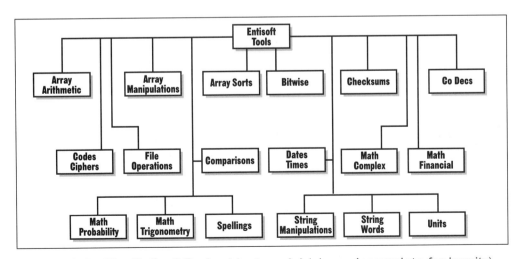

Figure 10.1 The Entisoft Tools object model (shown incomplete for brevity) places each group of functions at the root level.

OLE Automation **277**

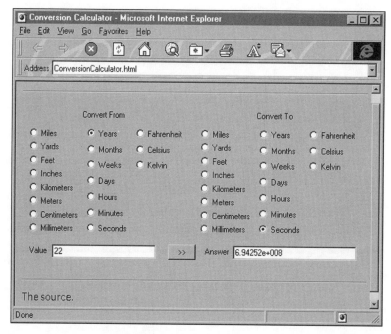

Figure 10.2 The Conversion Calculator applet encapsulates Entisoft Tools' **ConvertMeasure()** method.

Without Entisoft Tools, building the Conversion Calculator applet would have taken me more than a week. But because the **ConvertMeasure()** method handles all of the dirty work, I was able to create the applet in less than an hour. Plus, Entisoft Tools reduced the length and complexity of my applet many times over. I needed to add only 55 lines (see Listing 10.1) to the code skeleton generated by the Visual J++ Applet Wizard.

LISTING 10.1 THE CONVERSION CALCULATOR SOURCE CODE.

```
import java.applet.*;
import java.awt.*;
import com.ms.com.*;
import est10132.*;
import ConversionCalculatorFrame;

public class ConversionCalculator extends Applet
{
   private MainDialog m_dlgMain;
   private _Units m_estUnits;

   public void init()
   {
      m_dlgMain = new MainDialog(this);
      m_dlgMain.CreateControls();
```

```java
      m_dlgMain.IDC_FROMMILES.setState(true);
      m_dlgMain.IDC_TOMILES.setState(true);

      m_estUnits = new Units();
   }

   public void paint(Graphics g)
   {
      // No painting is necessary because we use a dialog box
      // template.
   }
   public boolean action(Event evt, Object obj)
   {
      if ( evt.target instanceof Button)
      {
         String  strValue = new String();
         Variant varValue = new Variant();
         Variant varFrom  = new Variant();
         Variant varTo    = new Variant();

         strValue = m_dlgMain.IDC_CONVERTFROM.getText();

         // Decide whether to treat the value text as
         // a double or a string...

         try
         {
            double d = Double.valueOf(strValue).doubleValue();

            varValue.putDouble(d);
         }
         catch (NumberFormatException e)
         {
            varValue.putString(strValue);
         }

         // Obtain the conversion units from the
         // radio buttons...

         varFrom.putString(
                  m_dlgMain.group1.getCurrent().getLabel() );
         varTo.putString(
                  m_dlgMain.group2.getCurrent().getLabel() );

         // Convert the value and display it...

         Variant varAnswer = m_estUnits.ConvertMeasure(
                                   varValue, varFrom, varTo);
```

```
        m_dlgMain.IDC_ANSWER.setText( varAnswer.toString() );

        return true;
    }

    return false;
    }
}
```

An Objective View Of The Object Viewer

*The OLE Object Viewer, located under the Visual J++ Tools menu, provides a peek at all of the OLE objects on your system. It can view the methods and properties of OLE automation servers that you might not have known were installed on your system. Try it out and see for yourself. (By the way, the Object Viewer that ships with Visual J++ is out of date. You can download the latest version at **www.microsoft. com/oledev/olecom/oleview.htm.**)*

Case Study: Microsoft Access

Microsoft Access is a relational database builder that ships with the Microsoft Office application suite. It creates tables, forms, queries, and reports combined into a single workspace. It also provides tools for sharing and distributing databases across networks.

The Object Model

The root of the Microsoft Access object model (see Figure 10.3) is the **Application** object. **Application** provides methods for opening databases, controlling the menu bar, and getting handles to child objects in the hierarchy.

The most important child object in Microsoft Access is **DBEngine**. By creating an instance of **DBEngine**, you can obtain information from a database, run queries, and add new data. To illustrate, Listing 10.2 shows how to open an Access database and obtain a handle to its first record. (For a complete reference to Microsoft Access' object model, consult its documentation.)

Listing 10.2   Opening an Access database from Java.

```
import msaccess.*;
import dao2532.*;
import com.ms.com.*;
```

```
        .
        .
        .

_Application access = new Application();
Variant varExclusive = new Variant();
varExclusive.putInt(0);
access.OpenCurrentDatabase("My Database.mdb", varExclusive);

Database database = access.CurrentDb();

Recordset recordset;
Variant varType = new Variant();
Variant varOptions = new Variant();

varType.putShort(dao2532.Constants.dbOpenDynaset);
varOptions.putShort((short)0);

recordset = database.OpenRecordset("My Table",
                                   varType,
                                   varOptions);

recordset.MoveFirst();
```

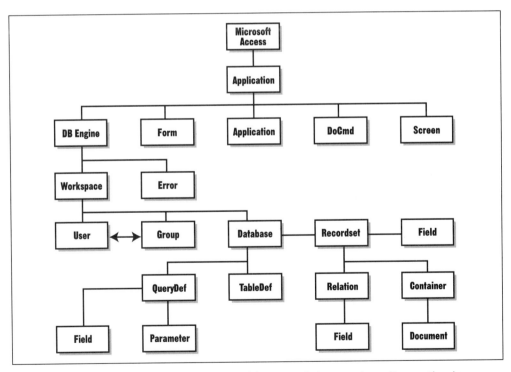

Figure 10.3 The Microsoft Access object model organizes its methods hierarchically.

Sample Code

To showcase the power of Microsoft Access, I've written a Java applet titled the Microsoft Access Driver. It creates an instance of the **Application** object and uses it to open a database of silly jokes (see Figure 10.4). It then obtains a **Recordset** object from the current **Database** object, as demonstrated in the previous listing.

Once the applet obtains the **Recordset** object, it can walk through each record in the database and display the record inside a Web browser. It allows the user to move to the first, last, next, and previous records simply by clicking the appropriate button (see Figure 10.5). It also allows the user to add jokes to the database.

Become One With The DAO

To work with databases in Visual J++, you don't need Microsoft Access. You could import the Data Access Objects (DAO) library that ships free with every copy of Visual J++. For a trivial example of linking Java to DAO, check out the DAOSample application inside the Visual J++ Samples folder. It demonstrates how to create a **Recordset** object and walk through records in a database.

The Microsoft Access code in this section is similar to DAOSample. It does, however, go beyond the example by showing you how to add records to the database (see the **addFields()** function in Listing 10.3.) In a real-world situation, harnessing the full strength of Microsoft Access would involve its **Report** and **Screen** objects, which are not provided by DAO alone.

For added power, you could use the Remote Data Objects (RDO) library, which also ships with Visual J++. RDO is a lightweight cousin of DAO and is designed to connect to remote databases through intranets.

See Chapter 11 for details on RDO, DAO, and a complete DAO application.

Figure 10.4 The sample Microsoft Access database.

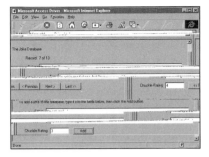

Figure 10.5 The Microsoft Access Driver applet encapsulates the **Recordset** object.

Listing 10.3 contains an abridged version of the source code to the Microsoft Access Driver.

LISTING 10.3   THE MICROSOFT ACCESS DRIVER SOURCE CODE.

```
import java.applet.*;
import java.awt.*;
import msaccess.*;
import dao2532.*;
import com.ms.com.*;
import MicrosoftAccessDriverFrame;

public class MicrosoftAccessDriver extends Applet
{
   MainDialog m_dlgMain;
   Database m_database;
   Recordset m_recordset;

   private static String strDatabaseName = "Joke Base.mdb";
   private static String strTableName = "Jokes";

   public void init()
   {
      m_dlgMain = new MainDialog(this);
      m_dlgMain.CreateControls();

      // Get the file name of the database according to the
      // current path...

      String strFilename;

      try
```

```java
      {
         java.net.URL urlFilename;
         urlFilename = new java.net.URL(getDocumentBase(),
                                       strDatabaseName);
         strFilename = urlFilename.getFile().substring(1);
      }
      catch(Exception e)
      {
         showStatus("Error: " + e.getMessage());
      }

      // Open the database...

      _Application access = new Application();

      Variant varExclusive = new Variant();

      varExclusive.putInt(0);

      access.OpenCurrentDatabase(strFilename, varExclusive);

      m_database = access.CurrentDb();
   }

   public void paint(Graphics g)
   {
      // No painting is necessary because we use a dialog box
      // template.
   }

   public void start()
   {
      createRecordset();
      displayFields();
   }

   public boolean action(Event evt, Object obj)
   {
      if (evt.target instanceof Button)
      {
         String label = ((Button)evt.target).getLabel();

         if ( label.equals("<< First") )
         {
            m_recordset.MoveFirst();
         }
         else
         {
            if ( label.equals("< Previous") )
```

```java
            {
               if ( m_recordset.getAbsolutePosition() > 0 )
                  m_recordset.MovePrevious();
            }
            else
            {
               if ( label.equals("Add") )
               {
                  addFields();
               }
               else
               {
                  if ( label.equals("Next >") )
                  {
                     if ( m_recordset.getAbsolutePosition()+1
                           <
                           m_recordset.getRecordCount() )
                     {
                        m_recordset.MoveNext();
                     }
                  }
                  else
                  {
                     m_recordset.MoveLast();
                  }
               }
            }
         }

         displayFields();

         return true;
      }

      return false;
}

// This function displays the current record in the three
// fields at the top half of the applet window.
private void displayFields()
{
   m_dlgMain.IDC_RECORD.setText(
               (m_recordset.getAbsolutePosition() + 1) +
                  " of " +
               m_recordset.getRecordCount() );

   Fields fieldList = m_recordset.getFields();
   _Field field;
   Variant varFieldValue = new Variant();
```

OLE Automation

```java
    Variant varFieldName = new Variant();

    // Get the Setup field...

    varFieldName.putString("Setup");
    field = fieldList.getItem(varFieldName);

    varFieldValue = field.getValue();
    m_dlgMain.IDC_SETUP.setText( varFieldValue.toString() );

    // Get the Tag field...
    varFieldName.putString("Tag");
    field = fieldList.getItem(varFieldName);

    varFieldValue = field.getValue();
    m_dlgMain.IDC_TAG.setText( varFieldValue.toString() );

    // Get the Chuckle Rating field...

    varFieldName.putString("Chuckle Rating");
    field = fieldList.getItem(varFieldName);

    varFieldValue = field.getValue();
    m_dlgMain.IDC_RATING.setText(
                            varFieldValue.toString() );
}

// This function obtains the three fields from the bottom
// half of the applet window and adds them to the database.
private void addFields()
{
    m_recordset.AddNew();

    Fields fieldList = m_recordset.getFields();
    _Field field;
    Variant varFieldValue = new Variant();
    Variant varFieldName = new Variant();

    // Add the Setup field...

    varFieldName.putString("Setup");
    field = fieldList.getItem(varFieldName);

    varFieldValue.putString(
                        m_dlgMain.IDC_SETUPADD.getText());
    field.putValue(varFieldValue);

    // Add the Tag field...
```

```
        varFieldName.putString("Tag");
        field = fieldList.getItem(varFieldName);

        varFieldValue.putString(m_dlgMain.IDC_TAGADD.getText());
        field.putValue(varFieldValue);

        // Add the Chuckle Rating field...

        varFieldName.putString("Chuckle Rating");
        field = fieldList.getItem(varFieldName);

        int nRating = Integer.valueOf(
                m_dlgMain.IDC_RATINGADD.getText() ).intValue();
        varFieldValue.putInt(nRating);
        field.putValue(varFieldValue);

        m_recordset.Update();

        createRecordset();

        displayFields();
    }

    // This function initializes the Recordset object.
    // It is called in start() and addFields().
    private void createRecordset()
    {
        Variant varType    = new Variant();
        Variant varOptions = new Variant();

        varType.putShort(dao2532.Constants.dbOpenDynaset);
        varOptions.putShort((short)0);

        m_recordset = m_database.OpenRecordset(strTableName,
                                               varType,
                                               varOptions);

        // Move the cursor around to update the record count...
        m_recordset.MoveNext();
        m_recordset.MovePrevious();
    }
}
```

SOUND OFF

Want to give Visual J++ a voice? Go to the Sounds icon in the Control Panel and find the Microsoft Developer item. Under this item, you can find entries for Breakpoint Hit,

Build Complete, Build Error, Build Warning, Error in Output, and *Warning in Output*. Assigning a sound file to one of the entries causes Visual J++ to play the sound at the appropriate event. (Whenever my Java code hits a breakpoint, Monty Python's Eric Idle calmly says, "We interrupt this program to annoy you and make things generally irritating.")

Creating Late-binding Automation Controllers

Entisoft Tools and Microsoft Access can be controlled either through late-binding or early-binding. Some OLE automation servers, however, allow only late-binding. You cannot create controllers in Java that bind to servers at runtime.

ActiveX To The Rescue

This sounds like a major problem. Let's take a step back and look at the big picture:

- Java can't handle late-binding.

- C++ can handle late-binding.

- Java can integrate with ActiveX controls.

- C++ can create ActiveX controls.

Put two and two together, and I think you'll come to the same conclusion I did: Create an ActiveX control in C++ to get around Java's late-binding restriction. Here's how it would work (see Figure 10.6):

1. Create a standard ActiveX control in C++.

2. Using the steps from "Driving From C++" in Chapter 8, import the automation server's type library into your C++ project, then add code that makes the control an automation controller.

3. Expose methods in the ActiveX control that match the methods in the automation server. For instance, if the server contained a method called **Print()**, you would expose a method in the ActiveX control called **Print()**. The ActiveX version would simply call the server's **Print()** method.

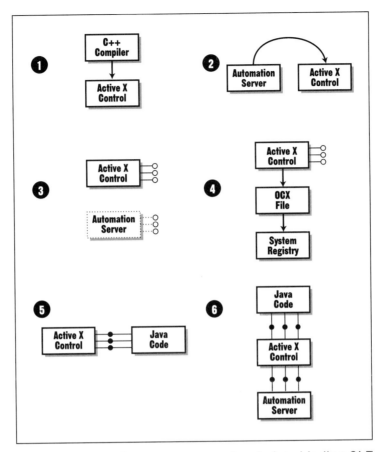

Figure 10.6 ActiveX controls can overcome Java's late-binding OLE automation restriction.

4. Compile and register the ActiveX control.

5. Import the ActiveX control into a Java project using the steps from the section "Harnessing The Wizard's Magic" in Chapter 7. Call the ActiveX methods in your source code as necessary.

6. Run the Java project. It will load the ActiveX control, which binds to the automation server and transfers method calls coming from the Java code.

By creating this type of ActiveX control, you can bridge the gap between late-binding and early-binding. The control will bind to the Java program at compile time and to the automation server at runtime. This technique is a brute-force workaround, but it still allows Java to control both types of automation servers.

ClassWizard Support For OLE Automation Controllers

Chapter 5 explained how to create ActiveX controls in Visual C++ using the OLE ControlWizard and the ClassWizard. With these same tools, you can easily convert an ActiveX control to an OLE automation controller for linking Java to late-binding servers.

First, use the ControlWizard to create a control as usual, then open the ClassWizard. Click the Add Class button, and select From An OLE TypeLib. Using the browse box that appears, find the file (a TLB file) that contains the automation server's type library. When you open it, ClassWizard will read the file and generate a C++ class wrapper for each object in the library.

At this point, calling methods and accessing properties in the server is simply a matter of calling functions in the class wrapper. The only tricky part is that you must first call the **CreateDispatch()** method (derived from the MFC's **COleDispatchDriver** class) and pass it the automation server's program ID. For example, if you imported Microsoft Word's type library, you could call its **FilePrintDefault()** method like this:

```
WordBasic* wb = new WordBasic();

if ( wb->CreateDispatch("Word.Basic") )
   wb->FilePrintDefault();
else
   AfxMessageBox("Error: Microsoft Word is not installed.");

delete wb;
```

For more information on ClassWizard's OLE automation support and the **COleDispatchDriver** class, see the Visual C++ documentation.

Case Study: Microsoft Word

Microsoft Word is the word processor that ships with the Microsoft Office application suite. It includes features for creating tables, importing graphics, and merging documents with mailing lists. It exposes these features through OLE automation, but they can be accessed only through late-binding.

THE OBJECT MODEL

The developers of Microsoft Word got a little lazy when they designed its object model. Instead of organizing features into logical groups, they dumped all of them into a single root object called **WordBasic** (see Figure 10.7).

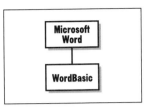

Figure 10.7 The Microsoft Word object model contains only one object: **WordBasic**.

As the name implies, **WordBasic** is an OLE automation wrapper for Word's macro language. Calling a method in Word's type library simply passes the call to the appropriate **WordBasic** function. This setup may sound easier than having to manage a formal object model, but it actually makes programming more difficult. The lack of structure means that finding a specific function takes longer, and you can seldom derive a function's purpose from its name. (Does **ToolsSpelling**() spell-check the document, or does it open the spell-checker's Options dialog box? If the function were part of a **Document** object—as it should have been designed—you would know immediately.)

SAMPLE CODE

Despite these drawbacks, Word's OLE automation still gives Java programs an advantage. For instance, a Java applet for online shopping could print an order form using Word. It could also format and sort the document before printing.

To demonstrate automation of Microsoft Word, I've written a Java applet titled the Microsoft Word Driver (see Figure 10.8). Java does not support late-binding, so instead of creating an instance of the **WordBasic** object, it creates an instance of an ActiveX control that wraps the **WordBasic** object. This control (whose source code you can find on the CD-ROM included with this book) exposes a small but valuable subset of **WordBasic**'s methods as ActiveX methods.

The Microsoft Word Driver applet displays a text box for inserting text. Clicking the buttons in the applet's window can send the text to Microsoft Word and sort it alphabetically, as shown in Figure 10.9. Listing 10.4 contains an abridged version of the source code to the Microsoft Word Driver.

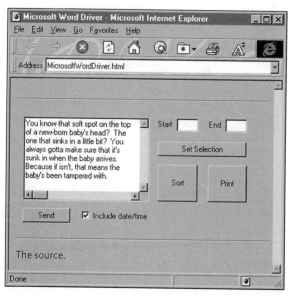

Figure 10.8 The Microsoft Word Driver applet encapsulates the **WordBasic** object.

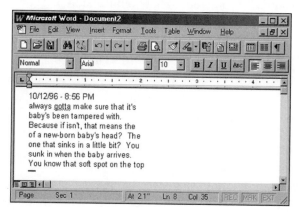

Figure 10.9 The results of sorting text sent to Microsoft Word.

LISTING 10.4   THE MICROSOFT WORD DRIVER SOURCE CODE.

```
import java.applet.*;
import java.awt.*;
import microsoftword.*;
import MicrosoftWordDriverFrame;

public class MicrosoftWordDriver extends Applet
{
   IMicrosoftWord m_word;
   MainDialog m_dlgMain;
```

```java
public void init()
{
   m_dlgMain = new MainDialog(this);
   m_dlgMain.CreateControls();
}

public void paint(Graphics g)
{
   // No painting is necessary because we use a dialog box
   // template.
}

public void start()
{
   m_word = new MicrosoftWord();
}

public boolean action(Event evt, Object obj)
{
   if (evt.target instanceof Button)
   {
      String label = ((Button)evt.target).getLabel();

      if ( label.equals("Send") )
      {
         m_word.Insert(m_dlgMain.IDC_TEXT.getText(),
                    m_dlgMain.IDC_DATETIME.getState());
         return true;
      }
      else
      {
         if ( label.equals("Set Selection") )
         {
            int nStart = Integer.valueOf(
              m_dlgMain.IDC_STARTSEL.getText()).intValue();
            int nEnd = Integer.valueOf(
              m_dlgMain.IDC_ENDSEL.getText()).intValue();

            m_word.SetSelRange(nStart, nEnd);

            return true;
         }
         else
         {
            if ( label.equals("Sort") )
            {
               m_word.Sort();          return true;
            }
```

```
            else
            {
                m_word.Print();
                return true;
            }
        }
    }
}

    return false;
    }
}
```

GIVE YOURSELF A TIP

Visual J++ presents you with a Tip of the Day each time it loads. Many of these tips are trivial, and others are simply arcane. To delete the ones you don't need and to add your own personalized tips, just edit the text file called vjtools.tip, located in Visual J++'s bin\ide directory.

Summary

You are a developer. You know that you must constantly improve yourself to stay ahead. You know that your customers want solutions to their problems—and they want them yesterday. Visual J++ can help you provide these solutions, but it can't handle every contingency. Sometimes, you must step outside the world of Java and into the world of OLE. OLE, through its automation features, can give your programs abilities that you might never have the chance to build yourself. It can harness the power of the world's best software and link it to your Java code. With OLE automation, you never have to reinvent the wheel.

Chapter 11

Data Access Objects

- DAO, RDO, and JDBC
- Building and browsing databases
- Adding, deleting, and modifying records
- Performing queries
- Example: Harmon Optical

My mom keeps a dusty old Rolodex on top of the fridge. It's the family's own white pages, stuffed with names and phone numbers of friends and relatives. Each card in the index is organized according to Mom's special system—one that only she can understand. See if you can figure it out: Last names that begin with *H* go under *H*, unless it's a grandma or a grandpa, in which case they go under *G*. Relatives from the Taylor side of the family go under *T*, but friends whose last names begin with *T* go to the *F* pile, as long as they're not doctors (who belong in the *D*s). All other relatives are sorted either by their last name or their title (i.e., aunt, cousin, etc.) on a random basis. Arrrgh!!

Luckily, most databases aren't as confusing as Mom's. Whether they hold bank accounts, scientific data, or a list of recipes, today's structured database systems are both powerful and relatively easy to use. They can store gigabytes of information while providing a convenient interface for searching and updating records. They can even share their data with anyone on the Internet.

With Visual J++, you can give Java programs access to the most popular database systems, including Oracle, Borland dBASE, and Microsoft Access. You can build a database front-end, complete with browse, query, and update features, by writing only a few dozen lines of Java code. Making the front end available to anyone on your company's intranet is simply a matter of posting it to the Web server.

This chapter shows you how to write database applications in Visual J++. It also provides an introduction to part of the Structured Query Language (SQL), which you'll need to perform queries from Java. In the final section, you can find a complete Visual J++ application that combines all of the topics from this chapter into a single program.

Database Support In Visual J++

Support for database access in Visual J++ is available only if you performed a Custom Install with its setup program. With Custom Install, Visual J++ provides a Database Options checkbox, allowing you to install the necessary drivers and automation servers. If you have not performed a Custom Install, run the setup program again, choose Custom Install, and make sure that the Database Options box is checked.

Once database support has been installed, Visual J++ provides two ways of accessing databases: Data Access Objects (DAO) and Remote Data Objects (RDO). Both sets of objects are proprietary to Microsoft and are supported by Visual Basic, Visual C++, and now by Visual J++.

As a third choice, you could write Java programs in Visual J++ that connect to databases through Java Database Connectivity (JDBC). JDBC—Sun's answer to Microsoft's database offerings—is based entirely in Java. When optimized, it is somewhat faster than DAO and RDO and provides tighter integration with Java. Visual J++ provides no built-in support for JDBC, so you'll have to look somewhere other than Microsoft to find examples, libraries, and drivers.

Data Access Objects

DAO allows programming languages to manipulate databases. It conforms to the ODBC protocol (see sidebar, "What Is ODBC"), so any database that you access through DAO must provide an ODBC driver. This requirement is seldom a problem, since all major database companies provide ODBC drivers.

DAO's power comes from the Microsoft Jet database engine, the same engine that drives Microsoft Access. Jet handles the dirty work of actually storing, retrieving, and updating the data. It sits between the DAO code and the ODBC driver manager, translating messages between the two (see Figure 11.1).

The job of DAO is to cover the Jet engine with an object-oriented interface. It exposes a hierarchy of classes that transforms a physical database into a logical code structure. DAO includes classes for the database itself, its tables, their fields, and so on (see Figure 11.2).

As you can see from the object model, you must drill down the hierarchy to obtain the object you want. For instance, to create a **Database** object, you must first create the **DBEngine** and **Workspace** objects.

After obtaining a **Database** object, you can access its properties and call its methods to manipulate the physical database. The other DAO objects expose properties and methods as well; the most important of these will be discussed later in this chapter.

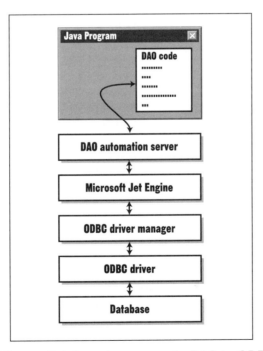

Figure 11.1 The Microsoft Jet engine connects DAO to ODBC.

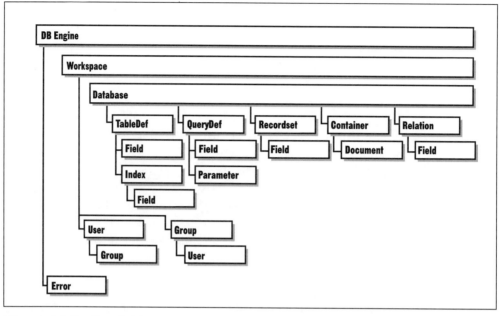

Figure 11.2 The DAO object model.

What Is ODBC?

further developments

Open Database Connectivity (ODBC) is a Microsoft standard that links database files to database drivers. The *open* means that any database vendor can write an ODBC driver that allows their file format to work with any ODBC-compliant application.

Despite criticisms of ODBC's slow performance, all major database vendors have jumped on the bandwagon. Oracle, Informix, Borland, and, of course, Microsoft offer ODBC drivers for their products. As long as you've installed the proper driver for a file format, all of your database applications—such as those you build with Visual J++—can recognize it.

You could bypass DAO and call into ODBC directly. This approach would give you higher performance and more flexibility, but it would also mean having to deal with the nitty-gritty functions of the ODBC API. You would be better off sticking to ODBC shells, such as DAO. They provide a reasonable balance of speed and simplicity.

Remote Data Objects

Visual J++'s other set of database classes, RDO, is similar to DAO in most respects. Both can manipulate databases and submit queries through the ODBC layer.

The key difference between DAO and RDO is that an RDO's database engine resides on a remote server (see Figure 11.3). Because the local computer offloads its work onto the remote server, users see an improvement in response time. They can continue browsing the database while the server performs queries, adds records, and handles other database chores.

Because RDO sits closer than DAO to the ODBC layer, its object model is somewhat harder to use. The methods are finicky, and if you don't call them with exactly the right parameters, they'll throw a confusing error back in your face. Also, RDO's low-level interface differs from DAO significantly; learning RDO is like learning database programming all over again.

These problems make RDO less capable than DAO for general use. This chapter won't go into the details of the RDO object hierarchy; for an example of using RDO in Java, see the SimpleRDO application that ships with Visual J++.

DSN-LESS RDO CONNECTIONS
The documentation for the SimpleRDO example states that you must register a Data Source Name (DSN) before using RDO. In fact, RDO does not require a DSN. You can skip the registration process by making a "DSN-less" connection

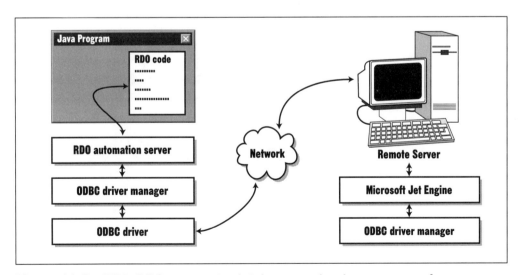

Figure 11.3 With RDO, a remote database engine increases performance.

> *directly through RDO. For example, to connect to a database called "mydb" on a server called "myserver", supply the rdoEngine.OpenConnection() method with the following string:*
>
> ```
> driver={Microsoft Access Driver (*.mdb)};server=myserver;
> database=mydb;uid=username;pwd=password;dsn=;
> For more information, see the Microsoft Knowledge Base article
> Q147875 at www.microsoft.com/kb/developr/vb/q147875.htm.
> ```

JDBC

JDBC is a low-level API for writing database applications in Java. Although it is in competition with Microsoft's DAO and RDO, it provides an ODBC interface for connecting to all database formats supported by DAO and RDO (see Figure 11.4). This interface uses native code, so it is not meant to be a long-term solution. It is mostly an attempt by Sun to garner industry support for JDBC. Over time, they will provide faster and more portable implementations of their database API.

From a programming standpoint, JDBC has an advantage over DAO and RDO. It is strongly typed, meaning that as much type information as possible is built into the function definitions. The strong typing allows the compiler to check that you're passing integers as integer parameters,

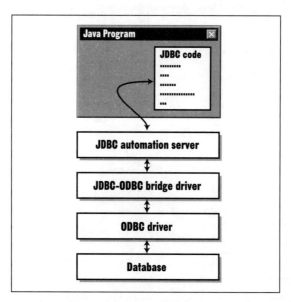

Figure 11.4 JDBC provides a bridge to ODBC for connecting to all major database formats.

strings as string parameters, and so on. In DAO and RDO, most parameter types are **Variant**s, so Visual J++ can't find your mistakes.

Like RDO, JDBC can connect to remote databases. It can open sockets to servers on either the Internet or a local network. This feature, however, raises security and performance issues that have yet to be resolved. (For instance, Java applets downloaded through the Internet cannot access local files or connect to arbitrary servers.)

Visual J++ provides no built-in support for JDBC, and this chapter won't go into the details of its API.

DAO Basics

The most popular ways of organizing databases are the indexed sequential access method (ISAM), the network model, the hierarchical model, and the relational model. In recent years, the relational model has become the accepted standard for database design, not just because of the model itself but because it defines an interface called the Structured Query Language, or SQL (pronounced *sequel*). SQL allows databases and tools from many different vendors to work together consistently and understandably. (You can find a tutorial on a subset of SQL in the "Searching For Records" section near the end of this chapter.)

The Microsoft Jet database engine is a relational database engine, so DAO—which sits on top of Jet—works best with relational databases. DAO can create, maintain, and modify any relational database that supports ODBC. Since DAO ships with Visual J++, your Java programs can also create, maintain, and modify relational databases.

This section provides an overview of DAO. It demonstrates how to write Java code for connecting to a relational database, browsing and modifying its records, and performing queries. For a complete DAO application, see the example at the end of this chapter.

Before You Begin

In Visual J++, the DAO library is treated like any other OLE automation server (see Chapter 10). This means you must import the library before you can use any DAO object. To import DAO, run the Java Type Library Wizard and select the item, Microsoft DAO 3.0 Object Library. The wizard will read the DAO type library and generate Java class files for it, placing them in the Java\TrustLib directory. To reference these classes in your project, insert the line

```
import dao3032.*;
```

at the top of your source-code file. DAO functions often take the **Variant** class as a parameter, so you should import the **com.ms.com.*** libraries as well. Once you have imported both sets of libraries, you're ready to write database code in Java.

Connecting To The Database

The art of database design could fill a book. For this chapter, then, I won't preach about primary keys, normalization, or one-to-many relationships. I'll just assume that you're connecting to an existing database or building one from scratch. Either way, you'll need to create an instance of the **DBEngine** object and obtain a **Database** object from it.

THE DBENGINE OBJECT

As shown earlier in Figure 11.2, **DBEngine** lies at the root of the DAO object model. You must create this object before creating any other. DAO is a licensed automation server, so you can't create **DBEngine** simply by calling **new**. Instead, you must call the **ILicenseMgr.create_WithLic()** function, passing it the license key of the DAO library and its class ID. For example:

```
ILicenseMgr mgr = new LicenseMgr();

_DBEngine daoEngine = (_DBEngine) mgr.createWithLic(
                "mjgcqcejfchcijecpdhckcdjqigdejfccjri",
                "{00025E15-0000-0000-C000-000000000046}",
                null,
                ComContext.INPROC_SERVER);
```

As discussed in Chapter 7, **createWithLic()** identifies your program as a legal user of a licensed library. You need to call this function only once when using DAO because all other DAO objects are obtained from **DBEngine**; they are not created explicitly. Just remember to save a copy of the **createWithLic()** return value so you can refer to it later.

THE DATABASE OBJECT

After creating the **DBEngine** object, you must link your code to a physical database—either an existing one or an empty one created on-the-fly. To open an existing database, call the **OpenDatabase**() function, which returns a **Database** object:

```
Variant varExclusive = new Variant();
Variant varReadOnly = new Variant();
Variant varSource = new Variant();

varExclusive.putBoolean(false);
varReadOnly.putBoolean(false);
varSource.putString("");

Database daoDatabase = daoEngine.OpenDatabase(
    "My Database.mdb", varExclusive, varReadOnly, varSource);

// Remember to close the database when you're done with it by
// calling daoDatabase.Close().
```

The first parameter is the file name of the existing database. (Remember to include the extension.) The next two parameters are **Variant**s holding boolean values. They open the database for exclusive (nonshared) and read-only access, respectively. The final parameter is a **Variant** string containing any parameters, separated by semicolons, that you wish to pass to the ODBC driver.

REMOTE DATABASES VIA DAO
Databases opened with DAO don't have to reside on the local computer. You can open a database anywhere on your intranet. Just place the name of the server before the file name, like this:

\\MyServer\MyServer's shared files\Databases\My Database.mdb

If you don't have an existing database to work with, DAO can create one for you. Call the **CreateDatabase**() function, specifying the database name, the language to be used for sorting, and the version number. For example:

```
Variant varVersion = new Variant();

// In Visual J++, always use Jet 3.0.
varVersion.putShort(Constants.dbVersion30);

Database daoDatabase = daoEngine.CreateDatabase(
        "My Database.mdb", "dbLangGeneral", varVersion);
```

Data Access Objects **303**

The general language setting applies to English, German, French, Portuguese, Italian, and modern Spanish. For other languages, consult the DAO documentation.

Browsing Records

Now that you've got a handle on the database, you can access its tables and the information they contain. (For adding new information to a blank database, see the section titled "Adding And Deleting Records" later in this chapter.) To open a table, call the **OpenRecordset()** function, a member of the **Database** object. The first parameter is a string containing the name of the table. The second and third parameters are **Variant** short integers that specify how to open the table, as described in Tables 11.1 and 11.2. (*Recordset*, by the way, is just DAO terminology for *table*.)

Table 11.1 Possible values for the second parameter (Type) of OpenRecordset().

Value	Description
dbOpenDynaset	Opens the table for browsing, searching, and updating. Only the primary key is loaded into memory.
dbOpenSnapshot	Loads the entire table into memory for faster performance, but it cannot be updated.
dbOpenTable	Like dbOpenDynaset, but works only on Jet databases, and the table cannot be searched.

Table 11.2 Possible values for the third parameter (Options) of OpenRecordset().

Value	Description
dbDenyWrite	Other users can't modify or delete records.
dbDenyRead	Other users can't view records (table-type recordsets only).
dbReadOnly	You can only view records; other users can modify them.
dbAppendOnly	You can only add new records (dynaset-type recordsets only).
dbForwardOnly	Allows only forward scrolling through the table for faster performance.
dbSeeChanges	Generates a runtime error if another user is changing data you are editing.

The following code, for example, opens a read-only, dynaset-type recordset for a table named "Employees":

```
Variant varType = new Variant();
Variant varOptions = new Variant();

varType.putShort(Constants.dbOpenDynaset);
varOptions.putShort(Constants.dbReadOnly);

Recordset daoRecordset = daoDatabase.OpenRecordset(
                        "Employees", varType, varOptions);

// Remember to close the recordset when you're done with it by
// calling daoRecordset.Close().
```

What's With All These Variants?

Most of the parameters in DAO functions are of a specific type, such as string, boolean, or integer. Why, then, does Visual J++ force you to use **Variant**s for these parameters? The reason is that most DAO functions—and most OLE functions in general—mark certain parameters as optional. If you don't specify them, DAO will use a default value.

Java, as you probably already know, does not support optional parameters. The nonvariation of **Variant**s is simply a means for making Java code compatible with DAO. For instance, omitting the call to **varType.putShort**() in the previous code fragment will open a table-type recordset, the default for the **OpenRecordset**() function.

After opening the table, you can walk through its records by calling member functions of the **Recordset** object, as shown in Table 11.3. (To search for a specific record, see the "Searching for Records" section.)

For example, the following code iterates through every record in the table:

```
daoRecordset.MoveFirst();

for (int i = 0; i < daoRecordset.getRecordCount(); i++)
{
   // Do something with the record...
   daoRecordset.MoveNext();
}
```

Table 11.3 Recordset functions for browsing records.

Function	Description
MoveFirst()	Moves to the first record in the table.
MoveLast()	Moves to the last record in the table.
MoveNext()	Moves to the next record in the table.
MovePrevious()	Moves to the previous record in the table.
Move(int, Variant)	Moves to the position specified by the first parameter, relative to the current record. Moves relative to the second parameter if it is specified.
int getRecordCount()	Returns the number of records in the table.
int getLastModified()	Returns the position of the last added or changed record.
int getAbsolutePosition()	Returns the position of the current record.
float getPercentPosition()	Returns the position of the current record as a percentage.
putPercentPosition(float)	Moves to the position specified as a percentage.

Getting And Setting Fields

Once you've moved to the record you want, you can access the information it holds. This step requires two objects:

- **Fields**—This object is a collection of the record's fields. You obtain it by calling the **getFields()** function of the **Recordset** object. You can get a handle to a specific field by calling **getItem(Variant)**, where the **Variant** parameter is the name of the field. (If you don't know the name, specify its zero-based ordinal position as a **Variant** integer.)

- **Field**—A **Field** object is returned by the **getItem()** function of **Fields**. It provides functions for getting and setting the field's value (**getValue()** and **putValue()**) and for getting the field's type (**getType()**). See Table 11.4 for a list of possible field types.

To illustrate the **Fields** and **Field** objects, the following code gets an integer value from a column called "Size" and adds 1 to it:

```
Fields fieldList = daoRecordset.getFields();
_Field field;
Variant varFieldValue;
Variant varFieldName = new Variant();
```

```
// Get the Size field...
varFieldName.putString("Size");
field = fieldList.getItem(varFieldName);

// Verify that the field is an integer...
if ( field.getType() == Constants.dbInteger )
{
   // Get the value of field...
   varFieldValue = field.getValue();

   // Change the value...
   varFieldValue.putInt( varFieldValue.getInt() + 1 );

   // Set the value back...
   field.putValue(varFieldValue);
}
```

Adding And Deleting Records

In addition to modifying records, the **Recordset** object can add and delete them. To add a record:

1. Open a table in a database by calling the **Database** member function **OpenRecordset()**. Be sure not to open it as read-only.

Table 11.4 Possible field types returned by getType().

Type	Value	Description
dbBoolean	1	True/False
dbByte	2	Byte (0-255)
dbInteger	3	Integer (-32,768-32,767)
dbLong	4	Long (-2,147,483,648–2,147,483,647)
dbCurrency	5	Currency
dbSingle	6	Single (-3.402823e38–3.402823e38)
dbDouble	7	Double (-1.79769313486232e308–1.79769313486232e308)
dbDate	8	Date/Time
dbGUID	9	Globally Unique Identifier
dbText	10	Text limited to 255 characters
dbLongBinary	11	Long Binary (OLE object; Variant string in Java)
dbMemo	12	Text limited to 2 billion characters

2. Call the **Recordset** member function **AddNew()**.

3. Using the technique described in the previous section, set each field in the record to an appropriate value.

4. Call the **Recordset** member function **Update()**. If you forget this step, your changes will be lost.

For sample code of adding a record, see the example program listed at the end of this chapter.

Dragging Windows Anywhere
While dragging Visual J++ windows with the mouse, hold down the Ctrl key to prevent automatic docking.

To delete the current record, simply call the **Recordset** member function **Delete()**. For example, to delete the last record in a table:

```
daoRecordset.MoveLast();
daoRecordset.Delete();
```

Searching For Records

In the early 1970s, E.F. Codd invented the relational database. A few years later, a programming language known as Sequel was developed for manipulating and searching (a.k.a. querying) relational databases. SQL is a modern version of the original Sequel language. Its use has become so widespread that the American National Standards Institute (ANSI) now controls its evolution.

SQL is not a traditional programming language, but rather a set of commands, clauses, and operators. These commands allow the programmer to add and delete records, change fields, and otherwise alter the structure of the database. DAO provides functions for performing these tasks, so you don't need SQL for most database work in Java. You do, however, need SQL for searching databases. This section explains how to use SQL for making database queries.

The WHERE Clause

WHERE is perhaps the most common keyword in SQL. Programmers use this clause to select records that match certain criteria. For instance, **WHERE** could search for all names that begin with the letter Z, or all orders greater than $100.

The syntax of the **WHERE** clause is similar to Java's **if** keyword. It can contain up to 40 logical and comparison operators (see Tables 11.5 and 11.6). Table 11.7 provides several examples of how to use these operators. For a complete reference to the **WHERE** specification, see Appendix C.

Table 11.5   Logical operators of the WHERE clause.

Operator	Meaning
AND	Record must contain both expressions
OR	Record must contain either expression
NOT	Record must not contain the expression

Table 11.6   Comparison operators of the WHERE clause.

Operator	Meaning
<	Less than
<=	Less than or equal to
>	Greater than
>=	Greater than or equal to
=	Equal to
<>	Not equal to
BETWEEN	Specifies a range of values
IN	Specifies a set of values
LIKE	Used for pattern matching

Table 11.7   Examples of using the WHERE clause.

Statement	Meaning
LastName = 'Cory'	Records whose LastName field is "Cory"
Salary BETWEEN 20000 AND 30000	Records whose Salary field is between 20,000 and 30,000 (inclusive)
LastName BETWEEN 'French' AND 'Saunders'	Records whose LastName field falls in alphabetical order between "French" and "Saunders" (inclusive)
FirstName IN ('Maria', 'Rachel', 'Lori')	Records whose FirstName field is either "Maria", "Rachel", or "Lori"

continued

Table 11.7 Examples of using the WHERE clause (continued).

Statement	Meaning
OrderDate < #9-7-96#	Records whose OrderDate field is earlier than September 7,1996
[Frame Size] <> 52	Records whose Frame Size field is not 52 (brackets necessary for fields containing spaces or punctuation)
FirstName LIKE 'Gen*' AND Age >= 20	Records whose LastName field begins with "Gen" and whose Age field is greater than or equal to 20
FirstName LIKE '?S[A-M]##'	Records whose value in the FirstName field begins with any letter, contains *S* for the second letter, any letter between *A* and *M* for the third letter, followed by two numbers

THE FIND FUNCTIONS

In DAO, you can send the database engine a **WHERE** statement by calling one of **Recordset**'s **Find** functions. These functions work the same as the **Move** functions, but rather than applying to all records in a table, they apply to only those you specify. For example, the following code searches for the next record whose Phrase field matches "I gotta vamoose, el pronto!":

```
daoRecordset.FindNext("Phrase='I gotta vamoose, el pronto!'");
```

Going the other direction, this code searches for the previous record whose ChocolateMilk field matches either "sweet" or "sour":

```
daoRecordset.FindPrevious("ChocolateMilk IN ('sweet',
  'sour')");
```

You can also call the **FindFirst()** and **FindLast()** functions to search for the first and last records matching the given criteria. After you call any of the four **Find** functions, the cursor is placed at the specified record and you can manipulate it as usual—but only if it can be found. If not, a flag is set to indicate a search failure. The flag is a boolean property called **NoMatch**, and you can obtain its value by calling **getNoMatch()**. This code, for example, iterates through every record whose **LastName** field matches "Oosterbaan":

```
String strSearch = new String("LastName = 'Oosterbaan'");

daoRecordset.FindFirst(strSearch);

while ( daoRecordset.getNoMatch() == false )
{
   // Do something with the record...

   // Find the next record...
   daoRecordset.FindNext(strSearch);
}
```

Putting It All Together: The Harmon Optical Example

After that whirlwind tour of the DAO library, you're probably ready for some thick 'n' hearty example code. Don't worry, I came prepared: I've built a complete DAO application around a database of eyeglass frames. The program is called Harmon Optical (named after my dad's optical shop in Kansas City), and it allows you to browse the database, search for specific eyeglass frames, and order the ones you want (see Figures 11.5, 11.6, and 11.7).

All of Harmon Optical's database features have been discussed earlier in this chapter, so I won't go over them here. I will mention, however,

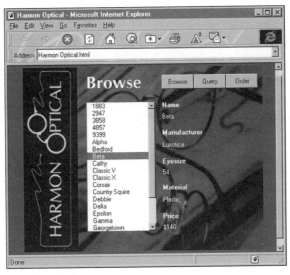

Figure 11.5 The Harmon Optical Browse layout.

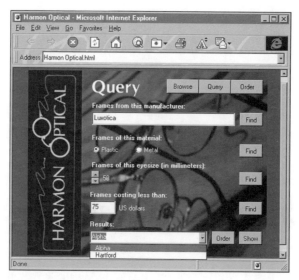

Figure 11.6 The Harmon Optical Query layout.

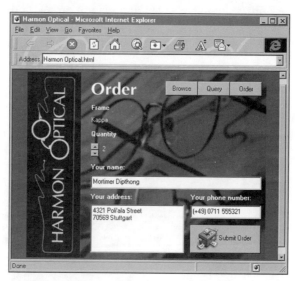

Figure 11.7 The Harmon Optical Order layout.

that the application uses Java only for driving the DAO database. For actually displaying the data and getting queries from the user, it relies on several ActiveX controls that ship with Internet Explorer (List Box, Command Button, etc.). Each control is arranged with an HTML Layout file and is connected to Java with an HTML script.

I hear you saying, "Wait a minute...ActiveX? HTML Layout? Isn't that Microsoft stuff? I want my application to be portable." Yes, HTML

Layouts are currently supported only by Internet Explorer. Then again, Java applications that use DAO also only run under Internet Explorer, so you're stuck either way. Besides, as long you're in the Microsoft universe, you may as well exploit it. HTML Layouts provide capabilities that would be difficult or impossible with Java alone (such as displaying AWT components on top of the Web page's background image). See the ActiveX Control Pad's online help to learn more about HTML Layouts.

Listing 11.1 contains the core HTML file for the Harmon Optical application; Listings 11.2, 11.3, and 11.4 contain the Browse, Query, and Order layouts; and Listing 11.5 contains the Java source code to the DAO driver. All listings have been abridged for easier reading. The complete source code and the eyeglass-frames database are on the CD-ROM that ships with this book.

LISTING 11.1 THE HARMON OPTICAL.HTML FILE.

```
<HTML>
<HEAD>

<SCRIPT LANGUAGE="VBScript">
<!--

Sub window_onLoad()

    'Hide the Query and Order windows
    Order_alx.Height = 0
    Order_alx.Width = 0
    Query_alx.Height = 0
    Query_alx.Width = 0

    ' Fill the Browse list with frame names
    Call document.DAODriver.fillBrowseList(
                            Browse_alx.Item("Frames"))

    Browse_alx.Item("Frames").ListIndex = 0

    ' Display the data for the selected frame
    Call document.DAODriver.updateBrowseWindow(
            Browse_alx.Item("Frames"),
            Browse_alx.Item("Name"),
            Browse_alx.Item("Manufacturer"),
            Browse_alx.Item("Eyesize"),
            Browse_alx.Item("Material"),
            Browse_alx.Item("Price"))
```

```
        ' Make the Order window match the Browse window
        Call document.DAODriver.updateOrderWindow(
                Browse_alx.Item("Frames"), Order_alx.Item("Frame"))

        ' Setup defaults for various controls...

        Browse_alx.Item("Browse").Value = 1
        Browse_alx.Item("Browse").Locked = 1
        Query_alx.Item("Query").Value = 1
        Query_alx.Item("Query").Locked = 1
        Order_alx.Item("Order").Value = 1
        Order_alx.Item("Order").Locked = 1

        Query_alx.Item("EyesizeSpin").Min = 52
        Query_alx.Item("EyesizeSpin").Max = 58
        Query_alx.Item("Eyesize").Caption = "52"

        Query_alx.Item("Plastic").Value = True

        Query_alx.Item("Results").AddItem("(none)")
        Query_alx.Item("Results").ListIndex = 0

        Order_alx.Item("QuantitySpin").Min = 1
        Order_alx.Item("QuantitySpin").Max = 10
        Order_alx.Item("Quantity").Caption = "1"

End Sub
-->
</SCRIPT>
<TITLE>Harmon Optical</TITLE>
</HEAD>
<BODY BGCOLOR=733173>
<CENTER>
    <OBJECT ID="Browse_alx"
     CLASSID="CLSID:812AE312-8B8E-11CF-93C8-00AA00C08FDF">
        <PARAM NAME="ALXPATH" REF VALUE="Browse.alx">
    </OBJECT>
    <OBJECT ID="Query_alx"
     CLASSID="CLSID:812AE312-8B8E-11CF-93C8-00AA00C08FDF">
        <PARAM NAME="ALXPATH" REF VALUE="Query.alx">
    </OBJECT>
    <OBJECT ID="Order_alx"
     CLASSID="CLSID:812AE312-8B8E-11CF-93C8-00AA00C08FDF">
        <PARAM NAME="ALXPATH" REF VALUE="Order.alx">
    </OBJECT>
</CENTER>
<APPLET
   CODE=DAODriver
   ID=DAODriver
```

```
   WIDTH=0
   HEIGHT=0>
</APPLET>
</BODY>
</HTML>
```

Listing 11.2 The Browse.alx (HTML Layout) file.

```
<SCRIPT LANGUAGE="VBScript">
<!--

Sub Query_Click()
   ' Show the Query window and hide the Browse window
   Window.Browse_alx.Height = 0
   Window.Browse_alx.Width = 0
   Window.Query_alx.Height = 253
   Window.Query_alx.Width = 335
End Sub

Sub Order_Click()
   ' Show the Order window and hide the Browse window
   Window.Browse_alx.Height = 0
   Window.Browse_alx.Width = 0
   Window.Order_alx.Height = 253
   Window.Order_alx.Width = 335
End Sub

Sub Frames_Change()
   ' Update the Browse and Order windows
   ' with the new selection...
   Call window.document.DAODriver.updateBrowseWindow(
         Frames, Name, Manufacturer, Eyesize, Material, Price)
   Call window.document.DAODriver.updateOrderWindow(
         Browse_alx.Item("Frames"), Order_alx.Item("Frame"))
End Sub

-->
</SCRIPT>

<DIV BACKGROUND="#733173" ID="HarmonOptical"
            STYLE="LAYOUT:FIXED;WIDTH:335pt;HEIGHT:253pt;">

   <OBJECT ID="Query"
   CLASSID="CLSID:D7053240-CE69-11CD-A777-00DD01143C57"
         STYLE="TOP:11pt;LEFT:239pt;WIDTH:45pt;HEIGHT:20pt;
               TABINDEX:9;ZINDEX:6;">
      <PARAM NAME="Caption" VALUE="Query">
   </OBJECT>
```

```
            <OBJECT ID="Order"
             CLASSID="CLSID:D7053240-CE69-11CD-A777-00DD01143C57"
                    STYLE="TOP:11pt;LEFT:284pt;WIDTH:45pt;HEIGHT:20pt;
                          TABINDEX:11;ZINDEX:7;">
                <PARAM NAME="Caption" VALUE="Order">
            </OBJECT>

            <OBJECT ID="Material"
             CLASSID="CLSID:978C9E23-D4B0-11CE-BF2D-00AA003F40D0"
                    STYLE="TOP:176pt;LEFT:194pt;WIDTH:137pt;HEIGHT:14pt;
                          ZINDEX:8;">
            </OBJECT>

            <OBJECT ID="Eyesize"
             CLASSID="CLSID:978C9E23-D4B0-11CE-BF2D-00AA003F40D0"
                    STYLE="TOP:139pt;LEFT:194pt;WIDTH:137pt;HEIGHT:14pt;
                          ZINDEX:9;">
            </OBJECT>

            <OBJECT ID="Manufacturer"
             CLASSID="CLSID:978C9E23-D4B0-11CE-BF2D-00AA003F40D0"
                    STYLE="TOP:101pt;LEFT:194pt;WIDTH:137pt;HEIGHT:14pt;
                          ZINDEX:10;">
            </OBJECT>

            <OBJECT ID="Name"
             CLASSID="CLSID:978C9E23-D4B0-11CE-BF2D-00AA003F40D0"
                    STYLE="TOP:63pt;LEFT:194pt;WIDTH:137pt;HEIGHT:14pt;
                          ZINDEX:11;">
            </OBJECT>

            <OBJECT ID="Browse"
             CLASSID="CLSID:D7053240-CE69-11CD-A777-00DD01143C57"
                    STYLE="TOP:11pt;LEFT:194pt;WIDTH:45pt;HEIGHT:20pt;
                          TABINDEX:13;ZINDEX:12;">
                <PARAM NAME="Caption" VALUE="Browse">
            </OBJECT>

            <OBJECT ID="Price"
             CLASSID="CLSID:978C9E23-D4B0-11CE-BF2D-00AA003F40D0"
                    STYLE="TOP:214pt;LEFT:194pt;WIDTH:137pt;HEIGHT:14pt;
                          ZINDEX:13;">
            </OBJECT>

            <OBJECT ID="Frames"
             CLASSID="CLSID:8BD21D20-EC42-11CE-9E0D-00AA006002F3"
                    STYLE="TOP:47pt;LEFT:88pt;WIDTH:97pt;HEIGHT:184pt;
                          TABINDEX:0;ZINDEX:15;">
            </OBJECT>
        </DIV>
```

LISTING 11.3 THE QUERY.ALX (HTML LAYOUT) FILE.

```vbscript
<SCRIPT LANGUAGE="VBScript">
<!--

Sub Order_Click()
   ' Show the Order window and hide the Query window
   Window.Query_alx.Height = 0
   Window.Query_alx.Width = 0
   Window.Order_alx.Height = 253
   Window.Order_alx.Width = 335
End Sub

Sub Browse_Click()
   ' Show the Browse window and hide the Query window
   Window.Query_alx.Height = 0
   Window.Query_alx.Width = 0
   Window.Browse_alx.Height = 253
   Window.Browse_alx.Width = 335
End Sub

Sub EyesizeSpin_SpinDown()
   ' Decrease the eyesize by 2
   if EyesizeSpin.Value - 1 >= EyesizeSpin.Min Then
      EyesizeSpin.Value = EyesizeSpin.Value - 1
   End If
   Eyesize.Caption = EyesizeSpin.Value
End Sub

Sub EyesizeSpin_SpinUp()
   ' Increase the eyesize by 2
   If EyesizeSpin.Value + 1 <= EyesizeSpin.Max Then
      EyesizeSpin.Value = EyesizeSpin.Value + 1
   End If
      Eyesize.Caption = EyesizeSpin.Value
   End Sub

Sub FindManufacturer_Click()
   ' Query for the specified manufacturer
   Call window.document.DAODriver.findManufacturer(
                             Manufacturer.Value, Results)
End Sub

Sub FindMaterial_Click()
   ' Query for the specified material
   Call window.document.DAODriver.findMaterial(
                             Plastic.Value, Results)
End Sub
```

```
Sub FindEyesize_Click()
   ' Query for the specified eyesize
   Call window.document.DAODriver.findEyesize(
                                EyesizeSpin.Value, Results)
End Sub

Sub FindPrice_Click()
   ' Query for the specified price
   Call window.document.DAODriver.findPrice(
                                Price.Value, Results)
End Sub

Sub ShowResult_Click()

  ' Show the selected queried item in the Browse window...

   If Results.Text <> "(none)" Then
      Window.Query_alx.Height = 0
      Window.Query_alx.Width = 0
      Window.Browse_alx.Height = 253
      Window.Browse_alx.Width = 335

      Browse_alx.Frames.Value = Results.Text

      Call window.document.DAODriver.updateBrowseWindow(
                        Browse_alx.Item("Frames"),
                        Browse_alx.Item("Name"),
                        Browse_alx.Item("Manufacturer"),
                        Browse_alx.Item("Eyesize"),
                        Browse_alx.Item("Material"),
                        Browse_alx.Item("Price"))
      Call window.document.DAODriver.updateOrderWindow(
              Browse_alx.Item("Frames"), Order_alx.Item("Frame"))
   End If
End Sub

Sub OrderResult_Click()

  ' Show the selected queried item in the Order window...

   If Results.Text <> "(none)" Then
      Window.Query_alx.Height = 0
      Window.Query_alx.Width = 0
      Window.Order_alx.Height = 253
      Window.Order_alx.Width = 335

      Browse_alx.Frames.Value = Results.Text

      Call window.document.DAODriver.updateBrowseWindow(
```

```
                                    Browse_alx.Item("Frames"),
                                    Browse_alx.Item("Name"),
                                    Browse_alx.Item("Manufacturer"),
                                    Browse_alx.Item("Eyesize"),
                                    Browse_alx.Item("Material"),
                                    Browse_alx.Item("Price"))

        Call window.document.DAODriver.updateOrderWindow(
                Browse_alx.Item("Frames"), Order_alx.Item("Frame"))
    End If
End Sub

-->
</SCRIPT>

<DIV BACKGROUND="#733173" ID="HarmonOptical"
            STYLE="LAYOUT:FIXED;WIDTH:335pt;HEIGHT:253pt;">

    <OBJECT ID="Query"
     CLASSID="CLSID:D7053240-CE69-11CD-A777-00DD01143C57"
            STYLE="TOP:11pt;LEFT:239pt;WIDTH:45pt;HEIGHT:20pt;
                    TABINDEX:17;ZINDEX:2;">
        <PARAM NAME="Caption" VALUE="Query">
    </OBJECT>

    <OBJECT ID="Order"
     CLASSID="CLSID:D7053240-CE69-11CD-A777-00DD01143C57"
            STYLE="TOP:11pt;LEFT:284pt;WIDTH:45pt;HEIGHT:20pt;
                    TABINDEX:19;ZINDEX:3;">
        <PARAM NAME="Caption" VALUE="Order">
    </OBJECT>
    <OBJECT ID="Browse"
     CLASSID="CLSID:D7053240-CE69-11CD-A777-00DD01143C57"
            STYLE="TOP:11pt;LEFT:194pt;WIDTH:45pt;HEIGHT:20pt;
                    TABINDEX:21;ZINDEX:4;">
        <PARAM NAME="Caption" VALUE="Browse">
    </OBJECT>

    <OBJECT ID="Manufacturer"
     CLASSID="CLSID:8BD21D10-EC42-11CE-9E0D-00AA006002F3"
            STYLE="TOP:56pt;LEFT:90pt;WIDTH:200pt;HEIGHT:18pt;
                    TABINDEX:0;ZINDEX:9;">
    </OBJECT>

    <OBJECT ID="FindManufacturer"
     CLASSID="CLSID:D7053240-CE69-11CD-A777-00DD01143C57"
            STYLE="TOP:56pt;LEFT:297pt;WIDTH:32pt;HEIGHT:18pt;
                    TABINDEX:1;ZINDEX:10;">
        <PARAM NAME="Caption" VALUE="Find">
```

```
        </OBJECT>

        <OBJECT ID="Plastic"
         CLASSID="CLSID:8BD21D50-EC42-11CE-9E0D-00AA006002F3"
                STYLE="TOP:99pt;LEFT:90pt;WIDTH:53pt;HEIGHT:18pt;
                       TABINDEX:2;ZINDEX:11;">
            <PARAM NAME="Value" VALUE="False">
            <PARAM NAME="Caption" VALUE="Plastic">
        </OBJECT>

        <OBJECT ID="Metal"
         CLASSID="CLSID:8BD21D50-EC42-11CE-9E0D-00AA006002F3"
                STYLE="TOP:99pt;LEFT:149pt;WIDTH:53pt;HEIGHT:18pt;
                       TABINDEX:3;ZINDEX:12;">
            <PARAM NAME="Value" VALUE="False">
            <PARAM NAME="Caption" VALUE="Metal">
        </OBJECT>

        <OBJECT ID="FindMaterial"
         CLASSID="CLSID:D7053240-CE69-11CD-A777-00DD01143C57"
                STYLE="TOP:99pt;LEFT:297pt;WIDTH:32pt;HEIGHT:18pt;
                       TABINDEX:4;ZINDEX:13;">
            <PARAM NAME="Caption" VALUE="Find">
        </OBJECT>
        <OBJECT ID="EyesizeSpin"
         CLASSID="CLSID:79176FB0-B7F2-11CE-97EF-00AA006D2776"
                STYLE="TOP:137pt;LEFT:90pt;WIDTH:11pt;HEIGHT:18pt;
                       TABINDEX:5;ZINDEX:14;">
        </OBJECT>

        <OBJECT ID="Eyesize"
         CLASSID="CLSID:978C9E23-D4B0-11CE-BF2D-00AA003F40D0"
                STYLE="TOP:142pt;LEFT:106pt;WIDTH:72pt;HEIGHT:14pt;
                       ZINDEX:15;">
        </OBJECT>

        <OBJECT ID="Price"
         CLASSID="CLSID:8BD21D10-EC42-11CE-9E0D-00AA006002F3"
                STYLE="TOP:178pt;LEFT:88pt;WIDTH:36pt;HEIGHT:18pt;
                       TABINDEX:7;ZINDEX:16;">
        </OBJECT>

        <OBJECT ID="Results"
         CLASSID="CLSID:8BD21D30-EC42-11CE-9E0D-00AA006002F3"
                STYLE="TOP:218pt;LEFT:88pt;WIDTH:164pt;HEIGHT:18pt;
                       TABINDEX:9;ZINDEX:17;">
        </OBJECT>

        <OBJECT ID="FindEyesize"
```

```
            CLASSID="CLSID:D7053240-CE69-11CD-A777-00DD01143C57"
                STYLE="TOP:137pt;LEFT:297pt;WIDTH:32pt;HEIGHT:18pt;
                    TABINDEX:6;ZINDEX:18;">
            <PARAM NAME="Caption" VALUE="Find">
        </OBJECT>

        <OBJECT ID="Label5"
          CLASSID="CLSID:978C9E23-D4B0-11CE-BF2D-00AA003F40D0"
                STYLE="TOP:182pt;LEFT:128pt;WIDTH:72pt;HEIGHT:14pt;
                    ZINDEX:19;">
            <PARAM NAME="Caption" VALUE="US dollars">
        </OBJECT>

        <OBJECT ID="FindPrice"
          CLASSID="CLSID:D7053240-CE69-11CD-A777-00DD01143C57"
                STYLE="TOP:178pt;LEFT:297pt;WIDTH:32pt;HEIGHT:18pt;
                    TABINDEX:8;ZINDEX:20;">
            <PARAM NAME="Caption" VALUE="Find">
        </OBJECT>

        <OBJECT ID="ShowResult"
          CLASSID="CLSID:D7053240-CE69-11CD-A777-00DD01143C57"
                STYLE="TOP:218pt;LEFT:297pt;WIDTH:32pt;HEIGHT:18pt;
                    TABINDEX:11;ZINDEX:21;">
            <PARAM NAME="Caption" VALUE="Show">
        </OBJECT>

        <OBJECT ID="Label6"
          CLASSID="CLSID:978C9E23-D4B0-11CE-BF2D-00AA003F40D0"
                STYLE="TOP:205pt;LEFT:88pt;WIDTH:232pt;HEIGHT:11pt;
                    ZINDEX:22;">
            <PARAM NAME="Caption" VALUE="Results:">
        </OBJECT>

        <OBJECT ID="OrderResult"
          CLASSID="CLSID:D7053240-CE69-11CD-A777-00DD01143C57"
                STYLE="TOP:218pt;LEFT:259pt;WIDTH:32pt;HEIGHT:18pt;
                    TABINDEX:10;ZINDEX:23;">
            <PARAM NAME="Caption" VALUE="Order">
        </OBJECT>
</DIV>
```

Listing 11.4 The Order.alx (HTML Layout) file.

```
<SCRIPT LANGUAGE="VBScript">
<!--

Sub Browse_Click()
    ' Show the Browse window and hide the Order window
```

```
        Window.Order_alx.Height = 0
        Window.Order_alx.Width = 0
        Window.Browse_alx.Height = 253
        Window.Browse_alx.Width = 335
    End Sub

    Sub Query_Click()
        ' Show the Query window and hide the Order window
        Window.Order_alx.Height = 0
        Window.Order_alx.Width = 0
        Window.Query_alx.Height = 253
        Window.Query_alx.Width = 335
    end sub

    Sub QuantitySpin_Change()
        ' Update the Quantity field with the new quantity value
        Quantity.Caption = QuantitySpin.Value
    End Sub

    Sub Submit_Click()

        ' Verify that all fields are filled, then add them
        ' to the database

        If Name.Value = "" Or
           Address.Value = ""
           Or Phone.Value = "" Then
           MsgBox("Please complete all fields before submitting an order.")
        Else
           Call window.document.DAODriver.submitOrder(
                                            Frame.Caption,
                                            Quantity.Caption,
                                            Name.Value,
                                            Address.Value,
                                            Phone.Value)

           MsgBox("Thank you for your order.")
        End If
    End Sub

-->
</SCRIPT>

<DIV BACKGROUND="#733173" ID="HarmonOptical"
            STYLE="LAYOUT:FIXED;WIDTH:335pt;HEIGHT:253pt;">

    <OBJECT ID="Query"
      CLASSID="CLSID:D7053240-CE69-11CD-A777-00DD01143C57"
            STYLE="TOP:11pt;LEFT:239pt;WIDTH:45pt;HEIGHT:20pt;
```

```
                    TABINDEX:12;ZINDEX:2;">
    <PARAM NAME="Caption" VALUE="Query">
</OBJECT>

<OBJECT ID="Order"
 CLASSID="CLSID:D7053240-CE69-11CD-A777-00DD01143C57"
        STYLE="TOP:11pt;LEFT:284pt;WIDTH:45pt;HEIGHT:20pt;
                TABINDEX:13;ZINDEX:3;">
    <PARAM NAME="Caption" VALUE="Order">
</OBJECT>

<OBJECT ID="Browse"
 CLASSID="CLSID:D7053240-CE69-11CD-A777-00DD01143C57"
        STYLE="TOP:11pt;LEFT:194pt;WIDTH:45pt;HEIGHT:20pt;
                TABINDEX:14;ZINDEX:4;">
    <PARAM NAME="Caption" VALUE="Browse">
</OBJECT>

<OBJECT ID="Frame"
 CLASSID="CLSID:978C9E23-D4B0-11CE-BF2D-00AA003F40D0"
        STYLE="TOP:59pt;LEFT:90pt;WIDTH:239pt;HEIGHT:14pt;
                ZINDEX:6;">
</OBJECT>

<OBJECT ID="QuantitySpin"
 CLASSID="CLSID:79176FB0-B7F2-11CE-97EF-00AA006D2776"
        STYLE="TOP:97pt;LEFT:90pt;WIDTH:11pt;HEIGHT:18pt;
                TABINDEX:0;ZINDEX:7;">
</OBJECT>

<OBJECT ID="Quantity"
 CLASSID="CLSID:978C9E23-D4B0-11CE-BF2D-00AA003F40D0"
        STYLE="TOP:99pt;LEFT:106pt;WIDTH:72pt;HEIGHT:14pt;
                ZINDEX:8;">
</OBJECT>

<OBJECT ID="Name"
 CLASSID="CLSID:8BD21D10-EC42-11CE-9E0D-00AA006002F3"
        STYLE="TOP:140pt;LEFT:90pt;WIDTH:239pt;HEIGHT:18pt;
                TABINDEX:1;ZINDEX:10;">
</OBJECT>

<OBJECT ID="Address"
 CLASSID="CLSID:8BD21D10-EC42-11CE-9E0D-00AA006002F3"
        STYLE="TOP:180pt;LEFT:90pt;WIDTH:131pt;HEIGHT:65pt;
                TABINDEX:2;ZINDEX:12;">
</OBJECT>

<OBJECT ID="Submit"
```

```
            CLASSID="CLSID:D7053240-CE69-11CD-A777-00DD01143C57"
                    STYLE="TOP:207pt;LEFT:230pt;WIDTH:99pt;HEIGHT:38pt;
                           TABINDEX:4;ZINDEX:14;">
        </OBJECT>

        <OBJECT ID="Phone"
         CLASSID="CLSID:8BD21D10-EC42-11CE-9E0D-00AA006002F3"
                    STYLE="TOP:180pt;LEFT:230pt;WIDTH:99pt;HEIGHT:18pt;
                           TABINDEX:3;ZINDEX:16;">
        </OBJECT>
</DIV>
```

LISTING 11.5 THE DAODRIVER.JAVA FILE.

```java
import java.applet.*;
import java.awt.*;
import dao3032.*;
import com.ms.com.*;
import fm20.*;

public class DAODriver extends Applet
{
   private Recordset m_recordset;
   private Database m_database;

   private static String strDatabaseName =
                                          "Harmon Optical.mdb";

   public void init()
   {
      resize(0, 0);
   }

   public void start()
   {
      // Start the DAO database engine...

      ILicenseMgr mgr = new LicenseMgr();

      _DBEngine daoEngine = (_DBEngine) mgr.createWithLic(
         "mjgcqcejfchcijecpdhckcdjqigdejfccjri",
         "{00025E15-0000-0000-C000-000000000046}",
         null,
         ComContext.INPROC_SERVER);

      // Obtain the database filename relative
      // to the current path...

      String strFilename;
```

```java
    try
    {
        java.net.URL urlFilename;
        urlFilename = new java.net.URL(getDocumentBase(),
                                      strDatabaseName);
        strFilename = urlFilename.getFile().substring(1);
    }
    catch(Exception e)
    {
        showStatus("Error: " + e.getMessage());
    }

    // Open the database...

    Variant varExclusive = new Variant();
    Variant varReadOnly = new Variant();
    Variant varSource = new Variant();

    varExclusive.putBoolean(false);
    varReadOnly.putBoolean(false);
    varSource.putString("");

    m_database = daoEngine.OpenDatabase(
            strFilename, varExclusive, varReadOnly, varSource);

    // Open the Frames table...

    Variant varType = new Variant();
    Variant varOptions = new Variant();

    varType.putShort(Constants.dbOpenDynaset);
    varOptions.putShort(Constants.dbReadOnly);

    m_recordset = m_database.OpenRecordset(
                            "Frames", varType, varOptions);
}

public void stop()
{
    m_recordset.Close();
}

// Obtains the names of all frames in the Frames table and
// adds them to the Browse list box.
public void fillBrowseList(Object fmList)
{
    IMdcList listFrames = (IMdcList) fmList;
```

```
        m_recordset.MoveFirst();

        // Iterate through each record in the table...

        for (int i = 0; i < m_recordset.getRecordCount(); i++)
        {
            Fields fieldList = m_recordset.getFields();
            _Field field;
            Variant varFieldValue;
            Variant varFieldName = new Variant();

            // Get the name of the frame from the Name field...

            varFieldName.putString("Name");
            field = fieldList.getItem(varFieldName);

            varFieldValue = field.getValue();

            // Add the name to the list box...

            Variant varListItem = new Variant();
            Variant varListIndex = new Variant();

            varListItem.putString(varFieldValue.toString());
            varListIndex.putInt(listFrames.getListCount());

            listFrames.AddItem(varListItem, varListIndex);

            m_recordset.MoveNext();
        }
    }
    // Obtains the current item from the Browse list box,
    // uses the name to get its data from the Frames table,
    // then updates the fields in the Browse window with
    // this data.
    public void updateBrowseWindow(Object fmList,
                                   Object fmName,
                                   Object fmManufacturer,
                                   Object fmEyesize,
                                   Object fmMaterial,
                                   Object fmPrice)
    {
        ILabelControl labelName = (ILabelControl) fmName;
        ILabelControl labelManufacturer =
                                (ILabelControl) fmManufacturer;
        ILabelControl labelEyesize = (ILabelControl) fmEyesize;
        ILabelControl labelMaterial = (ILabelControl) fmMaterial;
        ILabelControl labelPrice = (ILabelControl) fmPrice;
        IMdcList listFrames = (IMdcList) fmList;
```

```
// Get the current frame name from the list box...

Variant varListItem = listFrames.getValue();

// If there is no item selected, don't do anything...

if (varListItem.getvt() != Variant.VariantString)
   return;

String strFrame = varListItem.toString();

// Find the record in the database that
// matches the name...

m_recordset.FindFirst("Name = '" + strFrame + "'");

Fields fieldList = m_recordset.getFields();
_Field field;
Variant varFieldValue;
Variant varFieldName = new Variant();

// Get the Name field...

varFieldName.putString("Name");
field = fieldList.getItem(varFieldName);

varFieldValue = field.getValue();
labelName.putCaption(varFieldValue.toString());

// Get the Manufacturer field...
varFieldName.putString("Manufacturer");
field = fieldList.getItem(varFieldName);

varFieldValue = field.getValue();
labelManufacturer.putCaption(varFieldValue.toString());

// Get the Eyesize field...

varFieldName.putString("Eyesize");
field = fieldList.getItem(varFieldName);
varFieldValue = field.getValue();
labelEyesize.putCaption(varFieldValue.toString());

// Get the Plastic field...

varFieldName.putString("Plastic");
field = fieldList.getItem(varFieldName);
```

```
    varFieldValue = field.getValue();
    labelMaterial.putCaption(
            varFieldValue.getBoolean() ? "Plastic" : "Metal");

    // Get the Price field...

    varFieldName.putString("Price");
    field = fieldList.getItem(varFieldName);

    varFieldValue = field.getValue();
    labelPrice.putCaption("$" + varFieldValue.toString());
}

// Obtains the current frame from the Browse list box and
// changes the Order window to this name.
public void updateOrderWindow(Object fmList, Object fmName)
{
    ILabelControl labelName = (ILabelControl) fmName;
    IMdcList listFrames = (IMdcList) fmList;

    // Get the current frame name from the list box...

    Variant varListItem = listFrames.getValue();

    // If there is no item selected, don't do anything...

    if (varListItem.getvt() != Variant.VariantString)
        return;

    labelName.putCaption(varListItem.toString());
}
public void findManufacturer(String strManufacturer,
                            Object fmResults)
{
    findRecords("Manufacturer = '" + strManufacturer + "'",
            (IMdcCombo)fmResults);
}

public void findMaterial(boolean bPlastic, Object fmResults)
{
    findRecords("Plastic = " + (bPlastic ? "true" : "false"),
            (IMdcCombo)fmResults);
}

public void findEyesize(int nEyesize, Object fmResults)
{
    findRecords("Eyesize = " + nEyesize,
```

```
            (IMdcCombo)fmResults);
         }

         public void findPrice(String strPrice, Object fmResults)
         {
            findRecords("Price < " + strPrice, (IMdcCombo)fmResults);
         }

         // Finds all records in the Frames database that match
         // the search string and adds them to the Results list box.
         private void findRecords(String strSearch,
                                  IMdcCombo listResults)
         {
            listResults.Clear();

            // Find the first record in the database that matches
            // the search string...

            m_recordset.FindFirst(strSearch);

            // Iterate through each record until we can't find any
            // more that match the search string...

            boolean bRecordsFound = false;

            while ( m_recordset.getNoMatch() == false )
            {
               Fields fieldList = m_recordset.getFields();
               _Field field;
               Variant varFieldValue;
               Variant varFieldName = new Variant();

               // Get the Name field...
               varFieldName.putString("Name");
               field = fieldList.getItem(varFieldName);
               varFieldValue = field.getValue();

               // Add the name to the Results list box...

               Variant varListIndex = new Variant();
               varListIndex.putInt(listResults.getListCount());

               listResults.AddItem(varFieldValue, varListIndex);

               // Find the next record that matches
               // the search string...

               m_recordset.FindNext(strSearch);
```

Data Access Objects

```java
      bRecordsFound = true;
   }

   Variant varListIndex = new Variant();
   varListIndex.putInt(0);

   if (!bRecordsFound)
   {
      // Add an item that says "(none)" to the results...

      Variant varNone = new Variant();
      varNone.putString("(none)");

      listResults.AddItem(varNone, varListIndex);
   }

   // Set the current Results list box index
   // to the first item...

   listResults.putListIndex(varListIndex);
}

// Adds the given data to the Orders table
public void submitOrder(String strFrame,
                        String strQuantity,
                        String strName,
                        String strAddress,
                        String strPhone)
{
   // Open the Orders table for writing...

   Variant varType    = new Variant();
   Variant varOptions = new Variant();
   varType.putShort(dao3032.Constants.dbOpenDynaset);
   varOptions.putShort((short)0);

   Recordset m_recordsetAdd = m_database.OpenRecordset(
                              "Orders", varType, varOptions);

   // Add a new record...

   m_recordsetAdd.AddNew();

   Fields fieldList = m_recordsetAdd.getFields();
   _Field field;
   Variant varFieldValue = new Variant();
   Variant varFieldName = new Variant();

   // Set the Frame field...
```

```
varFieldName.putString("Frame");
field = fieldList.getItem(varFieldName);

varFieldValue.putString(strFrame);
field.putValue(varFieldValue);

// Set the Quantity field...

varFieldName.putString("Quantity");
field = fieldList.getItem(varFieldName);

varFieldValue.putInt(
                Integer.valueOf(strQuantity).intValue());
field.putValue(varFieldValue);

// Set the Name field...

varFieldName.putString("Name");
field = fieldList.getItem(varFieldName);

varFieldValue.putString(strName);
field.putValue(varFieldValue);

// Set the Address field...

varFieldName.putString("Address");
field = fieldList.getItem(varFieldName);

varFieldValue.putString(strAddress);
field.putValue(varFieldValue);

// Set the Phone field...
varFieldName.putString("Phone");
field = fieldList.getItem(varFieldName);

varFieldValue.putString(strPhone);
field.putValue(varFieldValue);
```

Chapter 12

- How to play in a sandbox
- The internals of Java security
- Code-signing and its benefits
- How to sign ActiveX controls
- How to sign Java applets

Security

Only one week after my arrival in Germany for a year of undergraduate study, I locked myself out of my dormitory at four in the morning. I spent the next three hours wandering the empty streets—nearly getting lost—and waiting at a bus stop for a bus that never came. Eventually, the Hausmeister opened the doors, and I sauntered, half-asleep, back to my room.

At the time, I cursed the very existence of locks and keys, wishing they had never been invented. I was ready to exchange peace of mind for a little extra freedom. But, of course, I know that security measures are a necessary inconvenience. Keys, locks, and strong oak doors keep the bad guys out and the good guys in. Less tangible—but just as solid—security methods, such as passwords, magnetic strips, and cryptography, protect sensitive data: bank codes, classified files, and credit card numbers.

As Internet commerce becomes a reality, more and more credit card numbers—not all of them encrypted—are zipping across fiber-optic cables and passing through alien computer systems. An unscrupulous eavesdropper needs just one number to turn a day of electronic sniffing into a week-long gold mine.

Credit card numbers are only part of the problem. With help from the Internet, computer viruses can replicate themselves across the globe, not just through diskettes as they have in the past. They can swipe sensitive data, disburse propaganda, or even bring entire computer systems to their knees. This new wired world could one day become a hive of villainy.

Thankfully, some companies—such as VeriSign, RSA Data Security, and Security Dynamics—are working hard to prevent such a catastrophe. They're concocting electronic vaccines and looking for new methods of ensuring security on the Internet. At present, the two most popular methods are:

- *Code-signing*—This stamps an electronic signature on computer programs. The signature tells you who created the program and how to contact them. If the software harms your computer in any way, you can hold the company accountable. You can warn other computer users of the dangerous software, and, with enough proof, you could even sue the company for damages.

- *Sandboxing*—This is an alternative to code-signing. It prevents accidents before they occur, shielding systems from harm. With sandboxed software, programs are unable to access files or perform other tasks that could endanger the security of your computer. It's like wearing a condom: You're not completely safe, but chances are good that viruses won't break through the barrier surrounding your sensitive equipment.

This chapter looks at both of these security methods and how they apply to Java and ActiveX.

Sandboxing

Sun Microsystems, in an intense effort to make Java a secure language, went a bit overboard. They hacked away at Java's C++ foundation and killed every possible feature that might threaten the safety of your computer. They abandoned such features as:

- *Pointers*—In C++, programmers can perform arithmetic on memory pointers and assign them to any value. For instance, a simple statement, such as **MyPointer = 0xAB124,** could give them direct access to the operating system. Recognizing this security threat, Sun removed pointers from Java entirely.

- *Direct array access*—Java programmers are not allowed to manipulate arrays directly. Instead, arrays are handled only through classes and their member functions. This security measure prevents access to out-of-bounds memory (and helps eliminate bugs).

- *Mutatable strings*—Strings in Java are immutable—that is, once assigned a value, they cannot be changed. This restrictive technique prevents runtime errors that could be exploited by hostile applets.

Sun took one more step in their crusade to liberate users from rogue programmers: They put Java applets in a sandbox.

How To Play In A Sandbox

Sandboxing is like saying, "I don't care who wrote this code because it can't do anything bad to my computer." No matter whose applet you download, it can't harm your system. The Java sandbox protects your computer and insulates your files.

In addition to preventing file access, sandboxing limits Java applets to their home server. They can't read files on other Web pages or Internet machines. At first, this approach may seem excessive. It bans potentially cool applets that use artificial intelligence to search the Internet for specific information. Also, most computer programs can't do anything really valuable unless they're able to input data from the file system.

Why Is Sandbox Security Important?

The importance of sandboxing becomes clear when you try to think like a criminal. What would you attack? Where would you find valuable information? Most criminals would conclude that a firewall—a system that prohibits access to private computer networks—is an excellent first choice. Once a firewall is broken, countless pages of sensitive data are available to anyone on the Internet.

Without sandboxing, Java applets could break through firewalls. A Web browser behind the wall could simply read an external Web page and bring a Java applet along for the ride. As shown in Figure 12.1, the applet could then scurry around the private network, gather information, and send the data back to its home server.

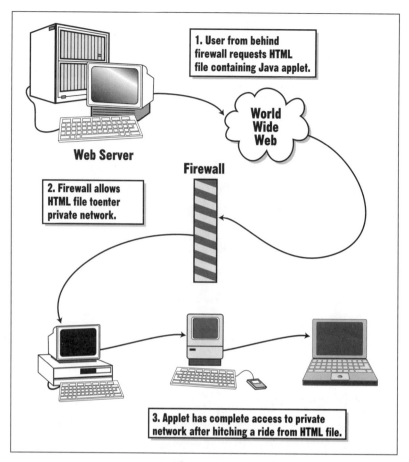

Figure 12.1 Without sandboxing, Java applets could break through firewalls.

Even though the Java sandbox is secure, it is not completely safe. Applets could still harm your computer just by hogging resources. These hostile programs, known officially as *denial-of-service applets*, could create one too many background threads, thereby exhausting your memory and possibly bringing down the entire system.

Still, sandboxing provides abundant security. You can feel certain that sandboxed applets from anyone, anywhere, will not violate your peace of mind.

Applets Vs. Applications

Sandboxing applies only to *applets*—Java code that you obtain through the Web. Another type of Java program, simply called a Java *application*, runs locally on your system. Because you install this program manually (as opposed to the automatic downloading of applets), the Java virtual machine assumes that you trust the program's author, and it allows the code to access files.

For example, to run the Java Lava Lamp from Chapter 3 as an applet (see Figure 12.2), you would choose Run from the Start menu and type:

```
LavaLamp.html
```

This command starts the Web browser and loads the applet, but it does not allow the code to read and write files. To run the Java code as a local application, you would type:

```
jview LavaLamp.class
```

This command starts Microsoft's Java interpreter and loads the application, allowing it to access files.

Standalone applications have a variety of privileges not available to applets. Table 12.1 provides a comparison of the basic differences between the two types of Java programs.

Applet Restrictions

Java's security model is strict. It says without ambiguity what your applet cannot do. The following sections describe the *cannots* in detail.

Access To Files On The Client

Applets have zero access to files on the client. They cannot:

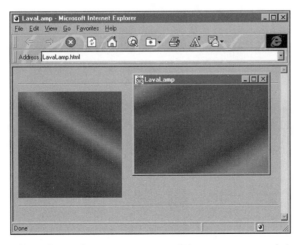

Figure 12.2 The Java Lava Lamp can run either as an applet or an application.

Table 12.1 Applets face harsher security restrictions than applications.

Feature	Applets	Applications
Read and write files on client	No	Yes
Read and write files on server	Yes	Yes
Delete files on client	No	Yes
Access native code	No	Yes
Create pop-up windows without warning	No	Yes
Jump the browser to another location	Yes	No
Connect to another location	No	Yes

- Check for the existence of a file
- Read a file
- Write a file
- Rename a file
- Determine the date or time stamp on a file
- Obtain a file's size
- Create a directory
- List the files in a directory

CONNECTING TO SERVERS

Applets cannot communicate with servers on the Internet. For example, trying to open a connection to **MyServer.com** by writing

```
Socket s = new Socket("MyServer.com", 25, true);
```

will fail with a security exception. Applets can, however, open a connection to the server from which they came. They can read and write files and start programs on their originating host (see the following section, "Applet Privileges").

NATIVE-CODE INTERFACE

Applets cannot load libraries or define native methods. They can use only their own Java code or code provided through the Java API. The API includes all classes defined in the **java.*** packages.

Reading System Properties

Applets can obtain information about their environment through *system properties*. By calling **System.getProperty("*key*")**, you can extract the value of any given key. Applets cannot read every system property, however. Table 12.2 contains a list of properties unreadable by applets.

See the following section, "Applet Privileges," for a list of properties that Java applets are allowed to access.

Displaying Windows

When an applet displays a window, the Java VM marks the window with warning text or a special color. This indicator helps users distinguish applet windows from trusted application windows. Figure 12.3 shows an applet window created under Microsoft's Windows VM.

Table 12.2 These system properties are unreadable by Java applets.

Key	Meaning
java.home	Java installation directory
java.class.path	Directory containing extra class files
user.name	User's account name
user.home	User's home directory
user.dir	User's current working directory

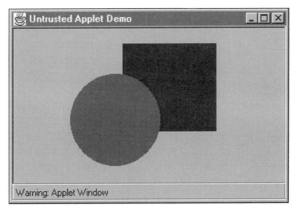

Figure 12.3 The VM warns users of untrusted applet windows.

Applet Privileges

Don't assume that applets are completely disabled. They have certain freedoms, carefully designed not to threaten the security of your system. The following sections describe what applets *can* do.

ACCESS TO FILES ON THE SERVER

Security restrictions on files do not apply to an applet's server. Listing 12.1 shows a Java code fragment that opens a file on the originating host.

LISTING 12.1   A JAVA CODE FRAGMENT THAT OPENS A FILE FOR READING.

```
import java.net.*;
import java.io.*;

    .
    .
    .

URL file;

try
{
   // Construct a pointer to the data file
   file = new URL(getDocumentBase(), "server_file.txt");
}
catch (MalformedURLException e)
{
   // Handle the exception...
}

try
{
   // Open the file for reading
   InputStream is = file.openStream();
   DataInputStream dis = new DataInputStream(is);

   // You can now read from file by calling methods of
   // the DataInputStream class (such as readByte).
}
catch (Exception e)
{
   // Handle the exception...
}
```

READING SYSTEM PROPERTIES

As described in the previous section, Java applets can obtain information about their environment by calling **System.getProperty("*key*")**. Table 12.3 provides a list of key values that are legal for applets.

BROWSER ENHANCEMENTS

Java applets are like little brothers and sisters. They get extra privileges by pandering to their parents. In Java, an applet's parent is the Web browser; it can display HTML documents and play sounds. Applets can access these features by importing the **java.applet.*** packages, which include the **AppletContext**, **AppletStub**, and **AudioClip** interfaces. See the Java documentation for information on calling these interfaces from your code.

The Internals Of Java Security

Security in Java comes from two sources: the compiler and the virtual machine. Both components put Java code under heavy scrutiny, running each line through a barrage of tests.

COMPILE-TIME CHECKS

As Visual J++ converts your Java source code to bytecode (i.e., from a source file to a class file), it performs certain security checks. It looks for operations that could be considered malicious, such as:

Table 12.3 These system properties are readable by Java applets.

Key	Meaning
java.version	Version number of the Java virtual machine
java.vendor	Manufacturer of the Java virtual machine
java.vendor.url	Location of VM manufacturer's Web page
java.class.version	Version number of the class file
os.name	Name of the operating system (e.g., "Windows 95")
os.arch	Architecture of the operating system (e.g., "x86")
file.separator	File separator (e.g., "\")
path.separator	Path separator (e.g., ";")
line.separator	Line separator (e.g., 0x0D0A)

- *Illegal type casts*—Java is a strongly typed language. Objects cannot be cast to a subclass without an explicit compile-time check. In addition, the compiler prevents casting of an object to Java's internal pointer type.

- *Illegal method invocation*—Before allowing code to call an object's method, the compiler checks that the object is of the correct type. For example, invoking **i.getInteger()** when **i** is not an **Integer** object produces a compile-time error.

- *Changing final variables*—When the **final** keyword (similar to the **const** keyword in C++) is used to initialize a variable, the value of that variable cannot be changed. The compiler prevents all attempts to modify **final** variables.

If the Java compiler finds any of these problems, it refuses to compile the source code.

Runtime Checks

The Java virtual machine includes a component called the *class loader*, which loads an applet into memory and prepares it for execution. This component ensures security by restricting the applet code to a unique, private area in memory. The VM uses only one class loader, established at start-up. It cannot be extended, overloaded, or replaced. Also, applets cannot reference the class loader or create a new one.

Another security component of the Java VM is the *bytecode verifier*. Before running an applet downloaded through the Web, this runtime system checks that the applet adheres to Java's language safety rules. The verifier is important because it can check bytecodes generated by any Java compiler, including rogue compilers that don't perform security checks when creating class files. The verifier ensures that the applet:

- Contains no stack overflows or underflows

- Accesses and stores registers properly

- Uses valid parameters for bytecode instructions

- Does not convert data illegally

Figure 12.4 shows the flow of bytecode through Java's security barriers.

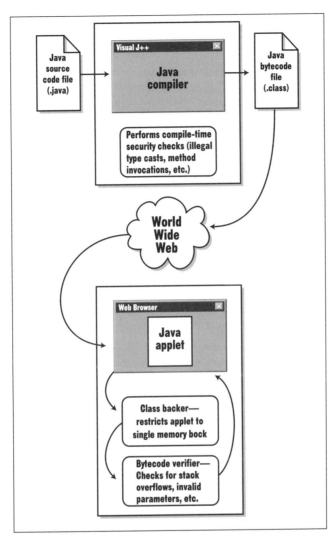

Figure 12.4 Java code must pass security tests before execution.

Java's Future Security

Almost a dozen computer scientists, working independently, have discovered holes in Java's security since its first release. Sun Microsystems fixed each problem immediately, and they distributed patches to all Java licensees. Because Java is still fairly new, more holes will probably be found in the coming months.

Some experts think that Java will always have security problems and will never be totally safe. They're correct, of course. No computer language can ever be 100-percent secure. Java is certainly safe enough, however. Its conservative measures come close to a true guarantee of security; and because the language is under such high scrutiny, few holes will go unnoticed.

As Sun continues to improve Java, they will expand the capabilities of applets—as long as those capabilities do not compromise security. Eventually, applets will be able to reach beyond today's Java sandbox. This expansion will most likely involve code-signing, a technique popularized by ActiveX controls, as explained in the following section.

Code-signing

My fingernails aren't very sharp. The simple task of opening packages is a momentous experience for me. Even the unassuming box of computer software, protected by an invisible shield of shrink-wrap, presents a major challenge. But I don't mind. Shrink-wrap is important, because it provides me with two guarantees:

- *Authenticity*—I know where the software came from, and I know who wrote it.

- *Integrity*—I know the software hasn't been tampered with since it was published.

On the Internet, these assurances don't exist. Software downloaded through the Web is dangerous: It doesn't have authenticity, and it doesn't have integrity. You simply can't send shrink-wrap through a modem.

Or can you? The technology of code-signing, which has been around for quite some time, offers the electronic equivalent of shrink-wrap. By stamping software with a digital signature, users can determine its author. They can also be certain that the code hasn't been tampered with since its original release. Code-signing gives software authenticity and integrity.

Why Is Code-signing Important?

As the Web enters a fourth dimension, software is becoming promiscuous. It loads directly into your system through an HTML file, often without your knowledge. You have no guarantee that this software is safe. It could be a virus or some other evil computer program.

With Java applets, lascivious code isn't a problem. The sandbox security model prevents the software from doing any harm—but it also prevents the software from doing anything truly useful. The Web demands a more practical method for distributing executable content.

Code-signing offers such a method. When a program is code-signed, it can access your files and any other information on your computer. It could even erase your entire hard drive. But because the code has a digital signature, you can hold its author accountable for any damage to your system. In other words, while code-signing does not prevent malicious code, it offers an excellent means to deter it.

As a developer, signing your code does not imply liability. It only proves to your customers that you are the author and that no one else has tampered with the code since it left your hands. Your liability comes from federal law, which prohibits the intentional distribution of malicious code.

How Code-signing Works

Code-signing doesn't copy-protect software, and doesn't make software bug-free or virus-free. It merely gives software an identity. This identity comes from a small chunk of data called a *certificate*, which is embedded directly into the software's executable code. It contains information about the publisher, such as the company's name, email address, and mailing address. When you have this certificate—a digital signature—you know that the software is what it claims to be.

CERTIFICATE AUTHORITIES

The inventors of code-signing knew that simply providing a certificate format would not make certificates secure. Anyone could forge a certificate just by running the signed code through a hex editor. For instance, I could write a disk-eating ActiveX control, certify it as coming from Microsoft, post it on the Web, and no one would be the wiser.

To prevent such forgery, software publishers cannot certify their own programs. They must obtain a certificate from a *certificate authority*, or CA. CAs are similar to notaries, but instead of handling signed contracts, they handle signed software. Any company can become a CA as long as it is trusted by the software industry and can provide the following services:

- Authenticating identities
- Providing, managing, and renewing certificates
- Publishing criteria for granting certificates
- Handling legal and liability issues for breaches of security

As soon as a company begins offering these services, it can begin granting certificates. Software publishers can go to the CA's Web site, provide the requested identity information, and download their certificates directly through the Internet.

ENSURING AUTHENTICITY

The process of granting certificates isn't quite as straightforward as I've described because it simply doesn't provide enough authenticity. For example, let's say I submit my credentials to a CA and receive my certificate. I could still change its identity information (illegally and unethically) to give the illusion that someone else signed my code.

To eliminate this problem, CAs encrypt their certificates. Here is how the encryption process works:

1. After the CA has verified a software publisher's identity, it encrypts the identity information using a *private key*. The private key is kept secret and secure so that no one but the CA itself can encrypt the CA's certificate.

2. The CA distributes a *public key*, which can decrypt their certificates, to makers of Web browsers and other software that needs to check for signed code.

3. To verify a certificate, the Web browser or other software tries to unlock it using the appropriate public key. If the public key successfully decrypts the certificate, then the certificate is valid. If it fails, the user is warned that the downloaded software contains an invalid certificate.

With this encryption process in place, distributors of software through the Web are no longer anonymous. They must take responsibility for harmful code just as they would take credit for good code. Like a brand name on packaged software, certificates give downloaded software authenticity.

In America, You Are Free...To Do As We Tell You

further developments

American software accounts for more than 70 percent of the global market, yet the federal government places severe restrictions on U.S. software exports. Under the International Traffic in Arms Regulations (ITAR), encryption software products that use keys larger than 40 bits—very small by today's standards—are considered munitions and cannot be shipped outside the U.S. or Canada.

This failed policy has been a thorn in the side of the software industry for many years. Not only is it unenforceable (free encryption software with

128-bit keys is available through the Internet to anyone in the world), but it is unwarranted (foreign software companies have built their own encryption algorithms using keys much longer than 40 bits). Despite the flaws in ITAR, it continues to allow foreign industries to fill the void left by Americans in the fast-growing encryption market.

You might wonder why the U.S. government is so interested in restricting encryption software. Does Big Brother want to listen in on our email conversations, or is this just another case of government being government, reminding you that you are free...to do as we tell you? Actually, the motives aren't that sinister. The government's fear is that, as powerful encryption becomes widespread, it won't be able to keep track of their money. Citizens will make encrypted transactions in secret, and the government will have no way of taxing them. Without taxes, the government—and the nation it supports—crumbles.

Fortunately, exporting signed code is not a problem. ITAR makes an exception for encrypted signatures, since they apply only to small amounts of data. Americans can freely export signed code anywhere in the world, and anyone in the world can obtain powerfully encrypted certificates (often with 512- or 1,024-bit keys) from America.

ENSURING INTEGRITY

Certificates are only part of the code-signing technology. Although they give programs *authenticity*, they do not give them *integrity*. Users have no way of knowing whether downloaded software has been tampered with. Unscrupulous hackers could swipe certificates or even reprogram the software so that it does something harmful.

Once again, the solution to the problem is encryption. Here is a summary of how public-key encryption ensures software integrity:

1. When the software publisher receives a certificate from a CA, a pair of keys is generated (the private key for encryption and the public key for decryption).

2. Ideally, the publisher would use the private key to encrypt the software. Because long chunks of code make public-key algorithms too inefficient, however, the publisher builds a small summary, or *digest*, of the program, as shown in Figure 12.5. (A digest is known technically as a *one-way hash*, which can take any code—no matter if it's two bytes or two gigabytes—and reduce it to a fixed length.) The digest, not the program itself, is then encrypted with the publisher's private key.

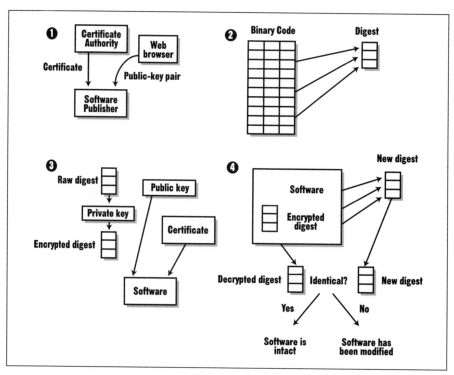

Figure 12.5 Encrypted digests ensure the software's integrity.

3. The publisher embeds the encrypted digest, the public key, and the certificate directly into the software. The software is distributed, but the private key remains safely and securely with the publisher.

4. When a Web browser or some other program downloads the code-signed software, it unlocks the digest using the embedded public key. It then creates a digest of the software on-the-fly and compares it to the decrypted digest. If the two digests match, then the code is intact. If not, the user is warned that the code has been tampered with.

This lengthy process is actually quite fast. Software publishers can produce a digest, encrypt it, and embed it in a program in only a few minutes. On the client side, Web browsers can produce a new digest, decrypt the original, and compare them in only a few seconds. These steps ensure that code-signed software has even more authenticity and integrity than shrink-wrapped, store-bought products.

Microsoft Authenticode

As Microsoft was inventing ActiveX controls, they realized that security would become a sticking point. They knew that controls would have complete access to their host and that the popularity of ActiveX would never take off unless Microsoft could provide better security. To address these issues, Microsoft created *Authenticode*, a technology founded on the principles of code-signing. Authenticode can stamp a digital, certified signature on any executable file, including ActiveX controls and Java applets.

Authenticode differs slightly from the traditional code-signing architecture. The following sections explain each difference and how it relates to you as a software developer.

COMMERCIAL CERTIFICATES VS. INDIVIDUAL CERTIFICATES

Code-signing is expensive: It requires several hundred dollars just to obtain the certificate and several hundred dollars more for adequate hardware protection of a private key. Hobbyists, college students, authors of freeware, and other individual software publishers can't afford the high cost of signing their code.

Microsoft, recognizing that the Internet thrives on these individual software publishers, didn't want the expense to exclude them from writing ActiveX controls. Thus, when designing Authenticode, Microsoft separated certificates into two types: *commercial* and *individual*.

Microsoft defines *commercial* publishers as any organization that sells software for profit. When applying for an Authenticode certificate, they must meet the following criteria:

- *Identity*—A representative of the organization must submit their name, address, and any other material that proves their identity.

- *Pledge*—Applicants must pledge that they will not knowingly distribute viruses or any other code that harms a user's computer or performs other malicious acts.

- *Dun & Bradstreet rating*—The organization applying for a certificate must have a rating with Dun & Bradstreet Financial Services (also known as a D-U-N-S number). This number proves that the company has released a financial statement and is still in business. If the organization does not already have a rating, it can apply for and receive one in about two weeks. D&B ratings are used because they are easy to obtain, even for international software publishers.

- *Private key protection*—Applicants must agree to store their private key on a dedicated hardware device, such as a magnetic stripe card, a plastic key with an embedded ROM chip, or a smart card. These devices cost anywhere from $150 for a PC Card device to $12,000 for a BBN SafeKeeper. The corporations can decide for themselves how much security they need.

After submitting credentials to a CA, commercial publishers can expect to receive their certificates in about one week. They can also expect to pay about $400 for the first year, and about $300 for annual certificate renewals. (One certificate can sign an unlimited number of programs.)

OPENING AUTHENTICODE'S TOOLBOX

Tools for signing code ship with every copy of Visual J++. To install them, run the setup program called CodeSignKit.exe, located in the Cab&Sign folder. You will need to run these tools after you receive an Authenticode certificate. For more details, see the section, "How To Sign ActiveX Controls," later in this chapter.

Microsoft defines *individual* publishers as any single software developer (not a company) or any nonprofit organization. When applying for an Authenticode certificate, they must meet the following criteria:

- *Identity*—Individuals submit their name, address, and any other material that proves their identity. CAs can usually handle this online by checking credentials with an independent consumer database.

- *Pledge*—Applicants must pledge that they will not knowingly distribute viruses or any other code that harms a user's computer or performs other malicious acts.

After submitting credentials to a CA, individual publishers can expect to receive their certificates in about 30 minutes. They can also expect to pay about $20 for the first year, and about $20 again for each annual renewal. Individuals can always upgrade to a commercial certificate by submitting the proper credentials and paying the higher fee.

Note: Don't confuse individual certificates with end-user certificates. End-user certificates (also called Class 1 certificates) allow people to sign their email and submit proof of identity to Web sites. They are not for publishing software.

Protecting Your Private Key

further developments

If you're an individual software publisher, you're not required to protect your private key with dedicated hardware. The CA simply recommends that you store the key on a floppy disk instead of your computer's hard disk. It is your responsibility to take any further steps necessary to safeguard your key.

Don't skimp on this responsibility. Anyone who obtains your private key can forge your digital signature and impersonate you. You could lose your reputation and face legal repercussions.

If you decide not to purchase security hardware for your private key, you can still give it adequate protection. Just use common sense: Put it in a secure place (such as a safety deposit box); bring it out only when necessary; and don't let anyone but you and the people you trust have access to it.

For an extra measure of protection, you should lock the key with standard encryption algorithms that use passwords instead of public keys. That way, even if someone steals the key, the thief won't be able to use it without the password. Make sure that the password is long and unusual so that brute-force searches (such as going through a dictionary) won't reveal it. Also, make it easy to remember and difficult to guess, but don't make it identical to any password that you've ever chosen.

For more information on choosing and protecting passwords, point your Web browser to **csrc.nist.gov/fips/fip112-1.wp**.

LOCAL REGISTRATION AGENCIES

The Authenticode specification makes an allowance for companies that are in a good position to authenticate identities, but don't wish to handle the liability issues of granting certificates. A university, for example, may want to provide students with digital IDs. Rather than investing money in an Authenticode certificate system, the university could simply verify the students' identities and pass the rest of the work to a private CA.

In this case, the university is a *local registration agency* (LRA). LRAs view enrollment requests, verify evidence, and transfer approved requests to the signing CA. The relationship among different CAs and LRAs may vary, but it is always specified in a binding contract.

THE UMBRELLA ORGANIZATION

Over time, Microsoft expects to establish an umbrella organization (see Figure 12.6) that will define the policies that Authenticode CAs must follow, as well as policies for commercial and individual software publishers. Such a group may consist of a consortium of industry partners, or it may become an independent organization, similar to the Software Publishers Association or the World Wide Web Consortium.

EXPIRED AND REVOKED CERTIFICATES

For added security, all Authenticode certificates are stamped with a *period of validity*: two dates between which the certificate is valid. Publishers cannot sign code with an expired certificate. This safety measure helps weed out compromised certificates. (Note that the period of validity applies to the *certificate*, not the *software*. Code-signed software can still be used even after the certificate has expired. The expiration date is checked only when signing new code.)

Another Authenticode security tactic is for CAs to maintain a list of revoked certificates, similar to a stolen credit card list. Whenever you discover (or even suspect) that your private key or certificate has been stolen or compromised, you should add your key to this list immediately. You must then re-sign and redistribute your software.

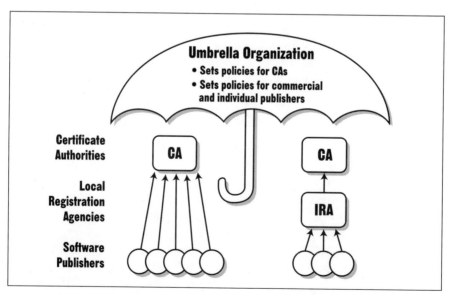

Figure 12.6 The umbrella organization will sit at the top of the Authenticode infrastructure.

Web surfers can freely check revoked certificate lists to make sure the software they download doesn't contain a revoked certificate. Microsoft and their Authenticode partners are investigating methods to allow Web browsers to check all lists automatically.

PORTABILITY: NOT A PROBLEM

Although Authenticode works with only the Windows 95 and Windows NT operating systems at the moment, it is designed for multiple platforms. Authenticode requires that signed code conforms to the *Portable Executable* (PE) format, and because PE files can run on any platform, Authenticode is portable. Microsoft will soon make it available to Windows 3.1, Macintosh, and Unix users.

Microsoft has also submitted a code-signing proposal, based on Authenticode, to the World Wide Web Consortium. If the proposal is accepted, Authenticode will become an open industry standard. Regardless of how the consortium handles Microsoft's submission, Netscape, JavaSoft, and more than 40 independent software vendors have pledged to support code-signing (though not necessarily Microsoft's standard).

INSTALLATION OF CERTIFICATES

Verification of Authenticode certificates happens only once: at install time. When a Web browser hits a page with a signed program, it checks for its embedded certificate. If the certificate is valid, the program is downloaded to the user's machine and is forever considered trusted. The certificate is never checked again, even if the user visits another page containing the same control. (The browser does, however, recheck the certificate when downloading a new version of the program.)

As of this writing, Internet Explorer is the only software capable of recognizing Authenticode certificates. The browser contains three settings (see Figure 12.7) for handling programs signed with Authenticode: High, Medium, and None.

On the High setting, IE never downloads unsigned code. When it discovers an unsigned program, it presents the user with the message box in Figure 12.8 and simply does not display the active content. Because High is the default setting, signing your code is extremely important if you want to distribute it.

Figure 12.7 The Safety Level dialog box, available from the Security Options tab, controls how Internet Explorer handles Authenticode certificates.

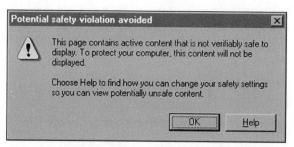

Figure 12.8 On the High setting, Internet Explorer displays this message when it discovers unsigned code.

If, on the other hand, the code has been signed, Internet Explorer calls the **WinVerifyTrust()** API function, which decrypts the certificate and displays a dialog box similar to the one in Figure 12.9. The certificate distinguishes between commercial certificates and the less-secure individual certificates, allowing the user to decide whether to download the program.

On the Medium setting, Internet Explorer downloads unsigned code only if the user allows it. To ask permission, IE displays the dialog box in Figure 12.10.

If the user decides to download the program anyway, IE then checks the Web page to see if an HTML script accesses the control. If the page contains a script *and* the control has not been marked as "safe for script-

Figure 12.9 Internet Explorer displays a dialog box similar to this one when it discovers signed code.

Figure 12.10 On the Medium setting, Internet Explorer asks permission to download unsigned code.

ing," the dialog box in Figure 12.11 appears. The Web page continues to load only if the user clicks Yes or Yes to All. (To learn how to mark an ActiveX control as safe for scripting, see the section "Marking Controls As Safe" later in this chapter.)

On the None setting, IE always downloads and runs active content, both signed and unsigned.

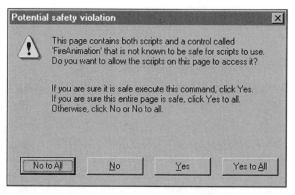

Figure 12.11 Even if a control has been code-signed, Internet Explorer warns the user if a script accesses it.

How To Sign ActiveX Controls

Now that you know the details of code-signing, you can fetch your Authenticode certificate. This section provides a step-by-step walkthrough of how to obtain a certificate and how to sign ActiveX controls using the tools in Visual J++.

Obtaining A Certificate From VeriSign

As of this writing, the only Authenticode CA is VeriSign Inc. Another CA, GTE, will begin providing Authenticode services within the next few months. More companies will likely follow VeriSign's and GTE's leads as ActiveX and code-signing become more popular.

Until then, your choice for Authenticode certificates will have to be VeriSign. It offers both the individual and commercial types of certificates, but refers to them as Class 2 and Class 3 certificates, respectively.

Class 2 Certificates

If you are an individual software publisher and want to obtain an Authenticode certificate, use IE to visit **digitalid.verisign.com**. Follow the prompts until you get to a page that looks like Figure 12.12. (Note: At this time, VeriSign offers Class 2 certificates only to residents of the U.S. and Canada. If you are located elsewhere, you must either obtain a Class 3 certificate or wait until VeriSign begins offering international Class 2 services.)

Before clicking on the Class 2 icon, be prepared to submit the following information:

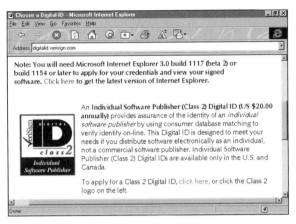

Figure 12.12 The VeriSign Web site allows you to choose between a Class 2 or a Class 3 certificate.

- Your name, address, phone number, email address, and date of birth
- Your previous address if you have moved in the past two years
- Your social security number and (if applicable) your driver's license number
- Your credit card number for paying the $20 fee

When you're ready, click the Class 2 icon. A form will ask you to submit your identity information (see Figure 12.13).

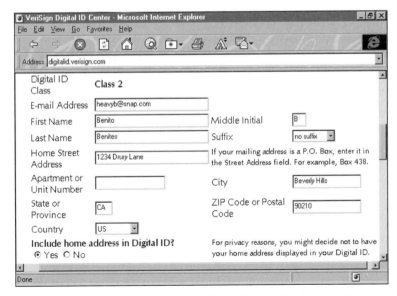

Figure 12.13 You can submit your identity information to VeriSign using an HTML form.

Security **357**

DON'T FORGET TO EXPAND!

My Class 2 application at VeriSign's Web site required six weeks, a half-dozen international phone calls, and three senior engineers. Eventually, the lead product manager at VeriSign tracked down the problem. My mistake? I had typed "St. Louis" instead of "Saint Louis" when entering my previous address into the form. When you're up to bat, remember to type the information exactly and to expand all abbreviations.

When you have entered the requested information into the form, continue with the next page. You will be asked for your credit card information and billing address. On the page after that, VeriSign will display all of the data you have provided. Make absolutely sure that all the information is correct before continuing.

The next page (see Figure 12.14) is the most important. Read it carefully, because this is where you pledge that any software you sign is not harmful or malicious and that VeriSign is not responsible for misuse of your certificate.

After all those steps, you're still not ready to receive your certificate. You must now submit your identity information, generate your private key, and allow VeriSign to run a background check on you. First, click on the Submit button, which transfers your information to VeriSign. While they're processing your data, their Web page installs on your machine a Microsoft-built ActiveX control called the Credentials Enrollment Wiz-

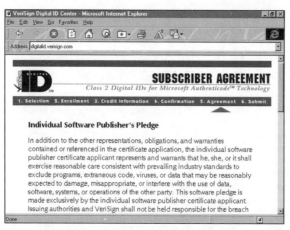

Figure 12.14 Before receiving your Class 2 certificate, you must accept the Individual Software Publisher's Pledge.

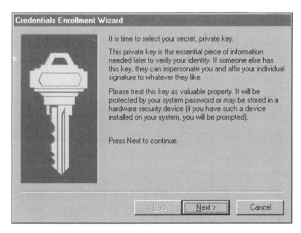

Figure 12.15 The Credentials Enrollment Wizard generates your private key.

ard (see Figure 12.15). This wizard generates the private key you will use to sign ActiveX controls (and any other signable programs).

After the wizard generates your private key and saves it to a floppy disk, you will return to the VeriSign Web site. Cross your fingers; this is the moment you've been waiting for: If your identity information checks out, you will see the page shown in Figure 12.16. Yes! Your Authenticode certificate is on its way. All you have to do now is check your email box in about 20 minutes, return to VeriSign's Web site, and enter the PIN you received. You can then download your certificate and skip to this chapter's next section, "Running The Authenticode Utilities."

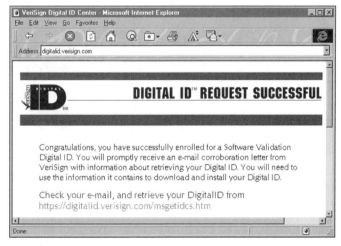

Figure 12.16 If your certificate enrollment is successful, VeriSign will present you with this Web page.

Security **359**

Error Codes Are "Veri" Bad

During my Class 2 certificate enrollment, I couldn't get past the dreaded "Status Code: 3009". This error indicates that the information I submitted does not match the information VeriSign obtained from an Equifax database. To fix this problem, I first started the enrollment process from scratch and made sure that all of the information I entered was accurate and complete. I still got the 3009 error, so I called Equifax's automated system at 770-612-3200 and requested a credit report. I received one in about two weeks and used it for double-checking the data I was entering. Unfortunately, that still didn't help. I was finally able to track down a number to the Equifax headquarters in Atlanta (404-885-8000). I called this number and gave the Equifax representative my current address (also called a verified address) and my previous address, since I had moved within the last two years. I learned that their information was the reverse of what it should be. If you receive that nasty 3009 error, follow the steps I took, and you should be able to get rid of it.

Class 3 Certificates

If you are a commercial software publisher and want to obtain an Authenticode certificate, use Internet Explorer to visit **digitalid.verisign.com**. Follow the prompts until you get to a page that looks like Figure 12.12. Before clicking on the Class 3 icon, be prepared to submit the following information:

- Your company's name, address, phone number, and D-U-N-S number

- The names, addresses, phone numbers, and email addresses of technical, organizational, and billing contacts

- Billing information (credit card or check)

Click the Class 3 icon. Several forms will ask you to submit the above information. After you have entered all the data and accepted the pledge, you can submit the information to VeriSign and run the Credentials Enrollment Wizard (see Figure 12.15). You must then wait about one week to allow VeriSign to validate your information, bill your company, and send you the certificate.

Running The Authenticode Utilities

Once you have your certificate, you can begin signing code. If you have installed either the ActiveX SDK or the Code Signing Kit that comes with Visual J++, you already have all the tools you need. The required files are:

- *WinTrust.dll*—Windows Trust Provider (located in Windows\System). Extracts certificates and allows the user to decide whether to install downloaded programs.

- *DigSig.dll*—Digital Signature Support Library (located in Windows\System). Contains algorithms for embedding certificates into executables and for generating one-way hashes.

- *SignCode.exe*—Code Signing Utility. Uses the Digital Signature Support Library to sign code. Also provides a wizard to automate the process.

- *PESigMgr.exe*—Signature Manipulation Utility. Determines whether a Portable Executable file contains a certificate.

- *ChkTrust.exe*—Trust Validation Utility. Checks the validity of a certificate.

PUT YOUR PENCILS DOWN; THE TEST IS OVER
The Authenticode utilities that ship with Visual J++ describe how to enable test certificates on your machine, but they forget to tell you how to disable test certificates. To do so, run the Windows Registry Editor and change the HKEY_CURRENT_USER\Software\Microsoft\Windows\Current Version\WinTrust\Trust Providers\Software Publishing\State key to 0.

THE CODE-SIGNING UTILITY

Your first step in the actual code-signing process is to run SignCode.exe. This program will display the Code Signing Wizard, which gathers the information required to sign one of your programs. (You can also sign code manually, using command-line parameters. To view them, run SignCode and specify "-?" as a parameter.)

In the first step of the wizard, select the program, type its formal name, and choose a Web site where users can find more information about it (see Figure 12.17).

In the next step, you must tell the wizard where to find your certificate and your private key (see Figure 12.18). You must also choose the digest (the one-way hash) algorithm that will be applied to the code. The choices are:

- *MD5*—The Message Digest Algorithm 5 was developed by RSA Data Security Inc. and hashes any byte sequence into a 128-bit value. MD5 is in wide use and considered reasonably secure.

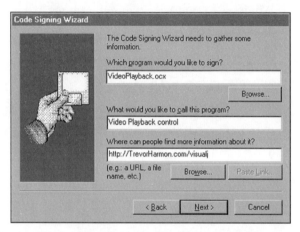

Figure 12.17 In the first step of the Code Signing Wizard, choose the program you wish to sign.

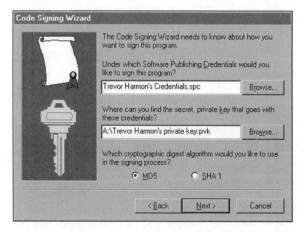

Figure 12.18 In the second step of the Code Signing Wizard, select the certificate, your private key, and a digest algorithm.

- *SHA*—The Secure Hash Algorithm, also known as the Secure Hash Standard, was developed by the U.S. government. It hashes any byte sequence into a 160-bit value and is not as common as MD5.

SECURE THE HASH!
For tighter security, use the SHA hash instead of the MD5 hash. SHA is 25-percent slower, but the digests it creates are less prone to attack.

The next step of the Code Signing Wizard asks you to confirm the information you just provided. Although you should be careful to make sure it's correct, you can always fix a mistake by running the wizard again. After you have verified your entries, click the Sign button to end the wizard. The SignCode program will then:

1. Create a digest of the file using the algorithm you specified.
2. Encrypt the digest with your private key.
3. Extract the X.509 structure (see sidebar) from your certificate.
4. Embed the encrypted digest and the X.509 structure into your program.

Your code is now signed and ready to distribute. You should, however, check the validity of the signature as described in the following sections.

The X.509 Structure

Authenticode certificates conform to an industry standard called the X.509 structure. This code-signing structure holds information, stored in separate fields, about your public-key certificate. The meaning of each field is as follows:

- *Version*—The version number of the certificate format
- *Serial number*—The serial number of the certificate, as defined by the CA
- *Algorithm identifier*—The algorithm and any necessary parameters needed to sign the certificate
- *Issuer*—The name of the CA
- *Period of validity*—The time period within which the signature is valid

- *Subject*—Your name

- *Subject's public key*—The algorithm and any necessary parameters needed to decrypt your program's digest

- *Signature*—The digital ID of the CA

THE SIGNATURE MANIPULATION UTILITY

To check whether SignCode was successful, run the PESigMgr program. You must specify the "-l" parameter, which lists the embedded certificate, and the name of your program. For example, at the command line you might type:

```
pesigmgr -l videoplayback.ocx
```

If the program contains a signature, you will see:

```
Certificate    0 Revision 256 Type    PKCS7
```

If not, PESigMgr won't print anything. Try running the SignCode program again, and make sure it's successful.

THE TRUST VALIDATION UTILITY

To verify further that you have successfully signed your program, run the ChkTrust program. It calls functions in the WinTrust library to:

1. Extract your certificate using the CA's public key

2. Decrypt your program's digest using your embedded public key

3. Compute a new digest of the program

4. Compare the decrypted digest with the new digest

If the digests are identical, you will see a dialog box like the one shown earlier in Figure 12.9. If not, you will see a dialog box like the one shown earlier in Figure 12.10. Try running the SignCode program again to make sure it's successful.

For example, at the command line you might type:

```
chktrust videoplayback.ocx
```

If you have signed your code successfully, you will see its certificate.

Marking Controls As Safe

Whew! After all that work, you're finally finished. You've built a control, obtained a certificate, and signed the code. Web surfers can download your control and know that it has authenticity and integrity.

Now, let's pretend one of those Web surfers has a little too much time on his hands. He discovers that your control exposes a method for deleting files, and he wants to have some prankish fun. By reading Chapter 9 of this book, he learns how to write an HTML script that calls your control's delete method. He then posts both the control and the script on a Web page, vanishes into cyberspace, and, since your name is on the certificate, lets you take the blame for the trouble he caused.

Fortunately, Internet Explorer is one step ahead of this mischief-maker. Whenever it encounters a script that accesses a control—signed or unsigned—it warns the user that the Web page may not be safe. (On the High security setting, IE refuses to run the control, and on the Medium setting, it asks the user's permission to run it.) IE uses the same security tactic when it encounters initialization of a control from parameters in an **<OBJECT>** tag.

This draconian safeguard isn't perfect. Most controls are perfectly suitable for scripting, and customers who have purchased your control will probably want to automate it with HTML scripts. To handle these situations, the ActiveX architecture provides an interface called **IObjectSafety**. By implementing the **GetSafetyOptions**() function of this interface, you can tell Internet Explorer that your control is safe for scripting and initializing. Alternatively, you could call the **CreateComponentCategory**() and **RegisterCLSIDInCategory**() functions as demonstrated in the WebImage sample from the ActiveX SDK.

If you have not installed the ActiveX SDK, you can still mark your control as safe for scripting and initializing. Just add the IDs of the "safe for scripting" and "safe for initializing" components to your control's entry in the System Registry.

I've written an MFC class, called **CMakeSafeCtrl**, which does this work for you. (You can find its source code included with the controls that ship on this book's CD-ROM.) To use the class, simply pass it the ID of your control and call the **MakeSafeForScripting**() and **MakeSafeForInitializing**() functions. For example:

```
CLSID clsid;
GetClassID(&clsid);

CMakeSafeCtrl* pSafeCtrl = new CMakeSafeCtrl(clsid);

pSafeCtrl->MakeSafeForScripting();
pSafeCtrl->MakeSafeForInitializing();

delete pSafeCtrl;
```

After rebuilding the control, it will make itself safe for scripting and initializing every time it runs. (Remember that recompiling a control destroys its signature, so you'll need to re-sign it after adding this code.)

How To Sign Java Applets

Although Sun has announced that Java applets will support code-signing, they have not yet delivered on this promise. In the meantime, a code-signing solution is available today from Microsoft. The trick is to place your Java applet in a *cabinet file*, or simply a *CAB file*. You can store as many Java classes as you like inside a CAB file, including such extraneous files as sounds and images. You can then sign this file (using the techniques described in the previous section) and distribute it safely through the Web.

Code-signed CAB files provide three benefits:

- *User assurance*—Your certificate assures users that your applet has authenticity and integrity.

- *Elimination of the sandbox*—Applets that originate from code-signed CAB files are considered trusted. Thus, they can look outside the Java sandbox and access files.

- *Compression*—Because CAB files are compressed, they download faster.

Note that although CAB files are inherently cross-platform, Internet Explorer is the only browser that supports them. Microsoft is working to provide Netscape Navigator and other browsers with cabinet compatibility.

Signing Standard Java Classes

To sign a Java applet and post it on a Web page, follow these steps:

1. Install the CABinet Development Kit by running CabDevKit.exe, located in the Visual J++ Cab&Sign folder.

2. At the command line, switch to the directory containing the Java applet you want to sign.

3. Build a CAB file by running the development kit's Cabinet Tool (cabarc.exe). Remember to leave 6K of extra space for the digital signature. For example, to insert all class files and all gif files into a cabinet called MySignedApplet, type the following at the command line:

```
\cabdevkit\cabarc -s 6144 n MySignedApplet.cab *.class *.gif
```

4. Sign the CAB file just as you would sign an ActiveX control. In other words, run the SignCode wizard and provide it the locations of your CAB file, certificate, and private key.

5. Check the validity of the CAB file's certificate by running ChkTrust. Remember to specify the -c parameter to indicate a cabinet file. For example:

```
\codesignkit\chktrust -c MySignedApplet.cab
```

If SignCode is successful, you will see the CAB file's certificate.

6. Insert an **<APPLET>** tag for the Java applet into an HTML file. Because you are specifying a CAB file, you must add the **CABBASE** parameter to the tag. For example:

```
<APPLET CODE="MySignedApplet.class" WIDTH=100 HEIGHT=100>
<PARAM NAME="CABBASE" VALUE="MySignedApplet.cab">
</APPLET>
```

Browsers that do not support cabinet files will ignore the **CABBASE** parameter and simply download the class directly.

For information on more advanced features of cabinet files, such as the ability to CAB and sign Java packages, see the CABinet Development Kit's readme.txt file.

Signing ActiveX-enabled Java Classes

If you want to sign and distribute a Java applet that is integrated with an ActiveX control, your work is much more involved. Not only must you sign the applet and the control separately, but you must also sign the control's Java interface classes (the ones created by the Java Type Library Wizard). You must then write a special text file, called an INF file, which tells Internet Explorer how to extract the classes from the cabinet and copy them to the user's Java\TrustLib directory. The following sections describe these steps in detail.

THE INTERNAL CABINET

Copying Java interface classes to a user's machine requires *two* cabinets: one to hold the classes and one to hold the INF file. The classes' cabinet is placed inside the INF's cabinet, as shown in Figure 12.19.

To create the internal cabinet for the interface classes, you can't use the Cabinet Tool (cabarc.exe) as you did in the previous section. Instead, you must run the Diamond Tool (diamond.exe), a low-level version of the Cabinet Tool. The Diamond Tool requires that parameters are placed in a DDF file, which is just a standard text file. The tool reads the names of the classes from this file, compresses them, and stores them in a cabinet. For example, if the Java Type Library Wizard created the following interface class files from your ActiveX control

```
MyControl.class
IMyControl.class
IMyControlEvents.class
```

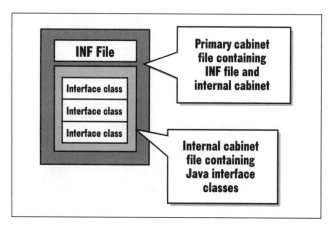

Figure 12.19 Before signing Java interface classes, you must place them inside two cabinet files.

you would create a DDF file that looks like this:

```
.OPTION EXPLICIT
.Set CabinetNameTemplate=MyControlInterfaces_.cab
.Set DiskDirectoryTemplate=
.Set Cabinet=on
.Set Compress=on
.Set MaxCabinetSize=0
.Set MaxDiskSize=CDROM
.Set DestinationDir=mycontrol
MyControl.class
IMyControl.class
IMyControlEvents.class
```

The first highlighted line sets the name of the cabinet file. Notice that in the example, I have appended an underscore character to the name. This avoids conflicts with the primary cabinet file name.

The second highlighted line sets the destination directory of the class files. This directory will descend from the user's Java\TrustLib directory. Make the name identical to the directory name created by running the Type Library Wizard on your machine.

The remaining highlighted lines contain a list of the class files to add to the internal cabinet. You can add as many class files as necessary. (Lines that are not highlighted in this DDF sample should remain unchanged.)

When you have finished typing the appropriate text, save it under a file name with a DDF extension. (For instance: MyControlInterfaces_.ddf. Again, the underscore prevents conflicts with the primary cabinet.) You may then run the Diamond Tool to create the internal cabinet file; for example:

```
\cabdevkit\diamond /f MyControlInterfaces_.ddf
```

BUILDING THE INF FILE

Your next step is to build an INF file. First, create a new text file and copy into it the template shown in Listing 12.2.

LISTING 12.2   A TEMPLATE FOR BUILDING INF FILES.

```
[Version]
signature="$CHICAGO$"
AdvancedINF=2.0
```

```
[Setup Hooks]
hook1=hook1
hook2=hook2

[hook1]
run=extrac32.exe /e /a /y /l %49000% InterfaceClasses_.cab

[hook2]
InfFile=INFFileName.inf

[Strings]
PackageName="Java Interfaces"

[RegistryData]
CustomDestination=MyCustomDestination

[PackageDestination49000]

"HKLM","Software\Microsoft\Java
VM","TrustedLibsDirectory","",""

[DefaultInstall]
CustomDestination=MyCustomDestination

[MyCustomDestination]
49000=PackageDestination49000,23
```

In this template, the two items in bold are the only ones you need to change. First, change **InterfaceClasses_.cab** so that it matches the name of your internal cabinet file (such as MyControlInterfaces_.cab). Next, change **INFFileName.inf** so that it matches the file name under which you will save the INF file (such as MyControlInterfaces.inf). Finally, save the INF file as a standard text file, making sure that its file name matches the name you specified.

THE PRIMARY CABINET

Now that you've built the internal cabinet and the INF file, you're ready to place them inside the primary cabinet. This step does *not* require the Diamond Tool. You can use the Cabinet Tool as you did in the previous section, "Signing Standard Java Classes." For example, if your internal cabinet is named MyControlInterfaces_.cab and your INF file is named MyControlInterfaces.inf, you would type at the command line:

```
\cabdevkit\cabarc -s 6144 n MyControlInterfaces.cab
   MyControlInterfaces_.cab MyControlInterfaces.inf
```

Notice that this command reserves 6K of empty space in the cabinet file. You must insert your Authenticode certificate into this space before distributing the interface classes. To insert a certificate, simply run the SignCode utility as explained in the previous section.

Setting Up The HTML File

After building the internal cabinet, the INF file, and the code-signed primary cabinet, you're finally ready to distribute your ActiveX-enabled applet on the Web. You only need to insert the appropriate tags into the HTML file. First, follow the steps from the previous sections to insert an **<OBJECT>** tag and an **<APPLET>** tag. Your HTML file might then look like this:

```
<HTML>
<BODY>

<OBJECT ID="MyControl" WIDTH=100 HEIGHT=100
   CLASSID="CLSID:D77B7824-1AAA-11D0-8512-0020AFC746E8"
   CODEBASE="http://myserver.com/MyControl.ocx">
</OBJECT>

<APPLET CODE=MyApplet.class NAME=MyApplet
   WIDTH=100 HEIGHT=100>
<PARAM NAME="CABBASE" VALUE="MyApplet.cab">
</APPLET>

</BODY>
</HTML>
```

You must now create a tag for the primary cabinet file containing your interfaces. To do so, use the **<OBJECT>** tag and specify the cabinet file name as the **CODEBASE** parameter. For example:

```
<OBJECT
   CLASSID="CLSID:474A4860-2B46-11d0-8512-0020AFC746E8"
   CODEBASE="http://myserver.com/MyControlInterfaces.cab">
</OBJECT>
```

The class ID you specify is irrelevant, as long as it is unique. (You can generate a unique ID by running the Create GUID utility found on the Visual J++ Tools menu.)

After inserting this final **<OBJECT>** tag (preferably somewhere between the **<HTML>** and **<BODY>** tags), you may post the HTML file on the Web so that anyone may safely download your ActiveX-enabled applet.

Summary

The next time you lock yourself out of your house or car, don't get too upset. Remember that keys and locks exist to protect you, not to annoy you. They're not perfect safety measures, but they do an adequate job of protecting your valuables.

Software that lives on the Web comes with an electronic version of locks and keys: sandboxes and signatures. Sandboxing provides security by restricting what programs can and cannot do. Unfortunately, this tactic also restricts the usefulness of those programs. Code-signing, on the other hand, places no restrictions at all on downloaded code. It relies on accountability and trust to ensure security. Neither method is perfect, but both provide adequate safety for the Web's fourth dimension.

Appendix A

Online Resources

Chapter 1: The Fourth Dimension

Web Sites

INTERNET EXPLORER
www.microsoft.com/ie

CLUBIE
www.clubie.com
A volunteer user group of computer professionals that assists and supports others using Microsoft Internet Explorer and its related technologies.

Trevor Harmon
TrevorHarmon.com
The author's home page.

The Web Developer's Guide To Visual J++ And ActiveX
TrevorHarmon.com/visualj
Get the latest book updates and information here.

HTML Specification
http://www.w3.org/pub/WWW/TR/WD-style

Email Addresses

The Web Developer's Guide To Visual J++ And ActiveX
visualj@TrevorHarmon.com
Report errors, ask questions, and offer comments here.

Chapter 2: Learn *More* Java Now

Web Sites

Pendragon Software
www.webfayre.com
Provides a comparison of various Java virtual machines.

Jamba
www.aimtech.com
A Java authoring tool from Aimtech Corporation for interactive multimedia applets.

Liquid Motion
www.dimensionx.com
An extensible Java tool from DimensionX for adding animation, sound, and interactivity to a Web site.

Mail Wizard
www.neural.com
A library from Neural Applications Corporation for building SMTP mail message dialogs.

Java Generic Library
www.objectspace.com
A library from ObjectSpace of containers and algorithms for Java.

Gamelan
www.gamelan.com
Earth Web's official index to Java applets.

Netscape
www.home.netscape.com
Netscape's home page with Java applications.

JDesignerPro
www.BulletProof.com
A tool from BulletProof Corporation for developing custom client/server database applications.

JavaSoft
java.sun.com
Sun's Java division.

Java User Resource Network
www.nebulex.com/URN
A meeting place for Java users.

JavaWorld
www.javaworld.com
An online magazine dedicated to Java.

The Java Pro
www.inquiry.com/techtips/java_pro/
The hiding place of a Java expert.

Java Applet Rating Service
www.jars.com

Provides ratings for the top 1%, 5%, and 25% applets of all time and for the top 10 and 100 applets of the month.

DIGITAL ESPRESSO
www.io.org/~mentor/jnIndex.html
A Java news magazine.

HOW DO I...
www.digitalfocus.com/digitalfocus/faq/howdoi.html
A tip sheet for Java programmers.

JAVA TUTORIAL
java.sun.com/books/Series/Tutorial/TOC.html

JAVA INFORMATION AND RESOURCES
www.microsoft.com/workshop/java/

Newsgroups

The following newsgroup is available from Microsoft's public server at **msnews.microsoft.com**.

MICROSOFT.PUBLIC.INTERNETEXPLORER.JAVA
Discussions of IE's Java support.

The following newsgroup should be available from any server.

COMP.LANG.JAVA
Discussions on any Java-related topic.

Chapter 3: Visual J++

Web Sites

JAVA SDK
www.microsoft.com/java/
Free downloading of Microsoft's SDK for Java.

BORLAND LATTÉ
www.borland.com/internet/latteinfo.html
Information on Borland's Java development environment.

SYMANTEC VISUAL CAFÉ
cafe.symantec.com
Information on Symantec's Java development environment.

MICROSOFT VISUAL J++
www.microsoft.com/visualj
Information on Microsoft's Java development environment.

MINDQ
www.mindq.com
Multimedia training for Visual J++.

MICROSOFT INDEPENDENT DEVELOPER
www.windx.com
A monthly publication that sometimes focuses on Visual J++.

Newsgroups

The following newsgroups are available from Microsoft's public server at **msnews.microsoft.com**.

MICROSOFT.PUBLIC.VISUALJ.INSTALLATION
Post installation and configuration issues here.

MICROSOFT.PUBLIC.VISUALJ.COMPILER
Post compiler syntax or code generation issues here.

MICROSOFT.PUBLIC.VISUALJ.DEBUGGER
Post debugger issues here.

MICROSOFT.PUBLIC.VISUALJ.DEV-ENVIRONMENT
Post issues with the editor, ClassView, and wizards here.

MICROSOFT.PUBLIC.VISUALJ.COM-SUPPORT
Post issues with COM support here.

MICROSOFT.PUBLIC.VISUALJ.DISCUSSION
Post product-wide Visual J++ issues here.

MICROSOFT.PUBLIC.VISUALJ.MISC-TOOLS
Post issues with command line tools here.

Chapter 4: ActiveX Fundamentals

Web Sites

ACTIVEX.COM
www.activex.com
News from the world of ActiveX.

ActiveX SDK
www.microsoft.com/intdev/sdk

ActiveX SDK for Macintosh
www.microsoft.com/intdev/sdk/mac/mactivex.htm

Microsoft Mailing Lists
www.microsoft.com/workshop/resource/mail.htm

Microsoft Mailing List Archives
microsoft.ease.lsoft.com/archives/index.html

Internet Development Toolbox
www.microsoft.com/intdev

ActiveX Info
www.microsoft.com/activex/

For Developers Only
www.microsoft.com/devonly
A Microsoft site catering to all types of developers.

ActiveX Plugin
www.ncompasslabs.com
A plugin from Ncompass Labs that gives Netscape Navigator ActiveX compatibility.

ActiveX Controls FAQ
www.microsoft.com/intdev/controls/ctrlfaq-f.htm

ActiveX Component Gallery
www.microsoft.com/activex/controls/

Chapter 5: Building ActiveX Controls

Web Sites

Microsoft Foundation Classes FAQ
www.stingsoft.com/mfc_faq/

Windows Developer FAQ
www.r2m.com/win-developer-FAQ/

C++ FAQ
www.quadralay.com/www/CCForum/CC_FAQ/CC_FAQ01.html

Win32 Information
www.microsoft.com/win32dev/wcnt.htm

Microsoft Visual C++
www.microsoft.com/visualc
Information on Microsoft's C++ development environment.

Visual C++ 4.2 ActiveX Patch
www.microsoft.com/visualc/v42/v42tech/42a

Chapter 9: Scripting

Web Sites

ActiveX Control Pad
www.microsoft.com/workshop/author/cpad/

JavaScript Handbook
home.netscape.com/eng/mozilla/3.0/handbook/javascript/
A JavaScript reference from Netscape.

JScript
www.microsoft.com/jscript
A JavaScript reference from Microsoft.

VBScript
www.microsoft.com/vbscript
A VBScript reference from Microsoft.

Internet Explorer Scripting Object Model
www.microsoft.com/intdev/sdk/docs/scriptom/

Newsgroups

comp.lang.javascript
General discussions of JavaScript.

Chapter 10: OLE Automation

Web Sites

Internet Explorer Object Model
www.microsoft.com/intdev/sdk/docs/iexplore/

OLE Development
www.microsoft.com/oledev/
Information on all aspects of OLE development.

OLEView
www.microsoft.com/oledev/olecom/oleview.htm
Download the latest copy of Microsoft's OLE interface viewer here.

OLE Broker
www.olebroker.com
A repository maintained by ObjectSoft for OLE components.

Java Beans
splash.javasoft.com/beans/
The latest news about Java's component architecture.

ENTISOFT TOOLS
entisoft.earthlink.net

MICROSOFT OFFICE DEVELOPER FORUM
www.microsoft.com/OfficeDev/TechInfo/TechInfo.htm
Find the Microsoft Word Type Library here.

DCOM BINARY PROTOCOL
www.microsoft.com/intdev/prog-gen/dcom-f.htm

Chapter 11: Data Access Objects

Web Sites

REMOTE SERVER CONNECTIVITY INFO
www.microsoft.com/vbasic/vbwhite/REMOTESERVERAB.HTM

HTML LAYOUT CONTROL DEMOS
www.microsoft.com/workshop/author/layout/

Chapter 12: Security

Web Sites

AUTHENTICODE FAQ
www.microsoft.com/intdev/security/authcode/signfaq-f.htm

CABVIEW
www.microsoft.com/windows/software/powertoy.htm
A utility for viewing cabinet files.

CABINET DEVELOPMENT KIT
www.microsoft.com/workshop/java/cab-f.htm
Updates will be posted here.

RSA DATA SECURITY
rsa.com

AUTHENTICODE
www.microsoft.com/intdev/signcode/

AUTHENTICODE CERTIFICATES
www.microsoft.com/intdev/signcode/certs/
Information on the latest CAs.

DUN & BRADSTREET
www.dbisna.com/dbis/aboutdb/dunsform.htm
Apply for a D-U-N-S rating here.

SECURITY FAQ
www.javasoft.com/java.sun.com/sfaq/index.html
Frequently asked questions of Sun about Java security.

Newsgroups

The following newsgroup is available from Microsoft's public server at **msnews.microsoft.com**.

MICROSOFT.PUBLIC.INTERNETEXPLORER.JAVA.CABDEVKIT
User support for the CABinet Development Kit.

Email Addresses

AUTHENTICODE
safecode@microsoft.com
General questions and comments about Authenticode.

Appendix B

com.ms.com Reference

This appendix provides a brief description of each class and interface in Microsoft's com.ms.com package.

Classes

ComContext

Defines constants for the **ILicenseMgr** interface.

```
final public class ComContext
{
   // Fields
   public static final int INPROC_SERVER;
   public static final int INPROC_HANDLER;
   public static final int LOCAL_SERVER;
   public static final int INPROC_SERVER16;
   public static final int REMOTE_SERVER;
   public static final int INPROC_HANDLER16;
   public static final int INPROC_SERVERX86;
   public static final int INPROC_HANDLERX86;
}
```

FIELDS

Specifies the context in which to run the COM object. Use **INPROC_SERVER** in almost all cases.

ComException

Provides information about runtime COM exceptions.

```
public abstract class com.ms.com.ComException
                  extends RuntimeException
{
   // Constructors
   public ComException();
   public ComException(int hr);
   public ComException(String message);
   public ComException(int hr, String message);
   // Methods
   public int getHResult();
}
```

CONSTRUCTORS

hr is the **HRESULT** for indicating success or failure. See Table 6.1 in Chapter 6 for common **HRESULT**s.

message is the string returned by **getMessage()**.

Methods

getHResult() returns the **HRESULT** value passed to the constructor.

ComFailException

Indicates failure in a runtime COM exception.

```
public class com.ms.com.ComFailException
        extends com.ms.com.ComException
{
   // Constructors
   public ComFailException();
   public ComFailException(int hr);
   public ComFailException(String message);
   public ComFailException(int hr, String message);
}
```

Constructors

hr is the **HRESULT** for indicating failure. See Table 6.1 in Chapter 6 for common **HRESULT**s. The default **HRESULT** is **E_FAIL**.

message is the string returned by **getMessage()**.

ComSuccessException

Indicates success in a runtime COM exception.

```
public class com.ms.com.ComSuccessException
          extends com.ms.com.ComException
{
   // Constructors
   public ComSuccessException();
   public ComSuccessException(int hr);
   public ComSuccessException(String message);
   public ComSuccessException(int hr, String message);
}
```

Constructors

hr is the **HRESULT** for indicating success. See Table 6.1 in Chapter 6 for common **HRESULT**s. The default **HRESULT** is **S_FALSE**.

message is the string returned by **getMessage()**.

LicenseMgr

An empty class designed for implementing the **ILicenseMgr** interface.

```
public class LicenseMgr implements ILicenseMgr
{
}
```

SafeArray

An empty class designed for holding placemarks to COM's **SAFEARRAY** data type.

```
public final class SafeArray
{
}
```

Variant

A class wrapper for COM's **VARIANT** data type.

```
public final class com.ms.com.Variant
{
   // Fields
   public static final short VariantEmpty;
   public static final short VariantNull;
   public static final short VariantShort;
   public static final short VariantInt;
   public static final short VariantFloat;
   public static final short VariantDouble;
   public static final short VariantCurrency;
   public static final short VariantDate;
   public static final short VariantString;
   public static final short VariantDispatch;
   public static final short VariantError;
   public static final short VariantBoolean;
   public static final short VariantVariant;
   public static final short VariantObject;
   public static final short VariantByte;
   public static final short VariantTypeMask;
   public static final short VariantArray;
   public static final short VariantByref;
   // Constructors
   public          Variant();
   // Methods
   public native  void     changeType(short vartype);
   public         Variant  clone();
   public         Variant  cloneIndirect();
   protected      void     finalize();
   public         short    getvt();
   public         void     getEmpty();
   public         void     getNull();
```

```
public            short    getShort();
public            int      getInt();
public            float    getFloat();
public            double   getDouble();
public            long     getCurrency();
public            double   getDate();
public   native   String   getString();
public   native   Object   getDispatch();
public            int      getError();
public   native   boolean  getBoolean();
public   native   Object   getObject();
public   native   byte     getByte();
public   native   short    getShortRef();
public   native   int      getIntRef();
public   native   float    getFloatRef();
public   native   double   getDoubleRef();
public   native   long     getCurrencyRef();
public   native   double   getDateRef();
public   native   String   getStringRef();
public   native   Object   getDispatchRef();
public   native   int      getErrorRef();
public   native   boolean  getBooleanRef();
public   native   Object   getObjectRef();
public   native   byte     getByteRef();
public            void     noParam();
public            void     putEmpty();
public            void     putNull();
public            void     putShort(short val);
public            void     putInt(int val);
public            void     putFloat(float val);
public            void     putDouble(double val);
public            void     putCurrency(long val);
public            void     putDate(double val);
public   native   void     putString(String val);
public   native   void     putDispatch(Object val);
public            void     putError(int val);
public            void     putBoolean(boolean val);
public   native   void     putObject(Object val);
public            void     putByte(byte val);
public   native   void     putShortRef(short val);
public   native   void     putIntRef(int val);
public   native   void     putFloatRef(float val);
public   native   void     putDoubleRef(double val);
public   native   void     putCurrencyRef(long val);
public   native   void     putDateRef(double val);
public   native   void     putStringRef(String val);
public   native   void     putDispatchRef(Object val);
public   native   void     putErrorRef(int val);
public   native   void     putBooleanRef(boolean val);
```

```
    public  native  void     putObjectRef(Object val);
    public  native  void     putByteRef(byte val);
    public  native  short    toShort();
    public  native  int      toInt();
    public  native  float    toFloat();
    public  native  double   toDouble();
    public  native  long     toCurrency();
    public  native  double   toDate();
    public  native  String   toString();
    public  native  Object   toDispatch();
    public  native  int      toError();
    public  native  boolean  toBoolean();
    public  native  Object   toObject();
    public  native  byte     toByte();
    public  native  void     VariantClear();
}
```

FIELDS

Specifies the data type contained in the **Variant**. Default is **VariantEmpty**.

CONSTRUCTORS

Constructs an empty **Variant**.

METHODS

changeType() coerces the current value to the given type.

clone() and **cloneIndirect()** make copies of the **Variant**.

finalize() destroys the **Variant** object.

getvt() gets the type of data contained in the **Variant**. See the Fields section for possible return values.

The **get** functions return the current value of the **Variant**, and the **set** functions change its value.

The **to** functions return the **Variant**'s value as the specified type.

noParam() specifies that the **Variant** should be passed as an optional parameter.

VariantClear() erases the data stored in the **Variant**.

Interfaces

ILicenseMgr
Allows the use of licensed COM components.

```
public interface ILicenseMgr
{
   // Methods
   public Object createInstance(String clsid,
                                Object punkOuter,
                                ComContext clsctx)
                          throws ComException;
   public Object createWithLic(String lic,
                               String clsid,
                               Object punkOuter,
                               ComContext clsctx)
                          throws ComException;
}
```

METHODS
createWithLic() uses the given license key, class ID, and context to create an instance of the COM object.

createInstance() should only be called for low-level COM programming.

WHERE Reference

This appendix lists the SQL-92 specification for the **WHERE** clause.

Where Clause

```
<where clause> ::= WHERE <search condition>
```

Search Condition

```
<search condition> ::=
    <boolean term>
  | <search condition> OR <boolean term>

<boolean term> ::=
    <boolean factor>
  | <boolean term> AND <boolean factor>

<boolean factor> ::=
    [ NOT ] <boolean test>

<boolean test> ::=
    <boolean primary> [ IS [ NOT ] <truth value> ]

<boolean primary> ::=
    <predicate>
  | <left paren> <search condition> <right paren>

<predicate> ::=
    <comparison predicate>
  | <between predicate>
  | <in predicate>
  | <like predicate>
  | <null predicate>
  | <quantified comparison predicate>
  | <exists predicate>
  | <unique predicate>
  | <match predicate>
  | <overlaps predicate>

<comparison predicate> ::=
    <row value constructor> <comp op> <row value constructor>
```

Predicates

BETWEEN

```
<between predicate> ::=
    <row value constructor> [ NOT ] BETWEEN
      <row value constructor> AND <row value constructor>
```

IN

```
<in predicate> ::=
   <row value constructor>
      [ NOT ] IN <in predicate value>

   <in predicate value> ::=
        <table subquery>
      | <left paren> <in value list> <right paren>

   <in value list> ::=
        <value expression> { <comma> <value expression> }...
```

LIKE

```
<like predicate> ::=
   <match value> [ NOT ] LIKE <pattern>
      [ ESCAPE <escape character> ]

   <match value> ::= <character value expression>

   <pattern> ::= <character value expression>

   <escape character> ::= <character value expression>
```

NULL

```
<null predicate> ::= <row value constructor>
    IS [ NOT ] NULL
```

QUANTIFIED COMPARISON

```
<quantified comparison predicate> ::=
   <row value constructor> <comp op> <quantifier>
                                     <table subquery>

   <quantifier> ::= <all> | <some>

   <all> ::= ALL

   <some> ::= SOME | ANY
```

EXISTS

```
<exists predicate> ::= EXISTS <table subquery>
```

UNIQUE

```
<unique predicate> ::= UNIQUE <table subquery>
```

MATCH

```
<match predicate> ::=
    <row value constructor> MATCH [ UNIQUE ]
        [ PARTIAL | FULL ] <table subquery>
```

OVERLAPS

```
<overlaps predicate> ::=
    <row value constructor 1> OVERLAPS <row value constructor 2>

<row value constructor 1> ::= <row value constructor>

<row value constructor 2> ::= <row value constructor>
```

Expressions

STRING

```
<string value expression> ::=
      <character value expression>
    | <bit value expression>

<octet length expression> ::=
    OCTET_LENGTH <left paren> <string value expression>
                                              <right paren>

<bit length expression> ::=
    BIT_LENGTH <left paren> <string value expression>
                                              <right paren>
```

DATETIME

```
<datetime value expression> ::=
      <datetime term>
    | <interval value expression> <plus sign> <datetime term>
    | <datetime value expression> <plus sign> <interval term>
    | <datetime value expression> <minus sign> <interval term>
```

INTERVAL

```
<interval value expression> ::=
      <interval term>
    | <interval value expression 1> <plus sign> <interval term 1>
    | <interval value expression 1> <minus sign> <interval term 1>
    | <left paren> <datetime value expression> <minus sign>
          <datetime term> <right paren> <interval qualifier>
```

CHARACTER

```
<character value expression> ::=
    <concatenation>
  | <character factor>

<concatenation> ::=
    <character value expression> <concatenation operator>
        <character factor>
```

BIT

```
<bit value expression> ::=
    <bit concatenation>
  | <bit factor>

<bit concatenation> ::=
    <bit value expression> <concatenation operator>
    <bit factor>

<bit factor> ::= <bit primary>

<bit primary> ::=
    <value expression primary>
  | <string value function>
```

Other Specifiers

```
<row value constructor> ::=
    <row value constructor element>
  | <left paren> <row value constructor list> <right paren>
  | <row subquery>

<row value constructor element> ::=
    <value expression>
  | <null specification>
  | <default specification>

<row value constructor list> ::=
    <row value constructor element>
        [ { <comma> <row value constructor element> }... ]

<value expression> ::=
    <numeric value expression>
  | <string value expression>
  | <datetime value expression>
  | <interval value expression>
```

```
<comp op> ::=
      =
    | <>
    | <
    | >
    | <=
    | >=

<truth value> ::=
      TRUE
    | FALSE
    | UNKNOWN
```

Index

A

Abstract keyword, 153
Abstract Window Toolkit (AWT), 69, 182
Access case study, 280
ActiveX, 11
   accessing properties, 164
   advantages over Java, 12
   architecture, 11
   color information, 130
   containers, 103
   control pad, 117, 251
   controls, 11, 50, 102
   data types available in Java, 180
   database access, 51
   distributed COM, 36
   function exception handling, 165
   integration with Java, 161
   interfaces, 158
   multimedia features, 36
   naming conventions, 131
   scripting, 244
   support for Macintosh, 174
   support for Unix, 174
   versus Java, 13
Add Method button, 128
Add Property button, 128
AddRef function, 160
ALIGN control, 112
Ambient properties, 130
AmbientFont function, 130
Animation
   sine waves, 83
   using the Applet Wizard, 62
Anonymous objects, 158
API functions, 182
APIs
   Java, 338
   JDBC, 300
   Win32, 199
App module, 126
APPLET tag, 30–32
Applet Wizard
   adding parameters, 63
   animation, 62
   changing applet window size, 62
   member mnemonics, 62
   multithreading, 62
   source file comments, 61
AppletContext interface, 341
Applets, 7
   access to client files, 337
   automation server integration, 182
   code signing, 174, 366
   debugging, 83
   denial of service, 336
   error text, 32
   Microsoft Word Driver, 291
   polling, 260
   privileges, 340
   readable system properties, 341
   restrictions, 337
   scripting, 258–262
   tag, 30, 189
   unreadable properties, 339
   untrusted windows indicators, 339
   using Visual J++, 15
   video playback source code, 191
   versus ActiveX controls, 105
   versus applications, 337
AppletStub interface, 341
Application object, 280
Audio Video Interleave (AVI), 190
AudioClip interface, 341
Authenticode, 349
   Class 2 certificates, 356
   Class 3, 360
   X.509 structure, 363

Auto tab (in Variables window), 78
Automation
  clients, 272
  controllers, 287–294
  using OLE automation, 272–276
  with OLE, 271–294
Automation server, 172, 181, 205
  binding, 273
  object model, 272
Auto-sizing columns, 79
AVI, 190
AWT, 182

B

Background color, 130
BASELINE of control, 112
Binding, 273
  early, 274
  late, 274
Bitmap Twirl, 149
Bitmaps
  creating, 73
  rotating, 149
  tiling, 149
Boolean, 134
BORDER width of controls, 113
Borland, 12, 125
  Delphi, 12
  Latté, 52, 97
Breakpoints, 74
  condition, 75
  dialog box, 75
  disabling, 75
  setting, 74
Browse button, 71
Browsers
  as an ActiveX container, 105
  HotJava, 7
  Internet Explorer, 10, 50, 173
  Netscape Navigator, 9
BSTR data type, 180
BSTR variable, 228
Build settings, 65
  debug tab, 65
  general tab, 65
Bytecode, 24, 64

interpreter, 25
verifier, 342

C

C++, 4, 207
  benefits, 4
  building ActiveX controls, 124
  driving a Java control, 224–229
  enumerated properties, 134
  exporting classes, 140
  memory leaks, 27
  multiple inheritance, 21
  saving pointers, 227
CA, 345
CAB, 174, 366
CABBASE parameter, 367
Cabinet file (CAB), 174, 366
Call
  keyword, 255
  stack, 50
  Stack window, 77
CENTER control, 112
Certificate authority (CA), 345
Certificates, 345
  Class 1, 350
  Class 2, 356
  Class 3, 360
  commercial versus individual, 349
  disabling test certificates, 361
  encryption, 346, 347
  end user, 350
  period of validity, 352
  private keys, 346
  public keys, 346
  revoked, 352
  verification, 353
CGI, 2
  communication method, 4
  drawbacks, 3
  server limitations, 3
Changed expressions, 75
Char data type, 180
ChkTrust program, 364
City selector example, 262
  with JavaScript, 266
  with VBScript, 263

Class
    class file, 64
    format definition, 66
    loader, 342
    view, 16, 53
    wizard, 15, 52
Classes (Java)
    classView icons, 53
    code signing, 367
    COleControl, 127
    COM, 206
    component, 211
    creating, 59
    IndexColorModel, 40
    naming and renaming, 71
    naming conventions, 208
    public, 208
    source code, 77
    stepping into, 77
    variant, 181
CLASSID parameter, 113
CLASSPATH, 222
CLASSPATH directories, 163
ClassWizard, 128, 289
    adding events, 139
    adding methods, 138
    adding properties, 132
CMakeSafeCtrl, 365
Coclasses (in ODL), 213
Code signing, 109, 334, 344–371
    classes, 367
    Credentials Enrollment Wizard, 358
    for ActiveX controls, 356
    for ActiveX-enabled Java classes, 368
    for applets, 366
    local registration agency, 351
    utility, 361
    wizard, 361
    X.509 structure, 363
CODEBASE parameter, 113, 147
Code-signing, 162, 174
COleControl class, 127
COleDispatchDriver class, 290
Color
    exchange property, 134
    in GIF images, 40
    palettes, 40
Columns
    auto-sizing, 79

COM, 30, 165
    class, 206
Common Gateway Interface. *See* CGI.
Compiled computer languages, 24
Component class, 211
Component gallery, 52, 140
Component Object Model. *See* COM.
Component software, 158
Computer languages
    compiled, 24
    interpreted, 23
Condition (breakpoints)
    skip breakpoint, 76
    skip true expression, 76
Condition button, 75
Conditions (breakpoint)
    changed expression, 75
    true expression, 75
Containers, 103
    versus applets, 105
Context list (in Variables window), 77
Control Pad (ActiveX), 117, 251
Control test container, 141
Controls (ActiveX), 102
    adding properties, 128, 132
    binary reuse, 102
    building using C++, 124
    code signing, 356
    compiling, 111
    containers, 103
    control pad, 117
    converting legacy code, 110
    creating, 104
    creating nonvisual controls, 145
    Ctrl module, 126
    debugging, 140
    defined, 102
    disabling, 130
    editor, 118
    error text, 114
    events, 105, 139
    exception handling, 166
    execution speed, 111
    fatal errors, 143
    file access, 109
    FormulaOne/Net Pro, 104
    in non-Internet applications, 110
    inserting on a Web page, 117
    licensing, 115, 197

methods, 105, 138
notification functions, 131
OLE support, 109
persistence, 114
portability issues, 107
properties, 105
property sheets, 119
scripting, 254–258
signature checking, 116
version checking, 116
version stamping, 146
visual controls and Java, 145
Controls (Java)
building the type library, 219
creating, 208–210
control driver, 222
creating, 208
creating object descriptions, 213
debugging, 210
defining interfaces, 213
displaying a user interface, 211
rebuilding the Java class, 220
registering, 220
ConvertMeasure method, 278
CORBA, 271
Create GUID program, 216
Create New Class dialog box, 59
CreateDatabase function, 303
CreateImage function, 40
Credentials Enrollment Wizard, 358
Ctrl module, 126
Currency, 134
Custom controls
defined, 6
Custom properties, 130
Customize dialog box, 57

D

DAO, 52
differences from RDO, 299
Jet database engine, 297
sample driver, 324
Data Access Objects (DAO), 282, 296
Data expansion, 82
DATA parameter, 113
Data structures
circular, 29

Data types, 180
exposed from Java, 209
Database
adding objects, 307
creating, 303
deleting records, 308
field types, 307
object, 281, 303
opening with DAO, 303
queries, 308
searching, 308
SQL, 308
Database Access Objects (DAO), 52, 295
DBEngine, 281, 302
DCOM, 36, 159, 274
DDF file, 368
Debug tab (in build settings), 65
additional classes, 66
browser, 66
general section, 66
standalone interpreter, 66
Debugging
Call Stack window, 77
controls, 140
controls in Java, 210
disassembly, 82
exceptions, 79
just-in-time debugger, 143
scripts, 250
stepping into standard classes, 77
threads, 81
Variables window, 77
Watch window, 78
with Visual J++, 74
without the debugger, 81
DECLARE a control, 113
Delete button, 129
Delphi, 97, 172
Denial-of-service applets, 336
Dependency information, 64
Developer Studio, 127
Dialog boxes
controls in Visual J++, 69
creating in Visual J++, 68
template, 126
Diamond Tool, 368
Digest of a program, 347
Digital signature, 109, 174
Digital Signature Support Library, 361

Direct image manipulation, 42
Disassembly, 82
DISP_E_ARRAYISLOCKED error, 168
DISP_E_BADCALLEE error, 168
DISP_E_BADINDEX error, 168
DISP_E_BADPARAMCOUNT error, 168
DISP_E_BADVARTYPE error, 168
DISP_E_EXCEPTION error, 168
DISP_E_MEMBERNOTFOUND error, 168
DISP_E_NONAMEDARGS error, 168
DISP_E_NOTACOLLECTION error, 168
DISP_E_OVERFLOW error, 168
DISP_E_PARAMNOTFOUND error, 168
DISP_E_PARAMNOTOPTIONAL error, 168
DISP_E_TYPEMISMATCH error, 168
DISP_E_UNKNOWNINTERFACE error, 168
DISP_E_UNKNOWNLCID error, 168
DISP_E_UNKNOWNNAME error, 168
Dispatch interfaces, 127
Distributed architecture, 163
Distributed COM (DCOM), 36, 274
    protocol, 159
Do While/Loop statements, 247
DoPropExchange function, 133
Double data type, 180
Double property exchange function, 134
Double-buffering, 36
Dun & Bradstreet Financial Services, 349
D-U-N-S number, 349

E

E_ABORT error, 168
E_ACCESSDENIED error, 168
E_FAIL error, 168
E_HANDLE error, 168
E_INVALIDARG error, 168
E_NOINTERFACE error, 168
E_NOTIMPL error, 168
E_OUTOFMEMORY error, 168
E_POINTER error, 168
E_UNEXPECTED error, 168
Early binding, 274
EarthWeb, LLC., 44
Edit Code button, 129
Editor window, 144
Enable Java Logging box, 81
Entisoft Tools, 277

Error
    codes, 168
    handling
        in a Java control, 210
    text, 114
Event handlers
    in applets, 259
    in JavaScript, 257
    in VBScript, 256
Events, 139
    catching, 143
    scripts, 249
Events (in ActiveX), 105
Exceptions
    debugging, 79
    dialog box, 79
    handling, 180
Exchange functions, 133
Executable files (EXEs), 33
ExitWindowsEx function, 182
Expressions
    changed, 75
    true, 75
Extends keyword, 153

F

Field objects, 307
FILEVERSION key, 146
FileView (in Visual J++), 54
Find functions, 310
Finish button, 71
Fire Animation control, 147
Firewall, 335
Flicker elimination, 37
Float data type, 180
Float getPercentPosition function, 306
Float property exchange function, 134
Fonts
    objects, 60
    property exchange function, 134
Formula One/NET Pro, 104
Frame windows, 212
Full Optimization box, 66
Functions
    AmbientFont(), 130
    createImage(), 40
    DoPropExchange(), 133

exposing, 208
get, 209
getAppletInfo(), 64
getFields(), 306
getImage(), 39
getParameterInfo(), 63
getSafety Options(), 365
getType(), 307
init(), 38, 61, 73
main(), 60
mouseDown(), 62
OnGetDisplayString(), 137
OnGetPredefinedStrings(), 135
OnGetPredefinedValue(), 136
paint(), 37
put(), 209
setCtrl(), 190
setIconImage(), 212
setTimeout, 260
start(), 179
ThrowError(), 131
TranslateColor(), 130
Fuzzy-state checkbox, 176

G

Gamelon, 44
Garbage collection, 13, 28
    mark-and-sweep algorithm, 29
    memory compaction, 28
    stop-and-copy algorithm, 29
General tab (in build settings), 65
Get function, 209
Get method, 131
Get property, 180
GetAppletInfo function, 64
GetFields function, 306
GetImage function, 39
GetParameterInfo function, 63
GetSafetyOptions function, 365
GetType function, 307
GIF images, 40
Globally unique identifier, 113, 216
Go, 76
Graphics
    editor in Visual J++, 71
    flicker elimination, 37
    index images, 39

    palette-based images, 38
    programming tricks, 36–44
GUID, 216

H

Harmon Optical example, 313
Header file (in C++), 224
HEIGHT parameter, 113
HotJava, 7
HRESULT, 209
HSPACE parameter, 113
HTML, 30, 64, 181, 371
    layout editor, 118
    layouts, 312
    scripts, 145, 189, 242. *See* Scripts (HTML).
    scripts. *See also* Scripts (HTML), 242
Hyperlinks, 2
Hypertext Markup Language. *See* HTML.

I

IDD_ABOUTBOX dialog box, 146
IDispatch interface, 159, 161
ILicenseMgr interface, 197
ILicenseMgr.createWithLic function, 302
Image editor
    creating bitmaps, 73
ImageObserver interface, 153
Images
    creating in Visual J++, 70
    direct manipulation, 42
    GIF, 40
    importing resources, 73
    palette-based, 38
    true color, 38
    zoom levels, 70
Implements keyword, 154
Import keyword, 177
Importing
    image resources, 73
    resources, 71
Indenting blocks of code, 56
Index images, 38
IndexColorModel class, 40
indexed sequential access method (ISAM), 301
INF file, 368

InfoView, 54
InfoViewer, 127
   event sink maps, 143
Init function, 38, 73
Int data type, 180
Int getAbsolutePosition function, 306
Int getLastModified function, 306
Int getRecordCount function, 306
INT64 data type, 180
Interfaces, 151
   as data types, 155
   capturing similarities among unrelated classes, 156
   declaring (Java), 152
   implementing, 154
   in ActiveX, 158
   in Java, 152
   keywords to avoid, 153
   multiple inheritance workaround, 157
   superinterfaces, 153
International Traffic in Arms Regulations (ITAR), 346
Internet. *See also* World Wide Web.
   debugging applets, 82
   newsgroups, 44
Internet Explorer, 173, 207
   advanced options tab, 81
Interpreted computer languages, 23
Intranets, 13, 174
IObjectSafety interface, 365
IsInvokeAllowed function, 188
ITAR, 346
IUnknown
   data type, 180
   interface, 159

J

Java. *See also* Visual J++.
   accessing hardware, 30
   advantages for programmers, 19
   applet restrictions, 337
   applets, 7
   Beans, 109
   bytecode, 24
   calling ActiveX functions, 163
   compiler security checks, 341
   control driver, 222
   controls, 206
   creating automation controllers, 271–294
   data types, 180
   exceptions, 79
   features, 21
   garbage collection, 28
   graphical front ends, 48
   history of, 7
   index images, 39
   integration with ActiveX, 161
   integration with Microsoft products, 10
   integration with Windows, 33
   interfaces, 152
   JIT compiler, 27
   late-binding constraint, 288
   multiple inheritance, 157
   native code interface, 13, 30
   networking, 21
   newsgroups, 44
   object orientation, 22
   overview, 21–23
   portability, 24
   potential, 19
   sample class declaration, 217
   tab (in build settings), 66
   Type Library Wizard, 175
   virtual machine, 24, 174
   virtual machine in Windows, 207
   versus ActiveX, 13
   weaknesses, 22
   Web page interaction, 22
   with Netscape Navigator, 9
Java Applet Wizard, 60
Java Beans, 276
Java Database Connectivity. *See* JDBC.
JavaMaker, 48
JavaReg utility, 221
JavaScript, 243
   event handlers, 257
   functions, 248
   random numbers, 256
   timer object, 260
JavaTLB, 182, 220
JDBC, 51, 296, 300
Jet database engine, 297
JIT, 27, 35
   compiler, 50

JScript, 244
Just-in-time compiler. *See* JIT.
Just-in-time debugger, 143

K

Keywords
    catch, 165
    extends, 153
    implements, 154
    import, 177
    public, 153
    try, 165

L

Late binding, 274, 288
Latté, 97, 162
Layout menu, 69
LEFT align control, 112
Legacy code
    converting with ActiveX, 110
License keys, 197
Licensed controls, 197
Licensing ActiveX controls, 115
Licensing demo, 198
Lingo Maker Driver program, 224
Lisp, 28
Local registration agency, 351
Locals tab (in Variables window), 78
Long data type, 180
Long property exchange function, 134
Long property type, 129
LRAs, 351

M

Macros, 58
Makefile, 64
Mark-and-sweep algorithm, 29
Marshaling, 159
MD5, 362
MDI, 142
MDP, 64
Member mnemonics, 62
Memory compaction
    system call, 29

Memory leaks, 27
Memory pointers, 334
Menu editor, 70
Message Digest Algorithm 5, 362
Methods
    adding, 128
    data type casting, 139
    get, 131
    set, 131
MFC, 125, 228
    AppWizard, 142
    COleControl class, 127
Microsoft Corporation, 5
    Access, 280
    Authenticode, 349
    Component Object Model (COM), 30
    Developer Studio, 127
    foundation classes. *See* MFC.
    Internet Explorer, 173, 207
    Jet database engine, 297
    strategy for Java, 21
    Visual Basic, 5
    Visual J++, 16
    Word, 290
Microsoft Developer Studio project workspace (MDP), 64
MIDDLE control alignment, 112
MkTypLib utility, 219
MouseDown function, 62
Move(int, Variant), 306
MoveFirst function, 306
MoveLast function, 306
MoveNext function, 306
MovePrevious function, 306
MSJAVA.DLL, 207
Multiple Document Interface (MDI), 142
Multiple inheritance, 21, 157
Multithreading, 62

N

Naming conventions
    get/set methods, 131
    in OLE, 208
    notification functions, 131
Native code interface, 13, 30, 162, 338
Netscape Communications, 9
    Navigator, 9

Netscape Navigator, 173
Network OLE, 274
New Project Workspace dialog box, 59
New Source File button, 59
Newsgroups, 44
No-compile browser information, 64
Notification functions, 131
    naming conventions, 131

O

Oak, 4
Object Description Language (ODL), 212
Object Linking and Embedding. *See* OLE.
Object model
    application object, 280
    DAO, 298
    Entisoft Tools, 277
    Microsoft Word, 290
Object models, 272
Object tag, 112, 147, 189
Object viewer, 280
Object-oriented programming (OOP), 151
Objects
    graphics, 36
ODBC, 51, 296, 298
    drivers, 298
    relational databases, 301
    with JDBC, 300
ODL, 212
    coclasses, 213
    commenting code, 215
    converting text to binary, 219
    equivalents of Java data types, 214
    interfaces, 213
    libraries, 213
    property declarations, 215
OLE, 5
    automation, 128, 271–294
    automation clients, 272
    automation servers, 172, 181, 207, 272
    control test container, 141
    Control Wizard, 125, 289
    controller, 222
    controls, 6
    enabling support for controls, 142
    history of, 5
    Internet adaptation, 11
    naming conventions, 208
OLE_COLOR data type, 130
OLEMISC_INVISIBLEATRUNTIME
    constant, 145
OnDraw function, 146
One-way hash, 347
OnGetDisplayString function, 137
OnGetPredefinedStrings function, 135
OnGetPredefinedValue function, 136
OOP, 151
Open Database Connectivity. *See* ODBC.
Open Software Foundation, 274
OpenDatabase function, 303
OpenDoc, 271
OpenRecordset function, 304
Output window, 56, 177

P

Packages (class libraries), 271
Paint function, 37
Palette-based images, 38
Parameters
    event, 139
Passwords, 351
PDA, 7
PE format, 353
Persistence, 114
Personal Digital Assistant. *See* PDA.
PESigMgr program, 364
Playground demo, 182
Plug-ins
    NCompass Labs, 112
Portability
    in Java, 21
Portable Executable format, 353
Primary cabinet, 370
Primary font, 130
Private keys, 346, 362
Private keyword, 209
Project workspace, 52, 208
    class view, 53
    creating, 58
    fileView, 54
    importing, 59
    infoView, 54
    text editor, 55

Properties
  get, 180
  pages, 148
  put, 180
  stock, 130
Properties (ActiveX controls), 129
Properties (ActiveX)
  accessing, 131
  ambient, 130
  custom, 130
  enumerated, 134
  exchange functions, 134
  long, 129
  read-only, 133
Property exchange function, 134
Property sheets, 119
PropPage module, 126
Public keys, 346
Public keyword, 153
  public, 208
Put function, 209
Put property, 180
PutPercentPosition(float), 306

Q

QueryInterface, 160

R

Rapid Application Development, 97
RDO, 283
  differences from DAO, 299
RdoEngine.OpenConnection() method, 300
Read-only properties, 133
Record Keystrokes, 58
Recordset, 304
Recordset functions, 306
Recordset object, 281
Redirect to Output window, 57
Reference count, 160
Relational databases, 301
Release function, 160
Remote Data Objects (RDO), 283, 296
Remote procedure call (RPC), 274
Remove button, 75
Resource Wizard, 57

creating resources, 68
dialog boxes, 68
how to run, 72
images, 70
importing resources, 70
valid resources in Java, 68
Resources
  32-bit files, 71
  importing, 70, 71
  template, 71
Return types, 138
RGB images, 38
RIGHT control alignment, 112
RPC, 274
RSA Data Security, 334
RSA Data Security, Inc., 362
Run to cursor, 77

S

Safety Level dialog box, 354
Sample code
  bitmap twirl control, 149
  city selector, 262–266
  class declaration in Java, 217
  conversion calculator, 277
  fire animation control, 147
  Harmon Optical, 311–332
  Java lava lamp, 82
  magnifying glass, 89
  Microsoft Access Driver, 281
  playground demo, 182
  plasma animation control, 148
  taskbar tray, 199
Sandboxing, 162, 182, 334–344
  importance of, 335
Scripts (HTML), 189
  applets, 258–262
  avoiding global variables, 254
  debugging, 250
  event pane icons, 251
  events, 249
  for ActiveX controls, 254–258
  functions, 248
  JavaScript, 243
  random number generator, 256
  Script Wizard, 251
  tag, 243

VBScript, 243
ScrollbarPeer interface, 153
SDI, 142
Searches
    with InfoViewer, 127
Secure Hash Algorithm, 363
Security, 333–372
    applet restrictions, 337
    certificate encryption, 346
    compiler security checks, 341
    Credentials Enrollment Wizard, 358
    features removed from Java, 334
    firewalls, 335
    passwords, 351
    private keys, 346
    unreadable properties, 339
    virtual machine restrictions, 174
    virtual machine security checks, 342
Security Dynamics, 334
Servers, 2
    applets, 21
Set method, 131
SetCtrl function, 190
SetIconImage function, 212
Set-top box, 4
SHA, 363
SHAPES of a control, 113
Short data type, 180
Short property exchange function, 134
Shortcut keys, 129
Signature checking, 116
Signature manipulation utility, 361
SignCode.exe, 361
Single Document Interface (SDI), 142
Skip
    true expression, 76
Smalltalk, 28
Sound files, assigning, 287
Source files
    comments, 61
Source-code file, 64
SQL, 301, 308
    comparison operators, 309
    logical operators, 309
    where clause examples, 309
STANDBY message of a control, 114
Start function, 179
Step Into, 76
Step Out, 76

Step Over, 76
Stock properties, 130
Stop-and-copy algorithm, 29
String property exchange function, 134
Structured Query Language (SQL), 301
Sun Microsystems
    set-top box, 4
Superinterfaces, 153
Suspend button, 81
Symantec, 125
Symantec Visual Café, 52, 98
System.gc function, 29

T

Tab characters
    converting, 275
Tables, 304
Tags, 30
    <APPLET>, 111, 189
    <BODY>, 118
    <OBJECT>, 111, 147, 189
    <SCRIPT>, 243
Taskbar tray sample, 199
Test certificates
    disabling, 361
Test container, 141
Text editor
    in Visual J++, 55
TEXTBOTTOM, 112
TEXTMIDDLE, 113
TEXTTOP, 113
This tab (in Variables window), 78
Thread debugging, 81
Three-state checkbox, 176
ThrowError function, 131
Timer object, 260
Tip of the day, 294
TLBs, 219
TranslateColor function, 130
True color images, 38
True expressions, 75
Trust Provider, 361
Trust validation utility, 361
Trustlib directory, 176
Type libraries, 219
Type Library Wizard, 57, 175, 220, 301

U

ULong property exchange function, 134
Universally unique identifier (UUID), 216
Unsigned char data type, 180
Untrusted applet windows, 339
URL, 32, 82
USEMAP image, 114
UShort property exchange function, 134
UUID, 216

V

Vaporware, 171
Variables
    changing values, 78, 79
    declaring, 178
    displaying values, 78
    exposing, 208
Variables window, 77
    auto tab, 78
    context list, 77
    locals tab, 78
    this tab, 78
Variant class, 181
VARIANT data type, 180
Variants, 305
VBScript, 243
    event handlers, 256
    functions, 248
    random numbers, 256
    timer object, 260
    while/wend statements, 247
VeriSign, 334
Version checking, 116
Version stamping, 146
Video files, 173
Virtual machine, 24–27
    bytecode interpreter, 25
    garbage collection, 28
    in Windows, 34
    security checks, 342
Virtual spaces, 147
Visual Basic, 12, 207
    creating a reference to a Java control, 222
    history of, 5
Visual C++, 12, 172
    as ActiveX container, 106

Class Wizard, 15, 52
    component gallery, 52, 140
Visual Café, 98
Visual debugger (Visual J++), 50
Visual J++, 14, 49
    ActiveX controls, 172
    ActiveX support, 15, 50
    applet restrictions, 337
    Applet Wizard, 60, 278
    bin directory, 82
    build settings, 65
    calling ActiveX functions, 163
    class view, 16, 53
    code-signing tools, 350
    competitors' features, 97
    compiler security checks, 341
    compiling speed, 15
    controls, 206
    converting ODL files to TLBs, 219
    debugging, 50, 74
    debugging Java code, 15
    debugging Java exceptions, 79
    dragging windows, 308
    external tools, 57
    feature limitations, 145
    help for compile errors, 56
    highlights, 49
    image editor, 71
    interface, 50
    late-binding constraint, 288
    layout menu, 69
    licensed visual controls, 198
    limitations, 51
    macros, 58
    native code interface, 338
    no-compile browser information, 64
    object viewer, 280
    organizing tools, 57
    output window, 56
    project workspace, 52
    resource editor, 52
    Resource Wizard, 67
    setting warning levels, 66
    tip of the day, 294
    tools, 56
    translating Windows fonts, 60
    tutorial, 165
    Type Library Wizard, 175
    using OLE automation, 272–276

virtual machine security checks, 342
warning levels, 67
wizards, 49
Void data type, 180
VSPACE of a control, 114

W

Warning levels, 67
Watch window, 78
Watches, 50
Web sites
    Visual J++, 240
Where clause
    comparison operators, 309
    logical operators, 309
    usage examples, 309
While/wend statements, 247
WIDTH of a control, 114
Window.onLoad event, 190
Windows
    getting the size of, 38
    integrating Java, 33
    obsolescence, 20
    output, 177
Windows System Registry, 220
Windows VM, 35

Wizards
    applet, 278
    class, 289
    code signing, 361
    credentials enrollment, 358
    java applet wizard, 60
    OLE Control, 179
    OLE control, 289
    script, 251
    type library, 175, 272, 301
    Visual J++, 49
Word case study, 290
WordBasic, 290
Workspace, 52. *See also* Project Workspace.
World Wide Web
    Gamelon, 44
    newsgroups, 44
    servers, 2

X

X.509 structure, 363

Z

Zoom level, 70

Get a Jump on Java
Visit the Coriolis Group's NEW Java Web site!

Visual Developer Online
The only magazine dedicated to the visual revolution. Read an article, grab a back issue, or review the editorial calendar to see what's coming next.

Developer's Connection
Jump into the "Developer's Connection," where you can stay up to date on hot topics, current articles, and the latest software, and browse the Developer's Club books and software.

Order a Book
Purchase a book online and save up to 20% off your total order. All orders are secure!

Search the Site
Know what you want but can't find it? Search the site quickly and easily.

News Flash
A quick peek at what's HOT on the Coriolis Web site and the Internet.

And the Winner Is...
Take a peek at the winners who won cool Coriolis products just by visiting the Web site.

Books & Software
Look through Coriolis' vast selection of books with topics ranging from the Internet to game programming. Browse through descriptions, tables of contents, sample chapters, and even view the front cover before you buy. Secure online ordering is now available.

What's Free
Grab the goods for free...including a free copy of *Visual Developer*, plus read about the upcoming giveaways available just for browsing our site.

What an Idea!
Do you have a cool topic that's not being addressed? Maybe an emerging technology that has not been tapped into? Check here if you want to write for The Coriolis Group.

Where have you been?

Stop wandering the Web and point your browser to http://www.coriolis.com. You'll find dozens of programming resources, books, and magazines that you can use to develop Web and intranet apps, databases, games, and more. In fact, we'll send you a FREE issue of *Visual Developer Magazine* just for stopping by and telling us what you think. Experience the world of software development with Coriolis Interactive.

Where you need to be.

http://www.coriolis.com
Coriolis Interactive

THE CORIOLIS GROUP

VBScript & ActiveX Wizardry

Uses clear, understandable language to teach you the latest special effects for creating eye-popping Web pages.

Only $39.99

Call 800-410-0192

Fax 602-483-0193

Outside U.S. 602-483-0192

If you're tired of the same old drab, static, text-only Web pages, use Visual Basic Script and ActiveX Wizardry to make your Web pages perform impressive tricks. You'll learn to create frames, animate graphics and text banners, play music or sound effects, create data entry forms, obtain and validate data from users, and use exciting new ActiveX controls. All the techniques are demonstrated with real-life projects that you can modify and incorporate into your own Web pages.

CORIOLIS GROUP BOOKS

http://www.coriolis.com

• JAVA • VB • VC++ • DELPHI • SOFTWARE COMPONENTS • OCX, DLL •

VISUAL DEVELOPER magazine

Give Yourself the Visual Edge

Don't Lose Your Competitve Edge Act Now!

1 Year $21.95
(6 issues)

2 Years $37.95
(12 issues)

($53.95 Canada; $73.95 Elsewhere)
Please allow 4-6 weeks for delivery
All disk orders must be pre-paid

The first magazine dedicated to the Visual Revolution

Join Jeff Duntemann and his crew of master authors for a tour of the visual software development universe. Peter Aitken, Al Williams, Ray Konopka, David Gerrold, Michael Covington, Tom Campbell, and all your favorites share their insights into rapid application design and programming, software component development, and content creation for the desktop, client/server, and online worlds. The whole visual world will be yours, six times per year: Windows 95 and NT, Multimedia, VRML, Java, HTML, Delphi, VC++, VB, and more. *Seeing is succeeding!*

1-800-410-0192

See *Visual Developer* on the Web! http://www.coriolis.com

7339 East Acoma Dr. Suite 7 • Scottsdale, Arizona 85260

• WEB • CGI • JAVA • VB • VC++ • DELPHI • SOFTWARE COMPONENTS •